Layman's
BIBLE
Commentary

D1467227

Layman's BIBLE Commentary

1 Chronicles thru Job

Volume 4

Contributing Editors:

DR. RALPH DAVIS
BOB DEFFINBAUGH, TH.M
REV. JOE GUGLIELMO

Consulting Editor:

DR. TREMPER LONGMAN

BARBOUR
PUBLISHING

Scripture quotations marked NIV are taken from the HOLY BIBLE, NEW INTERNATIONAL VERSION®. NIV®. Copyright © 1973, 1978, 1984 by International Bible Society. Used by permission of Zondervan. All rights reserved.

Scripture quotations marked NLT are taken from the *Holy Bible*, New Living Translation, copyright © 1996, 2004. Used by permission of Tyndale House Publishers, Inc. Wheaton, Illinois 60189, U.S.A. All rights reserved.

Scripture quotations marked CEV are from the Contemporary English Version, Copyright © 1991, 1992, 1995 by American Bible Society. Used by permission.

Scripture quotations marked NKJV are taken from the New King James Version®. Copyright © 1982 by Thomas Nelson, Inc. Used by permission. All rights reserved.

Scripture quotations marked MSG are from *THE MESSAGE*. Copyright © by Eugene H. Peterson 1993, 1994, 1995, 1996, 2000, 2001, 2002. Used by permission of NavPress Publishing Group.

Scripture quotations marked GWT are taken from God's Word, which is a copyrighted work of God's Word to the Nations. Quotations are used by permission. Copyright 1995 by God's Word to the Nations. All rights reserved.

Scripture quotations marked NRSV are taken from the New Revised Standard Version Bible, copyright 1989, Division of Christian Education of the National Council of the Churches of Christ in the United States of America. Used by permission. All rights reserved.

Scripture quotations marked ESV are from The Holy Bible, English Standard Version®, copyright © 2001 by Crossway Bibles, a publishing ministry of Good News Publishers. Used by permission. All rights reserved.

Scripture quotations that do not reference a specific translation use the same wording that is common to multiple translations

Quotations designated (NET) are from the NET Bible® copyright © 1996–2006 by Biblical Studies Press, L.L.C. www.bible.org. All rights reserved. Used by permission. The NET Bible is available in its entirety as a free download or online Web use at www.nextbible.org.

Published by Barbour Publishing, Inc., P.O. Box 719, Uhrichsville, Ohio 44683, www.barbourbooks.com

Our mission is to publish and distribute inspirational products offering exceptional value and biblical encouragement to the masses.

Member of the
Evangelical Christian
Publishers Association

Printed in the United States of America.

TABLE OF CONTENTS

1 CHRONICLES

INTRODUCTION TO 1 CHRONICLES

In the Hebrew, 1 and 2 Chronicles are one single book. The title means, "the events of the times." The book of 1 Chronicles covers the same time period and many of the same events as portions of 1 and 2 Samuel and the first chapters of 1 Kings, but has a unique perspective. While the books of Samuel and Kings focus more on the political history of Israel and Judah, the Chronicles dwell more on the religious history and stay focused primarily on Judah. The information included in the Chronicles helps the people of Judah understand their history so they can live well in the present.

AUTHOR

Many scholars believe that Ezra wrote 1 and 2 Chronicles, which is quite possible. The book of 2 Chronicles flows smoothly into the book of Ezra, and the time frame (450 to 430 BC) is reasonable. However, the author's identity cannot be proven beyond reasonable doubt, so it has become traditional to refer to him as "the Chronicler."

PURPOSE

In Jewish thought, genealogies were extremely important. The firstborn of each family was entitled to a double portion of the inheritance. The land was portioned out first by tribe, and then by family, and would never permanently leave that family. Levites had to prove their family credentials in order to serve in the temple. Priests had to show they were descendants of Aaron. Jewish people would consult these genealogies frequently, for various reasons. Genealogies were particularly important to post-exilic Judeans returning from exile after a disruption of their cultural history.

The Chronicler focuses his genealogies on the tribe of Judah, which eventually leads to the reign of David. Late in life, David is promised a "house" in which one of his offspring will reign forever (17:10–14). The Chronicler realizes the importance of such a promise and verifies the line of Judah both before and after David. For an audience who no longer has a temple or a Davidic king, 1 Chronicles is both a reminder of God's faithfulness in their past and an optimistic look toward the future.

OCCASION

The Israelites are captives of a powerful foreign empire, but some of the citizens are being allowed to return home. Their current status seems uncertain, so the Chronicler goes back to Adam (1:1) and reviews their history up to the current time (2 Chronicles 26:23). In doing so, he supports his outlook with various citations from the books of law, the Psalms, the prophetic books, and other sources. His repeated emphasis is on the covenants, the temple, and other reminders of how God has always provided for and delivered His people. As they look to return home and rebuild the temple that the Babylonians left in ruins, the Chronicler wants to assure them that God will continue to be with them.

THEMES

The Chronicler is fond of the term *all Israel,* and he uses it frequently, downplaying the divided kingdom of Israel/Judah, while highlighting the perspective that the kingdom is indeed intended to be a single nation.

Associated with Israel are the temple, priests, and Levites—all ongoing concerns of the author.

Most of 1 Chronicles, aside from a lengthy series of opening genealogies, focuses on David as God's chosen king over the united nation. In conjunction is the prominence of Judah over the northern tribes.

HISTORICAL CONTEXT

The Chronicles were written for a Hebrew audience no longer completely in control of their lives. They have recently undergone captivity at the hands of the Babylonians, but control has quickly shifted to the Persians. It is a time of uncertainty, if not despair, for the Jews, who have always taken for granted that they are God's chosen people. The book of 1 Chronicles, therefore, is a review of the best of their past history: the beginning of the kings, David's eventual rise to power, his desire and plans to build a temple for God, and the transition from his reign to that of Solomon.

CONTRIBUTION TO THE BIBLE

One of the interesting aspects of Chronicles is not so much what it adds to scripture but what it leaves out. (The translators of the Septuagint titled the book, "the things omitted.") While covering much of the same content as 1 and 2 Samuel, the author streamlines the story to make it a targeted look at God's ongoing involvement in honoring the covenants He had made with Abraham and David. The Chronicler has a distinct perspective. While the books of Samuel and Kings were written during the exile and answer the question "What did we do to deserve the exile?" Chronicles addresses the questions, "What do we do now?" and "What is our connection with the past?"

There are a few things unique to 1 Chronicles involving some of the names in genealogies (much of 23–27, for example) and a number of orations found nowhere else. The Chronicler identifies a Shalleketh Gate of the temple (26:16) that is mentioned nowhere else in scripture. And the Jabez who sparked a bestselling book in the early 2000s is not mentioned anywhere else in the Bible except 1 Chronicles 4:9–10.

OUTLINE

ORGANIZING PEOPLE TO SERVE IN THE KINGDOM

1 CHRONICLES 1:1–7:40

IMPORTANT FAMILY HISTORIES

Setting Up the Section

The first nine chapters of 1 Chronicles cover a number of genealogies going all the way back to Adam. While such lists of family histories are sometimes perceived to be insignificant (or even boring) to modern readers, the Hebrew mindset was quite different. Such lists helped define who they were as a people and were a reminder of the blessings of their past. In particular for this group of exiles returning home, the genealogies grounded them in their history. This section contains family lines for Noah, Abraham, and Israel.

⊕ 1:1–27

THE FAMILY OF NOAH

When approaching any section of biblical genealogy, many people automatically assume it will be dry and essentially meaningless. However, God does not place anything in His Word that is unimportant. With a little effort, the significance of many of these names will become both apparent and relevant to our modern faith. It has been said that some of the greatest treasure is found in the driest places.

The primary focus of the genealogies in Chronicles is the line of the Messiah. Other genealogies are included but usually run through a few names and are then dropped. Those that connect Adam to David to the ancestors of Jesus, however, will be much more prominent.

The sequence from Adam to Noah is brief but afterward becomes more detailed because it is the sons of Noah who are assigned to repopulate the earth after the Flood. Noah has three sons (1:4). Japheth (1:5–7) and his descendants live in the area of the north—what is now Europe and some of the former Soviet states. Ham's descendants (1:8–16) settle on the continent of Africa and the area known as Canaan. Perhaps the most prominent name in his progeny is Nimrod, a mighty hunter and warrior whose name is connected with both Babylon and Nineveh (Genesis 10:8–12). The Jewish Targum, a paraphrase of the Old Testament, attributes no small measure of wickedness to Nimrod, crediting him with creating the false religious system at the Tower of Babel.

The messianic line goes through Noah's remaining son, Shem (from where we get the word *Semites*). His descendants (1 Chronicles 1:17-27) take up residence in the Middle East.

The mention of the dividing of the earth during the days of Peleg (1:19) has created varying schools of thought. Some believe the reference is to the dividing of Earth's land masses into continents, but how could this be? They would have no knowledge of this in antiquity. Others feel it means that during the time of the Tower of Babel God divided languages, and thus people, into separate groups.

q 1:28-34

THE FAMILY OF ABRAM (ABRAHAM)

The final entry in Shem's list of descendants is Abram, and the genealogy picks up there with his families. Ishmael, the son Abraham had with Hagar, has a number of sons (1:29-31). Abraham himself has a number of additional children after Sarah dies (1:32-33). But the son whose line the Chronicler will follow is Isaac, the only son of Sarah.

Isaac has two sons: the twins, Jacob and Esau. However, Jacob's name isn't even used in this section of Chronicles. Instead, he is identified as *Israel*, the name he receives from God and by which the entire nation eventually comes to be known. (*Jacob* means "heel catcher"; *Israel* means something like "wrestling or struggling God.") Esau has several sons and many grandchildren. His line eventually comes to be called the Edomites (1:43). But it will be the children of Jacob—the Israelites—who will get the most attention in this genealogical list. And Judah will be the one of whom most is written because he is the one in the messianic line.

📖 2:1-4:23

THE FAMILY OF ISRAEL: JUDAH

Israel has twelve sons (2:1). Judah is fourth in birth order but rises to prominence after Jacob's oldest sons commit harsh actions that prevent them from receiving their father's blessing (Genesis 34:25-30; 35:22; 49:1-12). Still, Judah is hardly a perfect son or citizen.

Judah's first two sons, Er and Onan, are killed by the Lord for their wickedness (Genesis 38:6-10). Judah is reluctant to let his third son marry the same woman, Tamar, which was the tradition of the time. Tamar is therefore unable to remarry or have children. Seeing a unique opportunity, she poses as a prostitute and is approached by Judah himself, who unknowingly impregnates her without ever discovering her identity. Months later, when she is discovered to be pregnant, Judah wants to have her killed, but she produces some of his possessions as collateral. Only then does he realize he is the father of her child, which turns out to be *children*—twins (Genesis 38:13-30). One of the offspring is named Perez, and as it turns out, he is in the messianic line (1 Chronicles 2:3-9).

Another notorious member of Judah's family is Achar (2:7). Known in Joshua as Achan, he plunders Jericho after Israel's victory, in defiance of God's and Joshua's explicit instructions (Joshua 7). His life is summed up in Chronicles in one phrase: a troubler of Israel (1 Chronicles 2:7).

Other memorable names of a more honorable reputation are Boaz, the kinsman-redeemer and husband of Ruth, and his grandson, Jesse, who was the father of David (2:12). The account of Samuel anointing David as king in 1 Samuel 16:6–13 provides the names of David's three oldest brothers, but Chronicles provides the names of those three and three more (2:13–15). David has seven older brothers, but only six are listed in 1 Chronicles. Perhaps the difference is to promote David to seventh position, since seven is a significant number throughout scripture.

David's nephews (2:16–17) are decent warriors, yet they create a lot of unnecessary stress during David's conflict with Saul. Saul's commander, Abner, kills Asahel. Later, even though David has established a peace treaty with Abner, Joab kills Abner out of revenge. David tries to remove Joab as general, but Joab holds on to his job, although he is not a man to be trusted (2 Samuel 19:11–13). It is Joab who later kills David's son, Absalom, in direct disobedience to David's orders (2 Samuel 18:14–15).

Backing up a bit, the Chronicler records the family of Caleb (1 Chronicles 2:18–54). Caleb had represented the tribe of Judah when Moses selected one person from each tribe to spy out the promised land before entering (Numbers 13:3–16). Of the twelve spies, only Caleb and Joshua return with the recommendation to move ahead in faith. Sadly, they are outvoted. The other spies are terrified of the inhabitants of the land, and their fear spreads to the entire nation. As a result, all the tribes are forced to wander in the wilderness for forty years because of their unbelief. Caleb, however, has a strong and consistent faith throughout his lifetime (Judges 1:8–20).

Historically, perhaps the most famous Old Testament character who comes through the line of Judah is David. David's descendants are listed in this section (1 Chronicles 3:1–9), and after the opening genealogies of 1 Chronicles (1–9), most of the rest of the book reviews his life (11–29).

Even a brief mention of David's sons and daughters, however, tends to trigger recollections of tragic stories. David's daughter, Tamar (3:9), is raped by David's son, Amnon (2 Samuel 13:1–22; 1 Chronicles 3:1). In response, Tamar's full brother, Absalom (1 Chronicles 3:2), bides his time for two years before assassinating Amnon (2 Samuel 15:23–39). Absalom later leads a revolt against David in an effort to take the throne but is killed in the process (2 Samuel 18:1–18). Still later, another son named Adonijah (1 Chronicles 3:2) attempts a coup and is also put to death (1 Kings 1; 2:13–25). All these events follow the declaration of the prophet Nathan that "the sword will never depart from [David's] house" (2 Samuel 12:10 NIV), a prophecy that was delivered immediately after David's adultery with Bathsheba and his murder of her husband, Uriah (2 Samuel 11).

Yet the Chronicler's list of David's sons also includes Solomon (1 Chronicles 3:5), which serves as a reminder of God's grace and forgiveness. Even after David's sins, his son would sit on the throne of Israel during the most peaceful and prosperous era in their history.

Demystifying 1 Chronicles

After the kingdom is divided, the northern tribes will have eight different families/dynasties on the throne. The southern kingdom of Judah, however, had only one dynasty: David's. And it is from David's lineage that the Messiah will eventually come.

The kings of Judah who follow David are listed in 3:10–16. All the kings of Judah are descendants of David, up to Zedekiah, the last king before the majority of the people are taken away captive to Babylon. A curse is placed on Jehoiachin because of his great wickedness, averring that he will never have a descendant on the throne (Jeremiah 22:28–30). Zedekiah, who follows Jehoiachin, is a son of Josiah (Jeremiah 37:1), but Jehoiachin outlives Zedekiah to become the last surviving king in the line of David—until the arrival of Jesus.

The kingdom had originally been divided for a short time in the transition from Saul's kingship to David's (2 Samuel 2–5). During that time David reigned in Hebron for seven and a half years, with only Judah supporting him as king. Meanwhile, Saul's son Ish-bosheth ruled over Israel for two years. David continued to grow stronger and soon united the kingdom, after which he ruled over all of Israel for thirty-three years. He is the one who established Jerusalem as the capital city and planned the building of the temple.

Two of David's children born to Bathsheba, Nathan and Solomon (1 Chronicles 3:5), continue David's lineage in the messianic line. Nathan's descendants continue to the family of Mary, the mother of Jesus (Luke 3). Solomon's descendants go to Joseph, the adopted father of Jesus (Matthew 1), which links Jesus to the royal line of David, but avoids the blood curse that had been placed on Jehoiachin and his descendants (Jeremiah 22:28–30).

Hezron (1 Chronicles 4:1) is the father of Caleb, who had been an exemplary soldier and follower of God. Yet he is not included in the messianic line. The line runs through Perez instead. (The listing of Judah's descendants [4:1] is not a group of siblings, but rather a sequential series of families.)

The account of Jabez (4:9–10) is short but fascinating. He is a man in pain who seeks the Lord, and his prayers are answered. God honors his request and blesses him.

After spending much time detailing the family of Judah, the son of Israel through whose line the Messiah will eventually come, the Chronicler moves on to the other sons of Israel and their family lines. These non-messianic lines are considerably more abbreviated.

The Chronicler's extensive coverage of the family of Judah (2:3–4:23) is due to both David's involvement and the anticipation of the Messiah to come from that line. Reuben is actually the oldest son of Jacob (Israel), but he loses the privileges that were usually bestowed on the firstborn (5:1–2). He not only misses out on the birthright that would connect him with the Messiah, he also forfeits the double portion of the inheritance that traditionally would have been his. That honor goes to Joseph. (This is why there is no tribe of Joseph. Instead, there are two tribes named for Joseph's sons, Ephraim and Manasseh.) Reuben isn't even listed first after Judah in this genealogy. Next comes Simeon, the second oldest.

Critical Observation

When Jacob was blessing his sons, he made a somewhat cryptic statement that the scepter would not depart from Judah and that there would not cease to be a lawgiver until Shiloh comes (Genesis 49:10). The reference to the *scepter* brings to mind a king with the right to execute capital punishment. (Perhaps the best-known biblical example is King Xerxes in the book of Esther [see Esther 4:10–11].)

The Jewish nation eventually loses the right to govern themselves as they always had, which is why the Jewish leaders appeal to Pilate to have Jesus put to death. After the Romans deny Israel the right to pass a death sentence, rabbis walk through the streets of Jerusalem in sackcloth and ashes. They perceive that the scepter had been taken away before the Messiah had come, and they weep because they believe the Word of God has been broken. They do not realize that some seventy miles to the north, in a town called Nazareth, a young boy is working in his father's carpenter shop. The Messiah *has* come before the scepter departed, but He is not yet revealed to them.

📄 4:24–43

THE FAMILY OF ISRAEL: SIMEON

Simeon, along with his brother, Levi, had offended their father in an incident involving their sister, Dinah (Genesis 34). However, in this example provided by the Chronicler, the Simeonites are good models of faith and action. Their families have grown, along with their flocks and herds. They feel restricted and need more room, so they seek to destroy their enemies and enlarge their borders. Too frequently the problem with the Israelites (as well as with believers of all ages) was that they became complacent during good times. After they entered the promised land, they settled and stopped struggling as soon as they had acquired a little personal comfort—before they had dealt with the problems around them. Consequently, they remained vulnerable to the attacks of their enemies. The Simeonites are an admirable exception in this instance.

📄 5:1–26

THE FAMILY OF ISRAEL: REUBEN, GAD, AND MANASSEH

The tribes of Reuben and Gad and the half tribe of Manasseh have the common bond of settling on the east side of the Jordan River. In one account recalled by the Chronicler, these tribes go into battle and are victorious—not because of their own strength, but because they cry out to God (5:18–22). God gives them victory because they express confidence and trust in Him. In addition to their victory, they receive the spoils of battle, including land and numerous animals.

In time, however, this cluster of tribes became unfaithful to God. When the Assyrian army invades, led by Tiglath-pileser (or Pul), they are easily defeated and taken into exile. They had not crossed the Jordan River, a line of defense, to settle in Canaan, so they were easily the first to be taken away captive.

📖 6:1–81

THE FAMILY OF ISRAEL: LEVI

The Levites are placed in charge of the tabernacle and matters of worship, with each of the sons of Levi given a specific duty. Gershon and his descendants are responsible for the fabrics of the tabernacle, the coverings, tents, clothes, curtains, cords, and so forth. Kohath and his descendants (including Aaron) are to care for the ark, the table of show-bread, the oil-burning lamp, the altars of burnt offering and incense, the sacred vessels, the veil, and related furnishings. The Merarites (descendants of Merari) take care of the boards, sockets, walls, floors, and such.

Critical Observation

It was important for those who planned to work in the soon-to-be-built temple to trace their genealogy back to Levi to prove their authenticity. The Gershonites, Kohathites, and Merarites will be mentioned repeatedly throughout 1 Chronicles to identify those qualified to serve in various specific duties.

The assignment of specific responsibilities is akin to the Spirit's assignment of spiritual gifts in the New Testament. When everyone is doing what they have been assigned to do, worship goes smoothly. But it can be disastrous when someone attempts to be something he or she is not. When Korah and some of his followers rebel against the leadership of Moses (Numbers 16), God causes the earth to swallow them up.

The Gershonites, Kohathites, and Merarites are still going strong as David becomes king (1 Chronicles 6:31–48). David is a man of worship who is determined to provide qualified people to worship. Imagine being able to walk by the temple day or night and hear the worship of God being sung out.

The descendants of Aaron become the priestly line in Israel (6:49–53). The Levites do not inherit any land because the Lord is to be their inheritance. (It is important to note as well that Jacob cursed Levi's tribe in Genesis 49.) Instead, forty-eight cities are designated throughout Israel in which the Levites live and minister (6:54–81). Under this arrangement, no one in the other tribes is more than a day's journey from one of the Levitical cities.

📖 7:1–40

THE FAMILY OF ISRAEL: ISSACHAR, BENJAMIN, NAPHTALI, MANASSEH, EPHRAIM, AND ASHER

Biblical genealogies aren't altogether unlike the average family tree: Some members are going to be more prominent than others. In this section of Israel's family tree there are fewer familiar names. And while some of the tribes have lengthy sections with name after name and generation after generation, the tribe of Naphtali gets but a single verse with four names (7:13). But interesting tidbits are recorded for some of the biblical families, just as every modern family has its favorite stories that are told and retold. For example, two men in the line of Ephraim are killed in an altercation over livestock (7:21–24). The father grieves for them many days but then has other children and goes on with life.

One noteworthy name in Ephraim's family is Joshua, the assistant to Moses, spy of the promised land, and leader of the nation when the Israelites conquer Jericho and march triumphantly into the land. Here, however, he appears as just another name in the series (7:27).

In Manasseh's section (in this case, the western portion of Manasseh as opposed to the previously listed Transjordanian section) is mention of a man named Zelophehad, who had only daughters (7:15). More of that story is provided in Numbers 27:1–11, where the daughters go to Moses and the other leaders of Israel upon the death of their father, pointing out that the law made no provision for inheritances of families without sons. Moses took their case to the Lord, who determined that the daughters certainly did have a right to inherit their father's land.

The Chronicler has a few more lists of names to record (1 Chronicles 8–9), and then he moves into some history of Israel during the reigns of Saul and David.

Take It Home

How far back can you trace your family tree? Unless someone has an interest in genealogy, most people can't go back more than a generation or two. Aside from a relative who might be famous, notorious, or eccentric, we tend to forget our previous generations of family members. Yet Chronicles reveals in the ancient Hebrew mindset a devoted, intense commitment to trace one's ancestry back for dozens of generations. The importance placed on family lines might appear strange or useless to modern readers, yet it needs to be acknowledged in order to better understand Chronicles.

THE BEGINNING AND END OF THE ERA OF THE KINGS

Setting Up the Section

The lengthy opening list of genealogies in 1 Chronicles concludes in this section with an account of some of the people who return to Judah after being released from captivity. The author then backtracks to the first king of Israel and explains why, in spite of all his potential, King Saul falls far short of what God wants him to be.

📖 8:1–40

THE FAMILY OF SAUL

When Samuel first approaches Saul about being the first king of Israel, Saul's initial response is skepticism. He is well aware that he is not only from Israel's smallest tribe, but he is also from the least significant clan within the tribe (1 Samuel 9:21). Since that time, however, it appears that being the source of the first king of Israel had helped the tribe of Benjamin increase in status. The Chronicler has already included a short genealogy of the tribe, and here he inserts another, more detailed, family line.

The list begins with a background of the Benjamites in general (1 Chronicles 8:1–28). The note that they all lived in Jerusalem (8:28) indicates the author's awareness that David had eventually conquered the city and established it as Israel's capital. That act had not yet taken place during the lifetime of Saul.

The names that follow (8:29–40) are the Benjamites to whom Saul is specifically related. Similar lists of names are found elsewhere in scripture and do not always coincide exactly. Sometimes the term *son* might actually refer to a grandson or perhaps even a more distant relative. And depending on the writer's intent, he might be selective in how many names he provides. Not all lists will be complete. However, this particular section is more comprehensive than others of a similar nature (Genesis 46:21; Numbers 26:38–40).

📖 9:1–34

BACK FROM CAPTIVITY

After Solomon forsakes the worship of the Lord to pursue other gods (1 Kings 11:1–13), the kingdom begins a long spiritual deterioration. First it splits, with ten tribes forming the northern kingdom (Israel) and the remaining two comprising Judah. Each kingdom has a succession of kings, but very few show any kind of genuine devotion to God.

The northern kingdom is first to fall as the Assyrian Empire rises to power. More than a century later the Babylonian Empire begins making incursions into the southern kingdom, each time carrying away segments of the more trained and useful people. The first invasion was in 605 BC, the second in 597 BC. By 586 BC, they would tolerate no more of Judah's revolts and they level the city of Jerusalem, destroying the temple in the process. The invaders also take the majority of the leaders back to Babylon, leaving only the poor to take care of the land.

In 539 BC the Persian Empire conquers Babylon. The Persians allow the Israelites to go back to their homeland. However, by then not many of them *want* to return because they have become very comfortable in Babylon. The religious leaders are the first to return (9:2).

The priests (9:10–13) would normally have attended to and ministered in the temple, but the temple was no longer standing. They are assisted by the Levites (9:14–16). The gatekeepers (9:17–32) are a specified group of Levites in charge of opening and closing the gates of the temple. They ensure that only those who are permitted to be in the temple area are allowed in, and they keep out those who do not belong there.

Critical Observation

Although the official position of gatekeeper is not found in most churches today, that role has been assigned to the pastors and church leadership. The overseers of the church are not only to provide spiritual direction but also are to watch over and warn their congregations of danger, ensuring that "wolves" don't get in to harm the flock (see Acts 20:27–30). False teachers can be overt or subtle; either way, they need to be confronted and dealt with.

Some of the people in this group have no responsibilities other than being in the temple and singing worship songs to the Lord. Music and worship could be heard day and night. The Chronicler will have more to say about the priests, singers, gatekeepers, and other groups in chapters 23–26.

📖 **9:35–10:14**

A BRIEF LOOK AT SAUL

A portion of Saul's genealogy is reviewed as a prologue to the story that follows. First Chronicles 9:35–44 repeats 8:29–38.

Conflict with the Philistines escalates throughout Saul's lifetime, and they are victorious in the battle at Mount Gilboa. Saul's sons are killed, and Saul himself is severely wounded by an arrow. He knew he could not escape in his condition, and he did not want to be tortured and/or killed at the hands of his enemies. Saul appeals to his armor bearer, requesting to be killed, but the armor bearer refuses. As a last resort, Saul falls on his own sword, and the armor bearer follows suit. A young Amalekite takes credit for ending Saul's life in hopes of impressing David, and David has him killed as a result (see 2 Samuel 1:1–16).

Demystifying 1 Chronicles

The Chronicler covers only Saul's ancestry (1 Chronicles 9:35–44) and his death (10:1–14). A much more extensive account of Saul's life is found in 1 Samuel 9–31.

The Philistines are brutal. They cut off Saul's head and take his body, along with those of his sons, back to their town. Saul's head and armor are displayed as trophies in their temples (10:10). But one of Saul's first acts as king had been to rescue the men of the Israelite city of Jabesh-gilead from hostile Ammonites (1 Samuel 11:1–11). When the citizens of that city hear of the Philistines' despicable treatment of Saul and his family, they conduct a night raid, heroically retrieve the bodies, and carry them back to Jabesh for a decent burial (1 Samuel 31:11–13; 1 Chronicles 10:11–12).

The Chronicler adds an editorial note about Saul's life that isn't included in Samuel (10:13–14). The author of Samuel implies that Saul's consultation with a medium is entirely inappropriate. But here (10:13–14) the author provides three specific reasons why Saul falls short of what God wants him to be:

1) *Saul is unfaithful to God.* The Lord had instructed Saul to wipe out the Amalekites, but Saul uses his own discretion to determine who and what should be spared (1 Samuel 15:1–26).

2) *Saul disregards God's Word.* Only priests were permitted to sacrifice animals to God. Yet in a moment of desperation and panic, Saul makes an offering himself without waiting for Samuel, as he had been instructed (1 Samuel 13:5–14).

3) *Saul fails to seek God properly.* After the death of Samuel, Saul no longer receives direction from God. Again motivated by fear, he seeks counsel from a medium where he learns of his impending death (1 Samuel 28:4–25).

This section of 1 Chronicles recalls both the first king of Israel, who hadn't performed his duties very well, and the captivity of the people, which ended their long line of kings. Neither the beginning nor the end of the era of the kings in Israel is an exemplary time of spiritual faith or national security. But in between is the reign of David—a period when God blesses His people spiritually and in every other way. David's reign paves the way for Solomon to rule in an atmosphere of peace and prosperity, yet it is Solomon who begins the idolatry that eventually brings down the entire nation.

When Israel demands a king, God gives them Saul and promises to bless the new king if Saul will be obedient (1 Samuel 12:13–15). Saul, however, does not obey God. Consequently, his dynasty lasts only some forty years. He is replaced by David, a leader divinely ordained by God, whose dynasty lasts more than ten times as long—from 1011 BC until 586 BC.

Take It Home

It is easy to criticize someone like King Saul, who began his reign as king with God's full endorsement and a green light to lead, but ends up completely estranged from God. Yet Saul is not unlike many believers today. He was somewhat obedient—but not totally—and it was his lack of total commitment that eventually cost him his kingdom. What is recorded in 1 Chronicles is not his occasional courage or good intentions, but his ultimate failure. Believers will benefit by reminding themselves frequently that their spiritual journey is a lengthy race, and they need to pace themselves in order to *finish* (1 Corinthians 9:24).

1 CHRONICLES 11:1–12:40

THE RISE OF DAVID

Setting Up the Section

After providing all the opening genealogies and the brief account of King Saul, the Chronicler in this section turns his attention to the primary focus of this portion of his writing: the life story of King David. We need to remember that 1 and 2 Chronicles were originally a single book; the rest of what we know as 1 Chronicles (11–29) will be about David, concluding with his death.

📖 11:1–9

DAVID UNITES A NATION

By the time Saul dies, David is more than ready to be the next king. He had already been anointed years before, yet he was always insistent on leaving the timing of the transition in God's hands. He had had two ideal opportunities to kill King Saul, but refused each time (1 Samuel 24; 26).

In the meantime, he continues to serve God and his nation. His victory over Goliath and subsequent battles against the Philistines garner him national attention. It is not only evident that he is a great military figure, but the people also recognize the hand of God in David's life. Even as a shepherd, God had been training David to be king.

After Saul dies, the people in Judah immediately turn to David as their next leader, and he establishes a headquarters in Hebron (2 Samuel 2:1–4). The rest of the nation, however, recognizes Saul's son, Ish-bosheth. (They had wanted a king in order to be like the other nations, and the other nations tended to pass down their royal status through family lines.) For a long while, war rages between the supporters of David and the supporters of Saul (2 Samuel 3:1). As time passes, David's influence expands as the house of

Saul gets weaker. It takes seven and a half years, but finally the entire nation gathers to endorse David's leadership as king (1 Chronicles 11:1–3).

David's next step displays good political sense, insightful wisdom, and military courage. Rather than choose an established city in Israel as a capital (which would likely upset some of those in Judah) or a city from the south (that could reignite the still-delicate feelings of Saul's supporters), David chooses the city Jebus, located between Judah and the northern tribes. But unfortunately the city is inhabited by Israel's enemies.

The citizens of Jebus had withstood all former assaults for hundreds of years and were not worried about David's desire to conquer them (11:4–5). Entrenched as they were at the top of a hill, it was easy to pick off any enemy soldiers that approached. But they should not have been so complacent. David conquers Jebus, and from that point forward it is known better as the city of Jerusalem and will always be known as the City of David.

Critical Observation

Jebusites had inhabited the city of Jebus since before the Israelites had entered the promised land. If God's people had done as He instructed (Joshua 23:6–13) and driven out all their enemies before settling comfortably in the land, they could have avoided a lot of problems—including the one of a fortified city established on a hill that was thought to be impenetrable. But David accomplishes what all the Israelites before him failed to do.

David's victory at Jebus also allows someone else an opportunity to prove himself. As David steps into the role of king, his army is left without a commander-in-chief, so he promises the position to whoever leads the attack on the Jebusites. The challenge is accepted by one of David's nephews—a man named Joab. He is seen in scripture as a tough, though at times unethical, warrior.

Demystifying 1 Chronicles

Exactly how Joab is able to breach the defenses of Jebus when others could not is not fully explained. One possible scenario is that David knew of a 45-foot shaft from which the Jebusites brought water into the city, and Joab is able to climb up the shaft and open the doors for Israel's soldiers (see 2 Samuel 5:8).

📖 11:10–12:40

DAVID'S FIGHTING MEN

David had a reputation as a great warrior, and he seemed to attract others who were also noteworthy in battle. He collects a small army of about six hundred men while on the run from King Saul (1 Samuel 27:2). Several of their names are recorded (1 Chronicles 11:26–47). A sampling of their exploits is also provided (11:10–25), although few details are given.

Slight variations in names and details occur between the Chronicles account and the one in 2 Samuel 23, but the list is overall quite consistent. One soldier kills three hundred (or perhaps eight hundred) enemy soldiers in a single encounter. A small group takes a stand in a barley field, turning a potential defeat into a great victory. One man goes into a pit on a snowy day to kill a lion and later slays a giant Egyptian soldier. And there are more great accomplishments briefly recorded.

In one touching story, David expresses a desire for a drink from a particular well in a location where the Philistines are encamped. He is simply stating a wish, but he is overheard. Three of his very best soldiers break through the Philistine ranks, acquire the water, and take it back to David. Realizing the extent of their faith and commitment, David doesn't even drink the water; instead he pours it out as an offering to God, the One who really deserves that kind of devotion.

Ziklag (12:1) is a Philistine city that had been given to David. After David had been on the run from the relentless pursuit of King Saul for almost ten years, he had decided he would be just as safe among the Philistines as in Israel. He approaches the Philistine king Achish, asking for a city where he and his six hundred men can reside. Achish wrongly perceives that David will be his ally against Saul and Israel. He gives David and his men Ziklag, where they live for about sixteen months.

David uses Achish's misperception to his advantage. He and his men go out and destroy cities of Israel's enemies, but Achish assumes they are fighting against Israel. The setup works well until one day when Achish enlists the help of David and his men to march against Israel. David cannot refuse without exposing his actual feelings, so he starts out with Achish. God steps in to give David an out. The other Philistine leaders refuse to fight with David, suspecting that he might turn on them in battle. They force Achish to reluctantly send David back (1 Samuel 27:6–7; 29:1–11). As it turns out, this is the very battle where Saul and his sons are killed.

When David and his men return to Ziklag, they discover the Amalekites have burned it and taken all their wives and possessions. At this point, David's men are ready to stone him. David seeks the Lord, who assures him that they will defeat the Amalekites and retrieve everything that had been taken, which is exactly what happens (1 Samuel 30).

The author of Samuel provides much information about David's experiences in Ziklag. The author of Chronicles adds that it is during all these events that various groups of warriors come to Ziklag to join David. The soldiers in the first group mentioned (1 Chronicles 12:1–7) are Benjamites—relatives of Saul. This group must have been valuable on the battlefield because they were ambidextrous: They could use various weapons with either hand. A second group, from Gad, had a remarkable reputation. The least of them was equal to one hundred regular soldiers; the greatest of them could face one thousand. They wouldn't be stopped by flooded rivers or any human opponent (12:8–15). Another group came from Manasseh, defecting from Saul's army during the time that David had marched out with the Philistines. When David is sent back to Ziklag, they go with him (12:19–21).

As each group comes to David, he goes out to receive them. He welcomes all who come in peace to support him, but he warns against any attempt to betray him (12:16–18). It is only natural for him to be a bit suspicious, but God is with David in Ziklag, just as He had been all along the way.

People are coming to him day by day, and David soon has a great army. By the time Saul dies and David moves on to Hebron, they are joining his ranks by the thousands, from all the tribes (12:23–37). After all that David had been through—dodging Saul, negotiating with the Philistines, and leading all those who came to him—this was a relaxing and joyous time. Volunteers had provided plentiful supplies of food, and David and his group spend three days eating and drinking (12:38–40). It is a well-deserved break for the new king of Israel.

Take It Home

Reviewing the early life of David should remind us of the importance of waiting for God to act in His timing. Our first look at David is as a shepherd, and he is the best shepherd he could be. When he is a soldier, he serves his king and country with all his heart and courage. Even as a fugitive, David remains faithful to God and accomplishes all he can. As a result, people are drawn to him. When the opportunity finally arrives for him to step into the official leadership role, he has the support of those who know him. While you are hoping for some big opportunity to come along, are you being faithful in little things? Can you identify one thing you can do to make your (or someone else's) life better in the meantime?

1 CHRONICLES 13:1–16:43

DAVID AND THE ARK OF THE COVENANT

Setting Up the Section

Once anointed the next king of Israel, David had already waited a decade or so until God had determined King Saul's reign should come to an end. Saul tried persistently to capture and kill David, but it was Saul who died on the battlefield after drifting away from God. David was initially the king of Judah alone, but he eventually won over all the Israelites and received their endorsement as king. This section describes some of his early acts in his official leadership role.

13:1–14

AN EARLY MISSTEP

Throughout his writing, the author of Chronicles assumes that his readers are familiar with Samuel and Kings. Many in the twenty-first century, however, are not so knowledgeable, so a review of what happened to the ark of the covenant is in order.

The ark's usual location is in the tabernacle, the portable center of worship used by the Israelites as they traveled. At times, however, Moses had taken the ark into battles because it reminded the people of God's presence and power. They had no king, so it was the Lord Himself who led them out of Egypt, around the walls of Jericho, and into the promised land.

But after being in the land for a while, the people fail to acknowledge God's leadership and everyone did as they wanted (Judges 21:25). Consequently, God allows Israel's enemies to overpower them so they will turn back to Him. In one such instance, when the Philistines are the opposing force, the Israelites decide to carry the ark into battle with them as Moses and Joshua had done previously. But God was not fighting for his disobedient people that day, and the ark was captured (1 Samuel 4:1–11).

However, the newly acquired ark is the source of nothing but trouble for the Philistines, and they soon decide to send it back to Israel (1 Samuel 5–6). Some of the Israelites unwisely decide to look inside it while they have the opportunity, and a plague breaks out that kills many of them. Afterward the ark is taken to a nearby house, and a person is consecrated to care for it. There it remained for twenty years (1 Samuel 6:21–7:1).

Saul had shown little if any interest in the ark (1 Chronicles 13:3), but David has the highest respect for this holy object that symbolized the presence of God. Having had just established Jerusalem as the capital city of the nation, David wants to bring the ark there to be in the heart of the land and the hearts of the people.

David anticipates that moving the ark will be a time of great celebration and joy. He assembles the Israelites for the procession (13:5–6). The ark is placed on a new cart, and the journey begins as the people celebrate in music and song (13:8).

But a tragic event brings the festivities to an abrupt end. Crossing a threshing floor, the oxen stumbles and it looks as if the ark might topple. One of the two people accompanying the ark, a man named Uzzah, instinctively reaches out to steady it. But as soon as he touches the ark, he is struck dead (13:9–10).

The ark of the covenant had been designed to be carried by the priests on poles, which were not to be detached (Exodus 25:10–16). The Philistines, in returning the ark to Israel, had transported it on a cart—the method adopted by those in David's processional. Had the Israelites used the intended mode of transportation, instability would not have been an issue.

David becomes angry toward God. The name of the place where Uzzah died becomes Perez Uzzah. The usual translation, "outbreak against Uzzah," is mild compared to the original Hebrew, which suggests an attack on someone by an enemy. David was indeed angry, but he was also afraid of God (1 Chronicles 13:12)—not the reverential "fear of the LORD" that scripture frequently refers to, but a more literal sense of terror. This incident revised his concept of God.

Rather than continue toward Jerusalem, David has the ark rerouted to a nearby house, the home of Obed-edom (13:13–14), where it remains for three months. While the ark is there, the blessings of God are evident on Obed-edom and his entire household. It is evident that God did not object to the moving of the ark to Jerusalem, but He had been very clear about the penalty for breaching the holiness of the ark, the symbol of His presence. When properly transported, not even those assigned to moving the ark would look at it or touch it (Numbers 4:15, 20). Uzzah's action, though spontaneous and apparently well-intentioned, was still an offense to God that proved fatal.

📖 14:1–17

DAVID'S FAME BEGINS TO SPREAD

Before continuing the story of the ark, the Chronicler inserts a few interesting facts about David's early experiences as king. One of David's tasks was to build his living quarters. To help with the construction of the palace, David enlists the assistance of Hiram, king of Tyre (14:1). It is the beginning of an alliance that will carry on though the reign of Solomon.

Critical Observation

Some people use the example of David's association with Hiram as an illustration of how believers might benefit by going beyond Christian circles in their daily lives. By hiring the most qualified people to do the best possible work, God can be honored in a variety of ways.

At this point in his life, David is beginning to see things from God's perspective. He doesn't take for granted his position as king. Rather, he sees that God is using him for the good of the nation (14:2).

Still, this doesn't mean David is completely on track with God. The Chronicler notes that David continues to take more wives and have children by them (14:3–7). Because little, if any, editorial comment accompanies the statement, some people conclude that God must have endorsed David's behavior. This is not necessarily the case; however, the Mosaic Law does not prohibit polygamy. Instead, it regulates it (Exodus 21:7–11). God had specified, long before a king ever sat on a throne in Israel, that their king must not take many wives (Deuteronomy 17:17). God's model from creation had been to unite one man with one woman in a marriage relationship. The Chronicler is reporting the facts about David, but not necessarily endorsing them.

The Philistines continue to be a threat to Israel. Imagine the Philistines' surprise when David becomes Israel's king. It hadn't been so long before that David and his followers were living in a Philistine city and even going out to march (or pretending to) against Israel (1 Samuel 27:1–6; 29). Some had suspected his true convictions, while others had considered him a genuine ally. But they *all* knew his well-deserved reputation as a soldier and military leader, and now they are marching out to do battle against him.

David knew the Philistines and their tactics as well as anyone, but still he stops to consult God before deciding to fight. God gives him the go-ahead, and David and his men soundly defeat the Philistines (1 Chronicles 14:8–12). The Philistines had carried their gods into battle with them but left them behind when fleeing the Israelites, so David's men collect and burn them.

Later the Philistines regroup and attack again. David doesn't take anything for granted or make the assumption that he will again defeat them. He once more inquires of God. The Lord tells him to go ahead and fight, but He provides David with a completely different battle plan than before. David's army positions itself in an unexpected location, and God uses the sound of marching in the balsam trees in two ways: as a signal to attack and as a signal that God and His heavenly army are moving into the battle. David does just as God instructs and again wins a resounding victory. As a result, David's reputation spreads throughout the land—not just as a mighty warrior, but also as someone with a strong spiritual relationship with God.

📖 **15:1–16:6**

THE ARK IS CARRIED TO JERUSALEM

Prior to its capture by the Philistines, the ark had been located in Shiloh, tended to by Eli the priest and his family (1 Samuel 4:4). But now that Jerusalem had been established as Israel's capital, David sets up a temporary tent there to house the ark. The tabernacle that Moses had used in the wilderness was also still in use, located in Gibeon (1 Chronicles 16:39–40), a town in Benjamin, northeast of Jerusalem.

David had apparently used the interval of time since his first attempt to move the ark to determine what he had done wrong. This time he allows no one but the Levites to handle the transportation of the ark (15:2), using God's guidelines rather than his own.

He isn't going to make the same mistake twice. He recruits Levites from various families to participate (15:3–11).

David's anger toward and fear of God seem to have abated by now. He makes no excuses for his previous failure. He appears ready to right his mistake and move forward (15:12–15).

Again, worship is an integral element planned for moving the ark toward Jerusalem. Singers are appointed to sing joyful songs with musical accompaniment. And this is no ad hoc group; everyone has specific assignments, and the leader is skilled at what he does (15:16–24).

In addition to the worship music is the aspect of sacrifice. As the priests methodically progress toward Jerusalem with the ark, every six steps they stop and two animals are offered to God (2 Samuel 6:13).

David isn't just watching the processional; he is actively participating. The account in 2 Samuel says that David "danced before the LORD with all his might" (2 Samuel 6:14), to the dismay of one of his wives. Michal finds his behavior inappropriate for a king (2 Samuel 6:20) and despises David in her heart (1 Chronicles 15:29).

Demystifying 1 Chronicles

Michal was the daughter of King Saul, and David's first wife. Saul had given Michal to David as his wife, although Saul actually hoped that David would be killed attempting to acquire the unusual dowry asked for Michal (1 Samuel 18:20–27). When David was forced to flee Saul and leave Michal behind, Saul gave her to a man named Palti as his wife. Palti loved Michal, probably more than David ever did. But when David eventually gained the throne after Saul's death, he sent for Michal. Palti followed her, weeping all the way, but was sent back home alone (2 Samuel 3:13–16). After Michal's scolding of David for dancing, she remained childless for the rest of her life (2 Samuel 6:20–23).

But David's joy could not be contained. When the ark arrived and was positioned in the tent that David had provided, more offerings were made as the people gathered (16:1–2). David realized that he had been blessed by God, and he wanted to share those blessings with the people around him; so he gave everyone a gift of bread, dates, and a raisin cake (16:3).

Levites were appointed for regular petition, thanksgiving, and praise of God (16:4–6). In essence, their job was to remember and commemorate what God had done. Music would continue to be an essential element of worship.

DAVID'S EXPRESSION OF THANKSGIVING

David is credited with at least half of the songs in the biblical book of Psalms. Much of his psalm of thanks recorded in 1 Chronicles is also found in Psalms 96, 105, and 106:

1 Chronicles 16:8–22	Psalm 105:1–15
1 Chronicles 16:23–33	Psalm 96:1–13
1 Chronicles 16:34–36	Psalm 106:1, 47–48

David's challenge to his listeners isn't merely to be content with making a personal acknowledgment of God in their lives. Although one's worship should certainly entail thanksgiving, petition, and praise, it should also include telling the nations what God has done (1 Chronicles 16:8). In other places, God's people are called to be a light unto the Gentiles, and David confirms that goal here. For believers to proclaim the name of God means to interact with other people and explain what they have discovered about God's character and what it means to know Him.

Critical Observation

Bible translators help readers distinguish the original intent of the writers when referring to God. When the publishers print LORD (in small capital letters), it signifies the *name* of God (Yahweh). When they print *Lord*, it refers to God's *title* as lord or master. God's name indicates action: *Yahweh* means "the becoming one." When combined with other words, a variety of names for God are formed. For example:

Yahweh-Jireh	"God will provide"
Yahweh-Rophe	"God heals"
Yahweh-Nissi	"God, my banner"
Yahweh-M'Kaddesh	"God who sanctifies"
Yahweh-Shalom	"God is peace"
Yahweh-Tsidkenu	"The Lord our righteousness"
Yahweh-Rohi	"God my shepherd"
Yahweh-Shammah	"God is there"
Yahweh-Yeshua	"The Lord has become our salvation"

David expresses thanks for a number of things. He acknowledges Israel's inheritance of the land of Canaan. In another psalm he attests that the earth is the Lord's (Psalm 24:1–2), and he is thankful that God had provided the Israelites with their homeland (1 Chronicles 16:11–18). David is also thankful for God's protection of His people. They had been frequently outnumbered and occasionally displaced, yet they were still around and going strong, thanks to the provisions of the Lord (16:19–22).

When David tells the people to give God glory and strength (16:23–29), he is speaking of serving Him with all their ability. The day would come when everyone—all the earth, the nations, and the land (16:30–33)—would acknowledge the sovereignty of God. When David finishes proclaiming his psalm, all the people can do is endorse everything he has said (16:36).

With the ark in its new and special location in Jerusalem, and the tabernacle still in operation in Gibeon, there are now two primary centers of worship. David ensures that both places are staffed with competent and attentive spiritual leaders (16:37–42). Consequently, this is a period when two high priests are designated: Zadok is the priest in charge of the tabernacle, and David appoints Abiathar to attend to the ark in Jerusalem (18:16).

This had been big day for Israel. The ark was not only back in their land, but it had finally been reestablished in a place of prominence. Their new king was showing spiritual strength that the former king had lacked. And David would continue to inspire his people throughout the early years of his reign.

Take It Home

How often do you hear of someone rejecting God or walking away from his or her faith after a spiritual setback? It's as if any little disappointment becomes a justification for blaming God and giving up. Even David—a man after God's own heart—had similar moments. After Uzzah died while transporting the ark, David was devastated, and it was three months before he returned to the task. But because he did, he brought great joy to all of Israel. His example of willingness to humble himself before God, and his determination to serve, should inspire more people to persevere whenever their spiritual journey gets a little bumpy.

1 CHRONICLES 17:1–20:8

DAVID THE WARRIOR

Setting Up the Section

David has become king, united the nation, moved the ark to Jerusalem, and built his palace. He is becoming a popular leader, respected by the people. Now he has a desire to provide a more permanent and fitting home for the ark. It sounds like a good idea at first, but God has other plans.

📖 17:1–27

DAVID'S PLAN AND GOD'S RESPONSE

After David constructs a palace for himself and places the ark of the covenant in a special tent, he feels he needs to do more to honor God. He mentions his idea to Nathan the prophet, who thinks it is an admirable idea. In fact, it seems that Nathan automatically assumes God will endorse the idea, and he tells David to go ahead before he even consults the Lord (17:1–2).

That same night, however, God speaks to Nathan, telling him that David isn't the right person to build a temple to house the ark. Just because it appears to have been a good thing to do doesn't mean it is the will of God.

Later, as David recalls the story, he explains that God had declared that the one who builds His house should not be someone who had shed as much blood as David has (28:2–3). As a warrior, David had killed hundreds, if not thousands, of people (1 Samuel 18:27). Rather than having a temple constructed by those hands of violence, God reserves that right for a person of peace: David's son, Solomon. Keep in mind that this is not an ethical judgment on God's part. David is the one who completes the conquest at God's command, and it is only then that the temple which symbolizes stability can be built. Thus the son of the conquest completer, whose name means "Peace," should build it.

Besides, God shows little concern of having a house of cedar in which to live (1 Chronicles 17:4–6). The Lord had always been mobile, leading His people and living among them. He moved from one site to another as he led the Israelites. And just because they had settled in the promised land didn't mean that God would be any less active.

Critical Observation

The translation in some Bible versions may seem to suggest that God moved from one tent of worship to another, or from one tabernacle to another. That is not the intended interpretation. Rather, in the five hundred or more years that the tabernacle had been in existence, surely portions of it had worn out and had been replaced. But the Lord's presence with the Israelites had remained consistent.

In the first century, when John wrote that "the Word was made flesh, and dwelt among us" (John 1:14 KJV), his use of the word *dwelt* suggested a tabernacle or tent. So the presence of God has included, but has not been limited to, a tent in the wilderness, the temple that would replace the tabernacle, and the person of Jesus Christ. Today the residence of God is not in a building, but in believers (1 Corinthians 3:16).

Rather than expecting David to build Him a house, God said He would set David over a house (1 Chronicles 17:10–14). God had been with David all along, from shepherd to king (17:7–8). Under David's leadership, all of God's people were being blessed (17:9–10). And David's house would continue.

Like so many other prophetic passages, this promise of God has two intended fulfillments: one in the near future and a second that is more long-range. David's house will continue first through his son, Solomon, who will become the next king. In fact, the long series of kings of Judah will be from the Davidic line—an ongoing continuation of his "house." But beyond that, of course, is the anticipation of the Messiah who is to come from the lineage of David and who will sit on the throne and rule forever (17:14).

After Nathan delivers God's message (17:15), David is humbled. He realizes he has failed at times, and he feels unworthy to receive such abundant blessings from God. Yet David rightly acknowledges that the Lord is a God of grace who gives His people gifts, not because of their goodness, but because of *His* goodness (17:16–19).

God had chosen Israel to be His people, but not because they were more worthy than others. They were special only because the Lord chose to work through them. It had been clear from the beginning that the Israelites were a stiff-necked people (Deuteronomy 9:6) without adequate righteousness of their own, yet God graciously provided for them and lead them to the promised land.

If taken out of context, David's final response (1 Chronicles 17:23–27) might sound excessively bold. But David is only agreeing to the things that God has already promised him; he is affirming what God has said. It is because of his knowledge of God's will for his life that David can pray with such boldness.

DAVID'S MILITARY ACHIEVEMENTS

David's skill as a warrior is evident throughout his career. As king, he is a natural leader against Israel's enemies. One major accomplishment is his subjugation of the Philistines (18:1), who had been a recurring problem ever since Israel had entered the promised land.

The Moabites had also been an occasional enemy of Israel, even though their histories had frequently overlapped. The Moabites were descendants of Lot, originating from an incestuous relationship between Lot and his older daughter shortly after their narrow escape from the destruction of the city of Sodom (Genesis 19:36–37). David has strong ties to Moab: His great-grandmother is Ruth, who accompanied Naomi back from Moab. But since the Moabites continue to oppose Israel, David defeats them, and they offer tribute to him as his subjects (1 Chronicles 18:2).

The Edomites (18:12–13) are an opponent of Israel with a history going all the way back to the person of Israel (Jacob). The Edomites are Esau's descendants; the original tensions between Jacob and Esau continue between their offspring.

The Arameans are another adversary that keep afflicting the Israelites. David defeats them (again in great numbers) and erects garrisons in their territory (18:5–6), as he had done in Edom (18:13).

David was victorious over all these persistent foes of Israel because God was with him (18:6, 13). After conquering large numbers of enemy soldiers (18:3–4), David takes steps to minimize future conflict with the same groups. Establishing garrisons and demanding tribute kept such nations in line. He also hamstrung enemy horses—a practice that essentially eliminates their effectiveness in war yet allows them to live and serve a peaceful purpose.

David also begins to accumulate many valuable items from spoils of war, tributes received, and gifts from those who want to ally with him (18:7–11). He dedicates those assets to the Lord. Although David has not been allowed to build a temple for God, he is preparing for it. Solomon will later use the materials David is acquiring (18:8).

As the nation of Israel grows and prospers, the governmental structure begins to grow as well (18:14–17). David's nephew, Joab, is still over the army. Abishai's son, Ahimelech, has taken over as the high priest who attends to the ark; Zadok still serves at the tabernacle. The Cherethites (Kerethites) and Pelethites are David's royal bodyguards—the equivalent of a president's secret service personnel.

THE AMMONITE INCIDENT

David is a proven warrior, yet he doesn't see the need to fight when diplomacy will work just as well. He had formed an alliance with Nahash, the king of the Ammonites. When David hears of the death of Nahash, he sends a delegation of his men to express condolences to Nahash's son, Hanun.

Hanun's advisors, however, are suspicious and give Hanun some bad advice. They feel that the visit of David's men is only a ruse to allow Israel to spy on Ammon in preparation of overthrowing the country. The Ammonites treat David's men with the utmost disdain, utterly humiliating them by shaving off half of each man's beard and cutting off the bottoms of their garments so that the men's buttocks are exposed (2 Samuel 10:4; 1 Chronicles 19:4). A beard was a sign of masculinity at the time, which made the Ammonite insult intentional and personal.

David's delegation doesn't even want to return to Jerusalem out of shame. They send word to David about what has happened, and he sends back instructions for them to remain in Jericho until their beards have grown back (1 Chronicles 19:5). But David isn't going to ignore such an offense.

It doesn't take the Ammonites long to sense that they have riled David. They have become "a stench in David's nostrils" (19:6 NIV). They send immediately for Aramean (Syrian) mercenaries—thirty-two thousand additional chariots and charioteers to supplement their own large army. But David and his men are up to the challenge.

The Israelites divide into two forces: one led by Joab (the regular army commander) and a second commanded by his brother, Abishai. While Joab deals with the outer circle of Arameans, Abishai confronts the Ammonites. Each brother agrees to back up the other if the need arises (19:10–13).

As soon as the fighting starts, the Arameans quickly begin to flee, leaving the Ammonites on their own. The Ammonites immediately retreat into the safety of Rabbah, their capital city (19:14–15), while the Arameans recruit more of their countrymen to stand against the Israelites. The combined forces of the Arameans face off against David's army, and this time the entire Aramean army is defeated. They lose tens of thousands of their soldiers, including their army commander (19:16–19). As a result, they surrender and become David's subjects, effectively ending the Ammonite/Aramean alliance.

Meanwhile, the Ammonites remain within the protection of their city. They have weather on their side (for now) because fighting was usually suspended during the winter (rainy) season. (Chariots couldn't very well navigate in muddy terrain.)

But spring comes soon enough, and Joab begins a siege of Rabbah. The Chronicler provides a short note that David remains in Jerusalem (20:1), but this is an important fact in light of the account provided in 2 Samuel 11. It is during this time that David, while his men are all out on the battlefield, is passing time by walking on the palace roof and happens to see Bathsheba. And this is the battle where, after he unintentionally impregnates Bathsheba, David arranges to have her husband killed (2 Samuel 11:14–17).

Demystifying 1 Chronicles

Why does the Chronicler omit such a significant story as David's affair with Bathsheba? A couple of good reasons have been suggested. First, the focus of Chronicles is different than that of Samuel and Kings. And a second reason is simply that the people would have been well aware of David's story from the previous writings, and the repetition was not necessary. The Chronicler certainly isn't trying to gloss over or minimize the sins of David. He has already pointed out David's frustration while moving the ark (13:9–13) and his many wives (14:3–6), and he will soon detail an even more grievous sin (21:1–22:1).

David's sin has already been duly (and thoroughly) described in scripture. The Chronicler is not inspired to repeat it. Like a parent talking about a child, he chooses to dwell primarily on the positive qualities of his subject. David had sinned, repented, and confessed. God had forgiven him and no longer held his sin against him.

While David remained in Jerusalem, Joab had neutralized the threat of the Ammonite army. But when the city was ready to fall, Joab summoned David to come lead the final charge and receive credit for the victory. The Ammonite king had a magnificent (though hardly functional) crown made of gold and precious stones that weighed seventy-five pounds. The crown was removed from the Ammonite king and placed on David's head. David acquired much other plunder as well, and he put the conquered people to work doing common labor, thus adding the Ammonites to the list of peoples ruled by Israel.

📖 **20:1–8**

SUBJUGATING THE PHILISTINES

The Chronicler has already said that in time David subdues the Philistines (18:1). Here he provides a few brief details of that process.

No physical heights are recorded for the Philistine warriors singled out in this passage, but it is reasonable to believe that Goliath is not the only giant among the Philistines. Giants are mentioned prior to the Flood (Genesis 6:4) and afterward (Genesis 14:4–5; Deuteronomy 3:11). The group of Philistines are identified as Rephaites (1 Chronicles 20:4) or descendants of Rapha (20:8)—a line of large people who continued through the time of the early Philistines. It is conceivable that the two lines intermarried and produced others like Goliath, who stood more than nine feet tall.

Goliath's brother is one of the specific Philistines mentioned (20:5). The shaft of Lahmi's spear is likened to a weaver's rod, which is the same description given for Goliath's spear (1 Samuel 17:7). Another huge man taunts the Israelites, and David's nephew kills him.

When Goliath first challenged the Israelites, it had taken six weeks or so before he could convince even a single Israelite soldier to confront him (1 Samuel 17:16). After David kills Goliath, David's faith and courage became legendary. But more than that, it was also inspirational and motivational. The soldiers are no longer sitting around waiting for David to act on their behalf. In this passage, at least three others become legendary giant-killers in their own right.

Take It Home

Not everyone will have the exceptional levels of faith and confidence in God that David had as he went out to fight Goliath. However, more people in today's church should be inspired by David's men who, once they saw God at work, stepped up and got personally involved. It's far too easy to sit back and watch others deal with the "giant" problems that confront the church when it would be much more productive to take a step of faith and act personally. Can you think of a situation or opportunity where your personal involvement might make a significant impact?

1 CHRONICLES 21:1–22:19

THE SIGNIFICANCE OF THE TEMPLE SITE

David's Offense	21:1–8
The Immediate Consequence of David's Offense	21:9–17
The Long-Range Results of David's Offense	21:18–22:1
Plans for the Temple	22:2–19

Setting Up the Section

With only a few exceptions, everything the Chronicler has said about David so far has been positive and uplifting. He chose to omit the story of David's affair with Bathsheba and subsequent murder of her husband—the sin that most people appear to be familiar with. But David has another serious breach of faith that puts his nation at risk, and that event is included in this section.

📄 **21:1–8**

DAVID'S OFFENSE

When David first becomes king over all of Israel, it seems as if nothing can stand in his way. No enemy is too powerful for him, not even those who repeatedly defeated Israel in past battles. Under David's leadership, Israel's boundaries continue to expand and the people prosper. Yet even though David is stronger than any external enemy, he is still vulnerable internally. His affair with Bathsheba—not mentioned in Chronicles—is one example. The author chooses to record another as well.

At first it may be unclear as to what David has done wrong. As the leader of the nation, he takes a census of the people (21:1–2). Moses had previously numbered the people as they set out on their wanderings (Numbers 1:1–4) and again at the end of their journey (Numbers 26:1–4). Moses, however, was acting under a direct command of God. In contrast, the Chronicler attributes David's motive to the action of Satan (1 Chronicles 21:1). David is overseeing a time of unprecedented national security, and there is no real need to know the exact number of people. Joab's response to David's plan (21:3) confirms that it appears wrong. David's problem seems to be a matter of pride, of placing confidence in his military instead of in the Lord. Whatever David's inner motivation, it is clear that he later recognizes and acknowledges his sin (21:8).

Demystifying 1 Chronicles

Sometimes people point out the differences between the way this story is introduced in 2 Samuel to here in 1 Chronicles. The author of Samuel says that because God is angry with Israel (the reason was not provided), He tells David to take a census (2 Samuel 24:1). The Chronicler, however, writes that it is Satan who incites David's action (1 Chronicles 21:1). This is not actually a contradiction. Scripture clearly attests that God does not tempt anyone (James 1:13). But God can withdraw His control of a situation, allowing Satan to step in. In this case, David succumbs to temptation. As a result, God is then able to deal with David's pride as well as chasten the nation of Israel.

David had surrounded himself with good people, but in this case he does not take the advice of one of his closest counselors. It was against Joab's better judgment to go out to conduct the census. It is no small task, requiring almost ten months (2 Samuel 24:8). At last count, Joab has a total of 1,100,000 fighting men in the northern tribes of Israel and 470,000 men in Judah. (The numbers don't match exactly with the account in 2 Samuel 24:9, perhaps because they are rounded in one account, or because the count was never finalized.)

Yet even after all the time he devotes to the task, Joab does not complete it. He numbers most of the tribes, but does not count Levi or Benjamin. The Levites are omitted because their concerns are spiritual, not military (Numbers 1:47–53). And Joab apparently never got to the tribe of Benjamin because God confronted David before Joab finished (1 Chronicles 27:24). Besides, Joab never did feel quite right about conducting the census (21:6).

📖 21:9–17

THE IMMEDIATE CONSEQUENCE OF DAVID'S OFFENSE

Joab's opinion proves correct. God is indeed angry with David. One impressive characteristic about David, however, is how quick he is to repent and confess after being chastened by God. King Saul had looked for excuses and tried to blame others for his shortcomings, but David takes responsibility for his actions and immediately seeks to make things right with God again.

Even though David is sincerely sorry, and even though God will forgive him completely, sin has consequences. In this case, God allows David to *choose* which of three options he prefers. David could (1) withstand three years of famine in the land, (2) endure three months of defeat at the hands of his enemies, or (3) experience the angel of the Lord bringing plague on the people for three days (21:9–12). God presents these options to

David through the prophet Gad, someone who had advised David well in times past (1 Samuel 22:3–5).

David reasons that putting his future in God's hands is better than any other option (1 Chronicles 21:13). Still, three days under the judgment of God is a terrible thing. As soon as the plague falls on Israel, seventy thousand people die. The angel of the Lord then stands between heaven and earth, with a sword drawn to destroy Jerusalem (21:16). It is at this point that David's insight into God's character proves valuable. God deems that enough suffering has taken place, and He relents.

Critical Observation

Scripture says that God is not a man, so He does not lie nor repent, and He does whatever He says He will do (Numbers 23:19). Yet in this instance, God does not complete the entire three days of plagues that He said would happen. While we can count on every *promise* of God to come to pass, David's experience is an ideal example of the mercy of God. The Lord does not inflict on humankind all that it deserves. Scripture also reminds us that, "Through the LORD's mercies we are not consumed, because his compassions fail not. They are new every morning; great is [His] faithfulness" (Lamentations 3:22–23 NKJV).

When David sees the angel about to destroy Jerusalem, he takes full responsibility for the sin that has been committed and pleads with God to punish him rather than the people (21:17). David, it seems, still has the heart of a shepherd. He does not back down when faced with danger, because his sheep depend on him. In this case, the shepherd is attempting to protect the people under his leadership.

📖 21:18–22:1

THE LONG-RANGE RESULTS OF DAVID'S OFFENSE

God again communicates to David through the prophet Gad. This time the message is much better than the previous one. David is to build an altar on the spot where the angel had stopped (21:18). The trouble is that David doesn't own the land. The angel had been halted while standing on the threshing floor of a man named Ornan (or Araunah). In fact, Ornan and his four sons are in the process of threshing wheat when they see the angel, and the sons immediately run to hide (21:20).

When Ornan sees King David approaching, he quickly leaves the threshing floor and goes to meet him (21:21). David tries to buy the threshing floor, but Ornan offers it to him at no charge—not only the structure, but also oxen for the offering, equipment that can be burned for a fire, and wheat for an accompanying grain offering (21:22–23). David refuses, however, explaining that he will not offer God something that costs him nothing. So David arranges to pay Ornan for the site.

The amount that David pays is another discrepancy between the account in 2 Samuel (fifty shekels of silver) and the one in 1 Chronicles (six hundred shekels of gold). But it is reasonable to assume that, as specified in 2 Samuel 24:24, the lower amount only applies to the threshing floor and oxen. The greater total (1 Chronicles 21:25) is for the site, which likely included the surrounding land.

David builds an altar on the spot and makes offerings to God. When he calls on God, the Lord responds with fire from heaven falling on the altar (21:25–26). In conjunction with this miraculous sign, the angel returns his sword to its sheath (21:27–28).

David seems to realize that this is an appropriate place to worship God. Even though the tabernacle is still in Gibeon at this time, David is afraid to go there because of the judgment of God, so God tells him to make sacrifices right where he is. David continues to worship the Lord at the threshing floor of Ornan as he makes plans to construct a more permanent structure there (21:29–30).

▤ 22:2–19

PLANS FOR THE TEMPLE

David's isn't the first altar to be constructed in this location. As it happens, the threshing floor of Ornan is on the same spot where Abraham had traveled centuries earlier, intending to offer his son Isaac to God. It is the site where Solomon will soon build the temple (22:1). And roughly one thousand years later, Christ would be crucified approximately three blocks away at the location of Golgotha, in history's ultimate sacrifice.

David had been denied permission to build the temple for God. Some people might have taken that as a personal rejection and given up altogether, but David decides to do what he *could* do. He begins to gather the supplies he knows will be needed to construct the temple in order to give Solomon a head start. David's preparations are extensive (22:5). He collects enormous quantities of iron, bronze, and cedar logs, and he has stonecutters standing by, ready to go to work (22:2–4).

While the Chronicler continues to follow the life and exploits of David, from this point onward Solomon becomes a prominent figure as well. The building will come to be known as Solomon's Temple, but its construction was a team effort.

David is able to talk about his life's disappointments. Some people tend to dwell only on the things that have turned out well for them. But just as David is quick to confess his sins to God, he is apparently willing to also open up to others about his unfulfilled personal desires. His account to his son Solomon is one such example (22:6–10).

David is both supportive and encouraging as he charges Solomon to begin his task. He makes clear that as long as Solomon is careful to follow God's laws, he will find success in all he does.

Critical Observation

David's charge to Solomon (22:13) will not be the last challenge Solomon receives to be obedient. God Himself reminds Solomon of the importance of obedience on different occasions (1 Kings 3:14; 9:4–9; 2 Chronicles 7:17–22). But ultimately, Solomon will reject this wise advice, resulting in the deterioration of the kingdom that David worked so hard to establish and unite.

The quantities of precious metals that David gathers are overwhelming, translating roughly to be 3,750 tons of gold and 37,500 tons of silver. Other metals were so abundant they were not even measured (22:14–16).

David is a good leader. He doesn't just give Solomon the assignment of building the temple; he also enlists the support of all the people for his son's work. The people admire and support David, and he uses these good relationships to make things as smooth as possible for Solomon (22:17–19).

Take It Home

At this point it is a good idea to recall the opening lines of Psalm 127, a psalm attributed to Solomon: "Unless the LORD builds the house, its builders labor in vain. Unless the LORD watches over the city, the watchmen stand guard in vain" (NIV). Even though David and Solomon throw themselves wholeheartedly into the building of God's temple, they realize that God is the only one who deserves the credit. Can you think of things in your own life or ministry where you are actively involved, yet where the success cannot be explained other than the ongoing presence of God in what you are doing?

1 CHRONICLES 23:1–27:34

ORGANIZING PEOPLE TO SERVE IN THE KINGDOM

Organizing the Levites	23:1–32
Organizing the Priests	24:1–19
Organizing the Other, Non-Priestly Levites	24:20–31
Organizing the Singers	25:1–31
Organizing the Gatekeepers	26:1–19
Organizing the Other Temple Staff	26:20–32
Organizing the Soldiers	27:1–15
Organizing the Other National Leaders	27:16–34

Setting Up the Section

By this point in David's life, he is old and preparing to turn the kingdom over to Solomon. As plans for the temple construction are being completed, the human staffing is yet to be organized. In this section, David turns his attention to that job. While much of the content of 1 Chronicles has a corresponding version in Samuel or Kings, most of the content of this section is not found elsewhere.

📖 23:1–32

ORGANIZING THE LEVITES

The amount of work required at a permanent, full-time temple took a much larger staff than many realize. David has already gathered many of the physical materials Solomon will need to construct the temple, but he doesn't stop there. He next turns his attention to the human element—the people who will oversee the worship and day-to-day operations of the temple.

Solomon's ascension to the throne (23:1) will be more detailed in 1 Chronicles 28–29, but it is briefly mentioned here to show that David is not acting independently. The closing chapters of 1 Chronicles are not strictly chronological, but are laid out in a way to show that God's promise to build a house for David (17:10–14) is being fulfilled. To this end, the attempts of other family members to usurp the throne—and the resulting bloodshed (1 Kings 1–2)—are omitted by the Chronicler.

It may appear a bit strange to see David once again counting the people, because that same action had caused problems previously (1 Chronicles 21:1–8). This time, however, his motive is entirely different. Rather than lining up his fighting men to determine his military strength, now he is seeing how many people will qualify to serve in the temple. The Levites are one of the two tribes that hadn't been included in the previous census (21:6), so they are counted at this time—apparently late in David's life (23:27).

Traditionally, a priest or Levite had to be thirty years old before he was allowed to minister before the Lord, and he retired from service at age fifty (Numbers 4:1–3). David's count finds thirty-eight thousand Levites in that category. David assigns twenty-four thousand of them to supervise temple work. Six thousand others will serve as officials and judges; six thousand will be gatekeepers; and the final four thousand will be musicians. David even provides the instruments that are needed (1 Chronicles 23:5).

The Levites are subdivided into three smaller groups: the Gershonites, the Kohathites, and the Merarites (23:7–23). The Chronicler has already provided a similar breakdown in 6:16–30 and will do so again in 24:20–30. Each subgroup has specific duties to perform. The official priests, however, all come from the Kohathites—specifically, the line of Aaron. The other Levites assist the priests (23:28, 32).

A previous list of their jobs included guarding the facilities, opening the temple each morning, keeping up with the inventory, baking, mixing spices, playing music, and so forth (9:22–33). Here the Chronicler adds their ongoing responsibilities for caring for the temple's courtyards and side rooms, purifying the sacred objects, and offering praise to God every morning, evening, and during Sabbaths and festivals (23:28–32). The extent of the work is so demanding that David enlists additional help by lowering the age requirement from thirty to twenty (23:24–27).

📖 24:1–19

ORGANIZING THE PRIESTS

When the Chronicler begins to enumerate the line of people in the priesthood, beginning with Aaron (24:1–2), he briefly notes that Aaron's older sons, Nadab and Abihu, died before their father. Their deaths had been a tragic story from Israel's history, recounted numerous times in scripture. Nadab and Abihu had ministered in an inappropriate manner, and they were consumed by fire from the Lord (Leviticus 10:1–5). They had not yet had children of their own. Replacing Nadab and Abihu are two of Aaron's other sons, Eleazar and Ithamar (Leviticus 10:12; 1 Chronicles 24:2). Zadok, the priest who attends to the tabernacle, is a descendant of Eleazar. Ahimelech (son of David's other high priest, Abiathar) descended from Ithamar.

As it turns out, Eleazar has twice as many descendants as Ithamar, so lots are drawn to provide a fair and random assignment (24:3–5). A total of twenty-four families are available to serve (sixteen from Eleazar and eight from Ithamar). As the lots are cast, the assignments are duly recorded by Shemaiah, the scribe (24:6–19).

The priests' work is assigned in two-week shifts, so one full rotation lasts just about a year with each family serving once. (Later on, a shift is made to one-week commitments, with each family serving twice during the year.) The Chronicler provides no details as to the importance of the priesthood or the specific functions the priests perform, although his readers would have been familiar with such information.

Critical Observation

About half of the names of the family heads (24:6–19) are also names of priests who returned from the Babylonian exile or were active during the Maccabean era. The rest are found nowhere else in scripture. This observation, combined with the fact that the twenty-four-family division appears to be a later development of the Jewish priesthood (the date of its origin is uncertain), has given rise to the belief that Chronicles should have a date nearer the second century BC rather than during the time of Ezra (fifth century BC). There is no strong evidence for such an outlook, however.

📖 24:20–31

ORGANIZING THE OTHER, NON-PRIESTLY LEVITES

This list of the other descendants of Levi (24:20) is quite similar to the list in 23:7–23. For some unexplained reason, the author again lists the Kohathites (24:20–25) and Merarites (24:26–30), but not the Gershonites, and he adds one extra generation. Since this list follows the list of priests, these may have been the Levites specifically involved as priestly assistants.

Just as they had done for the assignments of the priests, David and his two high priests oversee the casting of lots to determine the responsibilities of the Levites. Every family receives equal treatment with no favoritism (24:31).

📖 **25:1–31**

ORGANIZING THE SINGERS

It's hard to miss the fact that music plays an integral part of Israelite worship. The Psalms (their hymnbook) are an extensive portion of scripture, centrally located in most Old Testaments. This portion of 1 Chronicles shows that such an emphasis on music is quite intentional. Much thought and planning went into the musical elements of Israel's worship life. The people weren't merely encouraged to sing; the music was modeled for them on a regular basis by gifted and well-trained Levites.

It might seem strange for David to work with the commanders of the army while assigning singing ministries (25:1). If indeed he did, it could indicate David's intent to combine the military and spiritual elements of his kingdom, with a goal of allowing each segment of his administration to influence and strengthen the other. However, a different usage of the Hebrew word would allow for a translation of "leaders of the Levites" rather than "commanders of the army"—a usage some scholars find more likely because of the preceding focus on the Levites.

Three key families are devoted to the music ministry: Asaph, Heman, and Jeduthun. The ministry of the singers/instrumentalists is clearly a musical one (25:1), yet their work is called *prophesying*. They are probably not foretelling the future as some of the prophets do, but rather forth-telling the mighty works of God through their music. Still, Heman is referred to as the king's *seer* (25:5), another word for *prophet*. (In other portions of scripture, the same title is applied to the other two: Asaph [2 Chronicles 29:30] and Jeduthun [2 Chronicles 35:15].)

Critical Observation

Of the three main families designated to serve as musicians, Heman appears to be the most prominent. In this section, only he is identified as a seer, and he has more than twice as many sons as either of the other two. Yet after the exile of Israel, references are found to the descendants of Asaph and Jeduthun, but there is no further mention of the descendants of Heman.

After being informed of the twenty-four divisions among the priestly families (24:7–18), it is interesting to note these three musical men have a total of twenty-four sons. Asaph has four sons (25:2); Jeduthun has six (25:3); and Heman has a whopping fourteen (25:4). Each of the twenty-four musical divisions is comprised of a twelve-person contingent (25:9–31), resulting in a total of 288 people (25:7). It appears likely that one group of musicians/singers is paired with one division of priests on each assignment at the temple.

Again, lots are cast to determine assignments. Perhaps singing didn't require as much training as some of the other areas of spiritual leadership. It is interesting to note that the musical positions are open to any qualified Levite—young or old, student or teacher (25:8).

ORGANIZING THE GATEKEEPERS

It is difficult to think of a contemporary job that compares to that of the temple gatekeepers. In one sense, they acted as ticket-takers at an amusement park or bouncers at a club. Entering the temple was a serious matter. There were sections where unauthorized people were prohibited from going, and the penalty for entering the forbidden areas was death (Numbers 3:10; 18:17). The gatekeepers not only served as security guards (9:22-27) but also as regular reminders to visitors and participants of the sanctity of the temple.

Compared to priests or the Levites who dealt with the holy items, the job of gatekeeper might not seem attractive, or even significant. But when viewed from a proper perspective, it is indeed a job that one might aspire to do (Psalm 84:10). The Chronicler never diminishes the roles of the gatekeepers in contrast to the groups he lists previously (1 Chronicles 26:12). He had already provided a list of the gatekeepers (9:17-27), and he reiterates their importance here.

Obed-edom (26:4) had been singled out in a previous story in scripture. After David first attempts to move the ark of the covenant to Jerusalem, and Uzzah dies trying to steady it on the shaky cart, David aborts his plans. The nearby home of Obed-edom had housed the ark for three months, during which time God blessed the people and possessions of the household (13:9-14). Obed-edom had also been blessed with many sons (26:4-5). Here Obed-edom heads up one of the three divisions of gatekeepers (26:4-8), the other two being overseen by Meshelemiah (26:1-3) and Hosah (26:10-11). As it works out, there are no representatives of the Gershonites involved in the temple gatekeeping, only Kohathites and Merarites (26:19).

Demystifying 1 Chronicles

Names that look odd to us may have been quite common in Old Testament times. Consequently, when we see a strange name that is used in different places, we may wrongly tend to presume that it is the same person, when instead it might be someone else with the same name. For example, the Asaph identified as one of the leaders of the singers in the previous chapter (25:1) *may* be the one mentioned in 26:1. Or the latter reference may be to a man named Ebiasaph, but using an abbreviation of his name. Similarly, some contend that one man named Obed-edom tended to the ark of the covenant (13:14), served as a musician (15:21), and was a part-time gatekeeper (15:18), while another man with the same name was a full-time gatekeeper (16:38; 26:4).

Casting lots is once more the method of determining which people will be assigned to each gate (26:13). The East Gate (26:14) is the primary entrance to the temple. It has two additional posts and requires more guards than the other sides (26:17). The Shalleketh Gate (26:16) is not mentioned anywhere else in scripture.

Only twenty-two jobs for gatekeepers are listed (26:17–18). However, these are probably the positions of the chief men (26:12). With four thousand gatekeepers available for service (23:5), each of the leaders probably had people who served *with* him.

📖 26:20–32

ORGANIZING THE OTHER TEMPLE STAFF

Unlike the unfamiliar and antiquated function of gatekeeper, the job of treasurer is more understandable to most people today. The Chronicler writes of two different areas requiring treasurers (26:20). The treasuries of the house of God refer to the usual storehouse of wealth for the temple.

The treasuries for the dedicated things are a collection of spoils of war that have been set aside for God (26:27–28). In the days of Joshua, God had given specific instructions that everything from the defeat of Jericho should be devoted to Him (Joshua 6:17–19, 24). Other of God's military leaders had apparently continued this practice on a voluntary basis. However, none of the specific examples from 1 Chronicles 26:28 are found in scripture, with the possible exception of Saul (1 Samuel 15:21).

A couple of places in this section raise questions of interpretation. The original Hebrew in 26:20 is translated: "As for the Levites, Ahijah was [in charge of the treasuries]." The sudden appearance of a man named Ahijah, with no explanation, seems too abrupt for some translators. When the passage was translated into Greek for the Septuagint, it was rendered, "Their fellow Levites were [in charge of the treasuries]." Scholars are still divided as to which is correct.

Another concern arises in 26:27, where the Chronicler speaks of repair to the temple. The passage still refers to David's involvement in conjunction with Solomon (26:31–32), so the temple would not even have been built at the time, much less be in need of repair. Some people suggest this is a clue that portions of the passage may have been added at a later date or perhaps that the word for *repair* requires a broader interpretation. (Some translations interpret the word as *upkeep*, or *maintenance*.)

What does come through clearly in the passage, however, is the leaders of the treasuries. There had been no Gershonites involved as gatekeepers, but the first recorded overseers of the temple treasuries are the descendants of Ladan (sometimes spelled Libni [6:17]), a Gershonite (26:21–22). The treasury leaders in the following list (26:24–26) are Kohathites. (A review of the list is previously provided in 23:12, 15–20.)

Four specific subgroups of Levites are mentioned in 26:23. No details are provided pertaining to the duties of the Uzzielites. The Amramites are in charge of the official temple treasuries (26:24–28).

The Izharites had similar responsibilities in areas out and away from the temple, in other parts of the nation. Some of their duties involved roles as judges (26:29).

The Hebronites were spread throughout the land in significant numbers: seventeen hundred in the western tribes and twenty-seven hundred on the east side of the Jordan River (26:30–32). This is one of the few times when Israel's theocracy works as it should—when the work of the king and the work of God are one and the same (26:30). David's fortieth year (26:31) will be his last as king.

ORGANIZING THE SOLDIERS

Some people examine 1 Chronicles 27 with a critical eye and point out that suddenly the writer says nothing about the temple and, for that matter, hardly mentions God. But in the context of all the lists of chapters 23–27, the concluding section about the military organization actually fits quite well. First David organizes the spiritual aspects of his kingdom, and then he turns his attention to the military.

The Lord had blessed David with a strong army that had made possible the current peace and prosperity in Israel and allowed anticipation of the temple. The army had played its part, but it couldn't take credit for all the victories—that credit went to God. The Babylonians had had one of the best armies on earth, and they had gone down in defeat to the Persians.

David had suffered by conducting a census of his army, perhaps out of military pride, but he had repented (21; 27:24). Now he places a proper perspective on his fighting men. As he gets closer to finalizing the plans for the temple, all of his leaders will be involved, both spiritual and military (28:1).

Many of the people David names to head divisions of the army are previously listed among the mighty men who had fought alongside him (11:10–47): Jashobeam (11:11; 27:2), Dodai (11:12; 27:4), Benaiah (11:22–25; 27:5), and others. Asahel and Joab (11:26; 27:7) had been close to David from the beginning. Twelve divisions are established, one to be on duty each month (27:1).

Twelve divisions of twenty-four thousand men each yields an army of 288,000 soldiers. That total may have been a potential maximum number, however, rather than the actual count. Based on the original language, it is appropriate, and perhaps preferable, to understand that each army division had twenty-four *units*, with each unit comprised of *up to* one thousand soldiers.

ORGANIZING THE OTHER NATIONAL LEADERS

Leaders of tribes weren't normally referred to as *officers* (27:16), and the exact job description that goes with the title is unknown. These people may have been appointees of David, initiating a transition between the former system of individual tribes to a more unified and centralized system of government. Most of those on the list are not mentioned elsewhere in scripture.

The tribal divisions are not traditional. Asher and Gad are omitted for some reason. The total remains at twelve, however, with the inclusion of Levi (27:17) and with Manasseh designated twice (27:20–21): once for the half-tribe on the western side of the Jordan River and again for the Transjordanian portion.

No numbers are designated for this section as had been done for previous sections. The Chronicler again brings up the problem of David's census, the consequences of which had prevented completion of the head count. Another of his reminders, however, is more positive—the promise God had made to Abraham to make his descendants (the Israelites) as numerous as the stars in the sky (Genesis 15:5). The Chronicler also clarifies that the soldiers he had previously mentioned (1 Chronicles 21:5) are all males older than twenty years.

Numerous historic journals are mentioned in scripture that have been lost to us today (or not yet discovered). For example, 1 and 2 Kings refer to the annals of the kings of Israel and the annals of the kings of Judah. The Chronicler mentions the annals of King David (27:24), which would have preceded those other books.

Last on David's series of lists (27:25–34) are overseers of various aspects of the king's business: storehouses, field hands, vineyards, herds and flocks, olive and fig crops, and so forth. One of the last names on the list, Ahithophel, needed to be replaced as the king's counselor (27:33–34), but the reason isn't explained here. Ahithophel had been one of the wisest people in Israel, and his advice was usually trusted without question (2 Samuel 16:23). Ahithophel also happened to be Bathsheba's grandfather (2 Samuel 11:3; 23:34). Even though he was David's top advisor, perhaps he harbored hard feelings after the affair between David and his granddaughter. Whether or not that was his motive, he sided with Absalom when Absalom tried to take the kingdom away from David. But after Absalom decided not to take Ahithophel's advice on a crucial matter, Ahithophel realized it would only be a matter of time until David regained control, so he went home and hanged himself (2 Samuel 17:1–14, 23).

The final name on the list, Joab (1 Chronicles 27:34), will also desert David eventually. Joab has a strong will and an ability to come out on top of any situation, even if his success requires someone else's demise. Sometime after Absalom's thwarted attempt to take over the kingdom (which Joab had personally ended [2 Samuel 18:9–15]), another of David's sons attempted to take control. This time Joab sides with Adonijah rather than respect David's wishes to pass the kingdom on to Solomon. As a result, Joab is eventually put to death (1 Kings 2:5–6, 28–35).

Take It Home

This section of 1 Chronicles shows an intentional and well-conceived plan to strengthen God's kingdom. All jobs are deemed important, whether spiritual or secular, public or private, urban or rural. David realizes that once the temple is built and becomes a center of Israel's life, support systems would need to be in place to ensure its success. The concept of the New Testament church, functioning as each member identifies and applies his or her God-given gifts, is similar. How does your job have the potential to contribute to the community of faith? Are your skills offered joyfully to God? Do you offer a service to fellow believers? How might you better serve God and others through your regular job?

1 CHRONICLES 28:1–29:30

DAVID'S FINAL DAYS

Setting Up the Section

David has put much thought and work into his organization of labor for the temple. In this section he is approaching the end of his life, so he calls together all the leaders he has appointed to gather their support for his son and Israel's next king, Solomon.

📄 28:1–21

CREATING SUPPORT FOR THE TEMPLE

As the Chronicler has shown, David is certainly not a perfect person. However, he is a person after God's own heart. He had made serious mistakes, but had repented and moved on with his life. His final words and actions in the closing chapters of 1 Chronicles show him to be, as always, someone with a desire to serve the Lord.

After all the appointments David had recently made (23–27), he gathers all the designated leaders (28:1) for a series of speeches. First he addresses the entire group (28:2–8). He was the greatest of Israel's kings, yet even at the close of his reign he considered the Israelites not his subjects, but rather, his brothers (28:2).

David had done much to prepare for the soon-to-be-constructed temple of the Lord, but he takes no credit for it. He makes it clear that God directed him all along the way. He wisely realizes that God is never confined to a building. The temple in Jerusalem would not be like other temples of the time, perceived as a residence for the god to which it was dedicated. Instead, it is built to honor God's name (28:3). God's throne and residence are in heaven, but the temple will be His footstool (28:2).

David reiterates his personal desire to build the temple and God's veto of his plans due to all the blood David had shed (28:3). Yet David feels honored and humbled to be a part of God's plan. Judah had not been the oldest son of Israel, David had not been the oldest son of Jesse, and Solomon is not the oldest son of David (28:4–5). But in each case, God chose the person for the task He had in mind. Solomon is God's choice to be the next king and the builder of His temple. After that, no subsequent king of Israel or Judah will be referred to as *chosen*.

The Chronicler had previously recorded a similar speech by David (22:5–19). In both cases, David addresses both Solomon and the leaders of Israel. In the prior instance, however, more of the emphasis was on Solomon. Here he spends more time attempting to prepare the Israelites to support their new king and new temple.

Critical Observation

Compared to the account in 1 Kings, the Chronicler's version of the transition between David and Solomon is extraordinarily different. Nowhere does he mention the frailty of David in his old age, the revolt by Adonijah, the desertion of Joab and others, the retribution of Solomon (as instructed by David), or any other negative aspect. The Chronicles account focuses on the Lord's designated chain of succession without including the human struggling involved.

David's speech repeatedly highlights obedience as a crucial element of the ongoing success of the kingdom. God will perpetuate Solomon's kingdom as long as the young king remains faithful (28:7, 9). Yet the imperative of obedience extends to the entire nation. As long as the people maintain their strong relationship with the Lord, He will bless their lives in the land He has given them, and the land will be an inheritance to their descendants (28:8).

The king turns his attention from the assembled crowd to address Solomon alone (28:9–10). He challenges his son to consider more than merely his actions. Solomon's success will depend on his wholehearted devotion to God, including his thoughts and motives. It appears, however, that later in life Solomon needs to verify this fact for himself. The book of Ecclesiastes, usually attributed to Solomon, describes the author's search for fulfillment through building projects, books, studies, material possessions, pleasure seeking, and more. None of those pursuits bring the joy he desires. The author's final conclusion is, "Fear God and keep His commandments, because this applies to every person" (Ecclesiastes 12:13 NASB).

David also reminds Solomon that he has been chosen for the task of building the temple. He challenges Solomon to be strong and to devote himself to the work (1 Chronicles 28:10). David will soon repeat these crucial imperatives to his son (28:20).

The plans David had prepared for the temple are not some vague, general concept. Just as God had given Moses detailed instructions for how to construct the tabernacle in the wilderness, the Spirit of God had worked through David to provide specifics for the temple to be built. The temple is far more than a one-room sanctuary. The plans include porches, storerooms, inner rooms, altars, treasury storehouses, and more. David has already seen to the divisions of the priests and Levites for all the areas of temple work (28:11–13).

The temple plans are so complete that David even specifies the designated weights of various implements: gold and silver lampstands, tables, forks, bowls, pitchers, dishes, and such (28:14–18). Especially important is the design of the golden angels with outspread wings that are to sit atop the ark of the covenant to shelter it (28:18). And lest there be any confusion about what David says should be done, he assures Solomon that everything is written down for him (28:19).

Demystifying 1 Chronicles

David's mention of "writing from the hand of the LORD" (28:19 NLT) sometimes gives rise to speculation. Since David's plans for the temple so closely parallel the plans Moses received for the tabernacle, it is interesting to note that some of the communication between Moses and the Lord was "written by the finger of God" (Exodus 31:18 NLT). There is no clear evidence to surmise that the *handwriting* in David's possession is God's, but what is certain is that the *content* of David's plans was received from the Lord and was written down for Solomon's benefit (1 Chronicles 28:19).

The construction of the temple is an enormous project, and Solomon is a young and inexperienced king, so David repeats his challenge to be strong and to get the work done (28:20). This time, however, he adds much assurance and encouragement. Far from being alone in this project, the entire nation is aligned behind Solomon—every willing person skilled in any craft (28:21). Much more importantly, however, is the confidence that God will be overseeing the project and will neither fail nor forsake Solomon until the work is complete.

29:1–9

FUNDING THE TEMPLE

David again appeals to the entire assembled group, imploring them to support their new, young, inexperienced king. No one in Israel had faced the magnitude of the task ahead of Solomon. This is no ordinary structure, no stately palace for a regal human occupant. More than that, this will be the temple of their unseen, all-powerful, loving, and merciful God (29:1).

No one knows better than David the scope of the project ahead of Solomon. In addition to the detailed plans David is handing over, he has also been accumulating incredible quantities of materials that will be needed. The kingdom treasuries are capable of providing great quantities of gold, silver, bronze, iron, wood, stone, and precious gems (29:2). In addition to such an impressive amount of national treasure, David donates his vast personal wealth: 110 tons of gold and 260 tons of silver (29:3–5).

David also encourages the people to contribute, and their response reflects their enthusiasm. Inspired by the example of their leaders, they give freely and sincerely, resulting in a one-day commitment of 5,360 tons of valuable materials needed for the temple (29:6–9). This is in addition to the staggering 41,250 tons of gold and silver (and bronze too abundant to count) that David had previously provided (22:14). (A *daric* [29:7] was a gold coin of Persia, first used around the reign of Darius I [522–486 BC].)

Critical Observation

The people's willing and generous giving is another parallel between the temple and the Old Testament tabernacle. After Moses made known the needs for the construction of the tabernacle, the people had come day after day with contributions until Moses had to issue an order for them to stop bringing their gifts (Exodus 36:2–7). Similarly, the Israelites pour out abundant financial support for the temple.

📖 29:10–20

DAVID'S RESPONSE

David is overjoyed to see such a response. He responds to all the giving with a prayer (29:10–19). Despite all David has done, and as important a project as the building of the temple, neither David nor the temple are prominent in the prayer. Indeed, David acknowledges his own insignificance (29:14) as he maintains a focus on the attributes of God. Certainly, without God's provision for His people, none of their gifts would have been possible (29:16).

David looks back with thankfulness to Abraham, Isaac, and Jacob (29:18) and at how God had established His people. Then David turns his vision to the future, asking for God's blessing on the reign of Solomon (29:19).

After leading the prayer, David instructs everyone assembled to join in praise to God. It has been a festive occasion, yet they all end the day's events by bowing low and offering their adoration to God (29:20).

📖 29:21–25

THE CORONATION OF SOLOMON

The worship continues the next day with a long series of sacrifices offered to God: one thousand bulls, one thousand rams, one thousand male lambs, and numerous other offerings (29:21). The sacrifices are accompanied with feasting, and it is a day of great joy.

Such is the mood as Solomon is anointed and acknowledged as their new king. David's high priest, Zadok, continues to serve in the position and is again anointed to acknowledge his role under Solomon (29:22). We know from 1 Kings 1–2 that the transition from David to Solomon is not as smooth as they may have wished, but the Chronicler chooses to focus on the support that Solomon receives, not the opposition (29:24).

It is soon clearly evident that Solomon is indeed God's choice as king based on the prosperity throughout Israel during his reign (29:25).

📄 **29:26–30**

THE DEATH OF DAVID

It is not known how long David continues to live after Solomon's coronation, but it probably isn't very long. His life is briefly summarized as 1 Chronicles concludes. He ruled a total of forty years, at first just as Judah's leader, but soon as the king of the united nation of Israel.

David had received three often-mentioned blessings of God: long life, wealth, and honor (29:28). And he lived to see Solomon begin to rule in his own right.

The sources cited by the Chronicler (the records of Samuel the seer, the records of Nathan the prophet, and the records of Gad the seer) most likely include the parallel account of 1 Samuel and possibly Kings. Samuel, Nathan, and Gad were all involved at various critical stages of David's life and rule as king.

The reign of Solomon will be impressive, but in the long line of kings until the fall of Jerusalem, no other leader will surpass David's lifelong reputation as a faithful king to his people and a devoted man of God.

Take It Home

David was a man who, during his lifetime, was guilty of sexual indiscretions, coped with intense family turmoil, and had his share of spiritual questions and dilemmas. Yet at the end of his life, those who had observed him had nothing but good to say about him. In spite of his shortcomings, David remained a person after God's own heart, quick to confess to the wrongs he had done and attempt to put them right. Too often people try to cover up the mistakes they have made and their transgressions against God and others. Can you think of any such instance in your own life, where an unresolved issue has resulted in guilt, embarrassment, or other undesirable emotions? If so, what steps can you take to deal with the problem and experience the freedom and joy that David came to know?

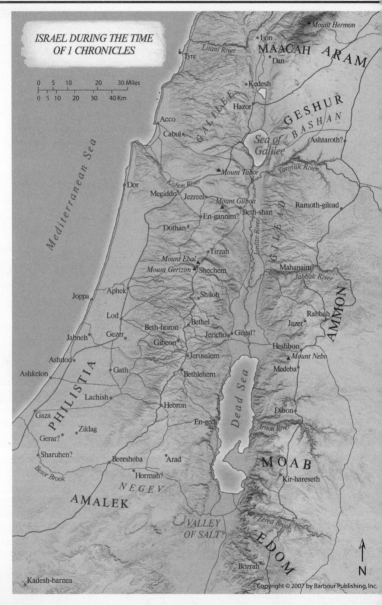

ISRAEL DURING THE TIME OF 1 CHRONICLES

0 5 10   20   30 Miles
0 5 10 20 30 40 Km

Mediterranean Sea

Mount Hermon
Ijon
MAACAH
ARAM
Tyre
Litani River
Dan
Kedesh
GALILEE
Hazor
GESHUR
BASHAN
Acco
Sea of Galilee
Ashtaroth?
Cabul
Yarmuk River
Mount Tabor
Dor
Kishon River
Megiddo
Jezreel
Mount Gilboa
En-gannim?
Beth-shan
Ramoth-gilead
Dothan
Jordan River
GILEAD
Tirzah
Mount Ebal
Mahanaim?
Mount Gerizim
Shechem
Jabbok River
Joppa
Aphek
Shiloh
Lod
Bethel
AMMON
Beth-horon
Jericho
Gilgal?
Jazer
Rabbah
Jabneh
Gezer
Gibeon
Heshbon
Ashdod
Jerusalem
Mount Nebo
Gath
Bethlehem
Medeba
Ashkelon
Dead Sea
PHILISTIA
Lachish
Hebron
Gaza
En-gedi
Dibon
Gerar?
Ziklag
Arnon River
Sharuhen?
Beersheba
Arad
MOAB
Besor Brook
Hormah?
Kir-hareseth
NEGEV
AMALEK
VALLEY OF SALT?
Zered Brook
EDOM
Bozrah
N
Kadesh-barnea

2 CHRONICLES

INTRODUCTION TO 2 CHRONICLES

The books of 1 and 2 Chronicles were originally written not as two books but as one continuous history. The majority of 2 Chronicles describes the history of Israel after Solomon's reign as the kingdom divided into northern Israel and southern Judah. This is not a history written as it was happening, however. Instead, it is a history written long after the fact to remind the people of Judah of the journey of their ancestors.

AUTHOR

The author of the books of 1 and 2 Chronicles is not explicitly stated in the text. Many scholars ascribe the work to Ezra, citing a unified authorship of the Chronicles and the books of Ezra and Nehemiah. However, there are parts of the book that are obvious additions and expansions on the original work, and it is difficult to date the entire book within Ezra's lifetime. The author was a wise and God-fearing person, writing with tremendous knowledge and insight into the significance of the community of God's people during this period.

PURPOSE

The book of 2 Chronicles is more of a commentary on a period of Israel's history than an exhaustive, chronological account of the events that took place during that time. The book is written to guide the remnant of God's people as they seek to reestablish their lives in the promised land.

OCCASION

While the accounts recorded in 2 Chronicles describe Israel's history during Solomon's reign and the fall of Israel afterward, the occasion of the writing is much later. It was written after the Jews had been exiled away from their homeland and had been given permission to return again. Therefore, it begins with Solomon, but it ends with Cyrus's decree that allowed the people passage back to Jerusalem.

THEMES

Beginning with the account of Solomon, and throughout this book, the Chronicler describes the dangers of religious compromise and demonstrates the vanity of seeking or serving anything besides God. He writes in order to help Jews returning to Jerusalem to know how they are connected to the past and how they should now live in light of their history. This is why negative stories about Israel are minimized here. The themes revolve around the temple, Judah, those who seek God, and a connection with past national history.

CONTRIBUTION TO THE BIBLE

This book is often considered one of the most unreadable of the Old Testament and therefore has been largely neglected and overlooked. Still, although at times the details seem mundane, the material supplements the stories told in Samuel and Kings and illuminates what was a very complicated and confusing period of Israel's history. From a broader biblical perspective, it emphasizes the continuance of the community of God and outlines how the Israelites are to interpret their history as a consistent reminder of God's faithfulness and love. The book also reminds them of the consequences of straying from the religious institutions God had established in order to help them honor Him and live well with one another.

OUTLINE

(SOLOMON'S KINGDOM)

(THE DIVIDED KINGDOM)

POWER SHIFT

FURTHER TROUBLE

CHANGING TIMES

JUDAH'S GODLY KINGS

SEEK GOD

THE BATTLE IS THE LORD'S

TURNING FROM GOD

HEZEKIAH: A GOOD KING

RAPID DECLINE

2 CHRONICLES 1:1–17

WISDOM AND WEALTH

Setting Up the Section

Following the end of King David's reign over Israel, his son, Solomon, begins his reign seeking and receiving God's blessing with boldness.

📖 1:1–12

SOLOMON SEEKS WISDOM

Solomon—who the text describes as exalted exceedingly by God—leads the assembled Israelites to Gibeon to visit the tabernacle of God. Historically, from other texts, we know that David had brought the ark up from Kiriath-jearim and placed it in a tent in Jerusalem (2 Samuel 6:2–17). But the tabernacle, the portable worship structure Moses had built some five hundred years earlier during their wilderness wanderings, was located in Gibeon.

With the tabernacle, besides the other temple articles, is the bronze altar in which the sacrifices were offered. Thus Solomon needs to go to Gibeon and offer his sacrifices to the Lord (Leviticus 17:11). It is only after that atonement is made that he can enter the presence of God, which the ark represents, and worship Him (2 Chronicles 1:1–5).

Demystifying 2 Chronicles

The burnt offering was given totally to the Lord, burned completely up, symbolizing the offerer's consecration to Him. On the other hand, the peace offering, also referred to in Leviticus 3 as the fellowship offering, was partly given to the Lord and partly eaten by those making the offering. It symbolized communion with the Lord. Historically, in this part of the world, when a person ate with someone, they formed an intimate relationship in a sense. Thus the connection between the names—peace and fellowship.

Solomon offers a thousand burnt offerings to the Lord before he approaches Him (1:6). When God speaks to Solomon, He is ready to grant him whatever he wants. Solomon's answer to this question reveals his heart (1:7).

Remember that Solomon is only fourteen years old at this time (David reminds him of his youth in 29:1). Solomon's prayers echo those of his father, David, who asked that God would give him wisdom and understanding to lead his people, for he rightly recognized he could not do it on his own. Solomon realizes that God had blessed his father, and at the outset of his own reign, he asks that God grant him wisdom and knowledge as well.

Critical Observation

Solomon's prayer can serve as a model prayer:

- He approaches God in a spirit of worship (1:6).

- He acknowledges God's history of kindness and leadership (1:8).

- He recognizes his own need for God's provision in order to obey and serve (1:10).

- He concerns himself with spiritual needs rather than material provision (1:10–11).

God honors the prayer of Solomon and gives him the desire of his heart, for it is what God wants for him. Solomon does not ask for his own personal gain, and since his heart is right, God blesses him abundantly (1:11–12). But unfortunately, Solomon does not apply all the wisdom God gives him to his own life.

📖 1:13–17

SOLOMON'S POWER

As Solomon takes power in Jerusalem, he begins to amass wealth—and the seeds of destruction for the nation of Israel are being sown. Solomon is gathering chariots, horses, and riches. He becomes an arms merchant as he traffics in chariots, even going to Egypt to obtain them, and he also takes multiple wives. This is precisely what God had warned the Israelites against when He brought them into the promised land (Deuteronomy 17:14–17). God knew that these harbingers of military and economic power would distract His people from worshiping Him (2 Chronicles 1:13–17).

Take It Home

The same cleansing that Solomon had to observe is mirrored for the modern believer in the cleansing blood of Christ, which, like the blood of the sacrifice in the Old Testament, enables us to enter the presence of the Lord (Hebrews 10:19–20). Despite his best intentions, Solomon is corrupted by the military and economic power that God blesses him with. His love of money competes with his love for God. What do you trust more than God? What will tempt you to become distracted and turn away?

2 CHRONICLES 2:1–18

PREPARATIONS FOR THE TEMPLE

Setting Up the Section

Solomon almost immediately begins an elaborate and extensive building project constructing his own palace and the temple of the Lord.

2:1–10

SOLOMON REQUESTS HELP

Solomon gathers together a tremendous group of forced labor gangs—mostly foreigners, probably prisoners of war—to build his own palace and the temple of God, according to David's plans (2:1–2). Solomon requests manpower and materials from a nearby neighbor, Hiram of Tyre. His letter of request begins by emphasizing how magnificent and great the house of the Lord will be. Before a God this great, even the mighty and powerful King Solomon pales in comparison (2:3–5).

Solomon understands that no temple or building can contain God, for the universe can't even contain Him. The temple that Solomon is building is indeed a place for worship, but Solomon realizes that the presence of God fills the universe (2:6).

Solomon needs fine wood and skilled craftsmen to build the temple. He plans to send 160,000 bushels of wheat and barley and 150,000 gallons each of wine and oil as payment for the work he is commissioning on the temple (2:7–10).

2:11–18

FOREIGN AID

Hiram begins his reply to Solomon by praising God for His provision of a wise king to lead His people (2:11–12). The king replies that he will also send along a skilled craftsman to help oversee the work. Huram-Abi is the son of an Israelite mother (from the tribe of Dan) and a Gentile father (2:13). While Solomon has sought to enlist the world's most skilled people, God ultimately provides an Israelite to do the job. The fact that this crafts-man is from the tribe of Dan creates a parallel with Moses' preparation of the tabernacle. In Moses' case, working in the wilderness, God appointed a Danite to oversee the work (Exodus 31:1–11).

Take It Home

God empowered these men to do the work by His Spirit. This is evidence that we can try to do the work of God in the flesh, but we will fail and come far short of what God intends to do. Or we can submit to God and be filled and lead by His Spirit, and God will do far above what we are able to do in the flesh. It is not by our might or by our strength but by God's Spirit working through us.

Hiram is going to send to Solomon the beautiful cedars of Lebanon. In order to do this, they have to tie logs together and float them down the Mediterranean Sea, some seventy miles, to the only seaport in the area, Joppa. From Joppa they are carried across land some twenty or thirty miles, to the city of Jerusalem, where they will be used in the construction of the temple (2:13–15). Solomon takes stock of the foreign labor force at his disposal and puts them to work according to the construction needs. Similar notes about aliens as laborers are made elsewhere in the Old Testament (1 Chronicles 22:2; 2 Chronicles 2:17–18; Isaiah 60:10–12).

2 CHRONICLES 3:1–4:22

TEMPLE BUILDING BEGINS

The Temple Structure	3:1–17
The Temple Furnishings	4:1–22

Setting Up the Section

Solomon begins construction on his temple at the site David had purchased for this very purpose (1 Chronicles 22:5).

📖 **3:1–17**

THE TEMPLE STRUCTURE

Solomon began this construction project around 966 BC, about 480 years after the Exodus (according to 1 Kings 6:1, which many use to date the Exodus around 1446 BC). The temple is being built on the threshing floor of Ornan, which is located on Mount Moriah, the place where Abraham went to offer his son Isaac a thousand years earlier (Genesis 22:2–14).

The temple is ninety feet long by thirty feet wide, roughly twice the size of the tabernacle, which was forty-five feet long by thirty feet wide and fifteen feet high. All the beautiful wood they have brought from Lebanon is overlaid with pure gold (3:3–7). The Most Holy Place, or Holy of Holies, is thirty feet long by thirty feet wide. This is where the ark of God resides. The Holy Place is sixty feet long by thirty feet wide. But the whole temple area is much bigger—some fifty acres in all. Thus, this area has to be built up and secured with various structures to help support it. Today the temple area still exists, with some additions that Herod made, and is an area that is claimed as a holy site by Jews, Muslims, Christians, and Catholics (3:8).

Inside the Holy of Holies, standing above the ark of the covenant and the mercy seat, are two giant cherubim with a wing span of fifteen feet each. One of their wings touches the wing of the other, and their other wing touches the wall, thus filling the whole place (3:9–14).

The veil (3:14) separates the Holy Place from the Most Holy Place, for only the high priest is allowed to enter the Most Holy Place, and only once a year after a ceremonial cleansing. According to Jewish legend, even then the priest entered with a rope around his feet and bells on his robe; for if the bells stopped ringing, it meant God had struck him dead for being unclean.

Take It Home

In the New Testament, when Christ gives up His spirit and pays for our sins, the veil described here (3:14) is torn from top to bottom, signifying that God had opened the way into the Most Holy Place to all people (Mark 15:37–38). Now we can boldly come before God anytime we need to. There is no longer a priest who needs to intercede for us.

Two freestanding pillars flank the entrance of the temple. One pillar is named *Jachin*, to the south side, and the name means "He shall establish." The other is *Boaz*, to the north side, and the name means "In Him is strength." Thus, every time someone came to the temple, before he or she entered, they were reminded that God had established this nation, and it is only by His strength that this nation will stand. This would help the worshiper have the right perspective of things before entering the temple (3:15–17).

Critical Observation

It is unclear from the information here whether the pillars are load-bearing elements of the construction or if they are simply a part of the aesthetics. Some have imagined them as freestanding pillars with bowls at the top that could be filled with oil and thus used for lighting (much like large oil lamps).

THE TEMPLE FURNISHINGS

The bronze altar of sacrifice is thirty feet long by thirty feet wide and about seventeen feet high. It stands in the courtyard directly in front of the temple. The twelve bulls mentioned are probably symbolic of the twelve tribes of Israel but also demonstrate how Solomon had adopted the Phoenician symbol of fertility (the bull), representative of God's life-giving rain (4:1).

The sea of cast bronze, or the laver, is Solomon's version of the laver of bronze in Moses' tabernacle (Exodus 30:18). It is fifteen feet across, forty-five feet in circumference, and seven and a half feet deep. It can hold between twelve and fifteen thousand gallons of water. It is used by the priests for ceremonial cleansing and is located to the south side of the temple, or on the left as you walk in (2 Chronicles 4:2–5).

The ten portable lavers are used for washing. Each laver is able to hold some 230 gallons of water, and they are placed on carts for mobility. These are located on the sides of the temple, five on each side (4:6). The tabernacle only had one menorah and one table of showbread. Solomon makes ten of each, placing five on each side of the temple (4:7–8).

The court of the priests and the great courts are both mentioned in Kings (1 Kings 6:36; 7:12). The larger court is intended for the laity (2 Chronicles 4:9). The descriptions here are general.

Huram heads up the production of various articles for the temple. The casts for the temple articles are made of clay obtained in the plain of Jordan (4:10–17).

Note that they have so much bronze for use in the temple that they do not bother to weigh it (4:18). Solomon completes the work on the temple, a seven-year building project, and what a sight it must have been (4:19–22).

2 CHRONICLES 5:1–14

THE ARK ARRIVES

Setting Up the Section

With the help of a foreign king and a massive conscripted labor force, Solomon has completed the construction of the temple. Now it is time to bring the ark of the covenant into the new temple of the Lord.

MOVING THE ARK

The first verse of chapter 5 is a kind of transition. Once construction is complete, as described in chapter 4, Solomon moves the consecrated gifts of David to the treasuries (5:1).

The massive temple building project took seven years to complete. And now it is time to bring the ark of the covenant up from the city of David and place it in the temple. The city of David, also called Zion, was actually the easternmost hill in what we now know as Jerusalem. It was there that David had placed the ark in a tent (5:2). During the time of David, Zion was only about half of a city block wide and about two city blocks long, built upon the lower ridge of Mount Moriah.

The ark arrives at the area Solomon has built up as a site for the temple (among other structures). This area was previously known as Ornan's threshing floor. The account given here in 2 Chronicles follows almost verbatim the account given in 2 Kings 8:1–13.

The moving of the ark of the covenant takes place during the Feast of Tabernacles, which is on the fifteenth day of the seventh month (September–October), and lasts eight days. The festival proclaims God's kingship over His people and His world. The whole celebration ends with a seven-day feast as the temple is dedicated; thus, it is a fifteen-day celebration in all. As is the custom, the elders of Israel come, and the Levites take the ark according to strict rules established by God in the days of Moses (5:3–5).

Demystifying 2 Chronicles

The transportation of the ark was to be done by the Levites, the Kohathites specifically. When it was time for the children of Israel to move, the tabernacle was to be dismantled, and the Kohathites had the responsibility of caring for the ark and the other temple implements. They would walk into the Holy of Holies backwards, carrying a covering for the ark. Next they would place the covering over the ark and then lift the ark by two poles that were inserted through four rings located on the sides of the ark. The poles were then placed upon the shoulders of the Kohathites (see Exodus 25:10–16).

As the ark approaches, Solomon and the congregation of Israel assemble and make sacrifices—too numerous to count—to honor the arrival of the chariot-throne of God (5:6). The temple proper consists of two main rooms: The Holy Place is sixty feet long by thirty feet wide, and the Most Holy Place is thirty feet long by thirty feet wide. It is in the Most Holy Place, or the Holy of Holies, where the ark is to be placed (5:7). The wings of cherubim form a canopy for the ark within the Holy of Holies. Above the ark are two cherubs with their wings extending and filling the room. Each cherub has a wing span of fifteen feet (5:8).

Unlike David, whose first attempt at transporting the ark had gone awry because he failed to follow God's instructions (2 Samuel 6:6–11), Solomon transports the ark exactly as outlined in the Law of Moses. This is underscored in the events of the coming verses (2 Chronicles 5:9).

Earlier on, the ark contained the two tablets of stone in which the covenant was written, the rod of Aaron that had budded miraculously (Numbers 17:1–11), and the jar of manna (Exodus 25:16; Deuteronomy 10:2; Hebrews 9:4–5). Now only the two tablets of stone remain (2 Chronicles 5:10). The ark is relatively small: three feet nine inches long by two feet three inches wide by two feet three inches tall. The box is overlaid with gold, and the mercy seat covers the top of it. The ark contains the law of God, but God does not meet with us in the ark. Instead God meets with His children between the cherubim. This is symbolic of the fact that we cannot enter the presence of God by the law, only by His mercy. We deserve death, but God has offered us eternal life (Hebrews 9:22, 28).

5:11–14

THE COMING OF GOD'S GLORY

David had divided the priests into twenty-four divisions, each serving two weeks. After their work is done, they return to their city until the time of their next service. The priests have forty-eight Levitical cities spread throughout the land of Israel in which to live. Here, for the dedication of the temple, all who were present during this time of celebration to assist in the sacrifices (5:11).

Take It Home

As the people came together to worship the Lord, it was neither chaotic nor free-form. They sang in one accord, with one voice, and the focus was the Lord! God wants our full attention both in the silence of our own individual hearts and in the cacophony of the community. In a corporate setting, and in our own lives, worship is a reflection on God's faithfulness that refreshes us and fills us with His presence.

It is after this time of worship and praise that the Shekinah glory, the presence of God, fills the temple. In this tremendous moment for Israel, God inhabits the praises of His people (5:12–14).

The words of praise recorded in verse 13 are used at other times in the accounts of 2 Chronicles (7:3; 20:21).

2 CHRONICLES 6:1–42

TEMPLE DEDICATION

Setting Up the Section

The glory of the Lord has just filled the temple, and in response, Solomon speaks to the people and to the Lord. The account here parallels 2 Kings 8:14–21.

📖 6:1–11

SOLOMON SPEAKS TO THE PEOPLE

Throughout the scriptures, the full glory of the Lord is shrouded from the people, because it would consume those unworthy (Exodus 33:20). The Bible says that God allows His children to see His presence through a veil, like looking through dark glasses, but one day we will see Him face-to-face, in all His glory, as we go to be with Him (1 Corinthians 13:12). Solomon explains this when he turns to address the people—that the Lord has said (see Leviticus 16:2; Psalm 97:2) He will dwell in the dark cloud (2 Chronicles 6:1–2).

When God chose David to be the first king of the Israelites, He also declared that Jerusalem would be the place for the temple. Solomon honors God by building the temple according to His instructions and choice (6:3–6). God does not allow David to build the temple because he is too busy with war. Yet God, and Solomon in this speech, honors David for having a desire to build a place that centers on the purpose of worship (6:7–8).

Take It Home

God rewards the desires of a person's heart, even those that are not realized. Jesus reminds His disciples that God will bless their hearts' desires, but He also cautions that the attitudes of their hearts will be judged. As the prophet Samuel declared when he anointed David as Israel's first king, "The LORD doesn't see things the way you see them. People judge by outward appearance, but the LORD looks at the heart" (1 Samuel 16:7 NLT).

God's faithfulness, Solomon declares, is demonstrated when He brings His promises to pass. God has honored His covenant with the children of Israel (6:9–11).

📖 6:12–42

SOLOMON SPEAKS TO THE LORD

The picture of Solomon turning from the people to offer a prayer of dedication is striking—imagine the newly completed temple in all its beauty. Solomon takes confidence in God's future faithfulness by reflecting on His past provision (6:12–15).

Solomon asks for a conditional blessing. If Israel follows after the Lord, Solomon prays, God will bless Israel by maintaining the line of kings on the throne (6:16–17). Solomon understands that the heavens cannot contain God, and yet he asks that God look upon this city and this temple, that it will be a place where people can come together with God and repent of their sin; and when they do, God will forgive them (6:18–21).

God alone is a righteous judge—knowing the hearts and minds of people (6:22–23). Solomon considers the consequences of turning from the Lord: loss of His power and defeat by the enemy (6:24–25). Next Solomon considers how God often uses disasters to get His children's attention—such as a drought or famine, which forces people to awaken out of spiritual slumber and turn to God. Of course, in a fallen world, not all disasters are instances of God's judgment or results of sin. Sometimes the brokenness of this world reminds us of nothing else except our longing for the healing of the world to come. God is warning His people, through Solomon, that these things will come to pass if they fail to repent of their sins and cling to Him (6:26–31).

God opens the door for all to come to Him, not just the Israelites—an invitation not typically found in the Old Testament. Solomon asks the Lord to forgive all who come in repentance, even the foreigners (6:32–33). He prays that no matter where the people may be that God will hear their prayer and sustain them (6:34–35). Solomon's prayer is for mercy, because there is no one who does not sin, an idea that Paul repeats often in the New Testament (6:36).

Solomon not only foresees Israel's rebellion and exile but also hopes for her repentance. As Solomon closes his prayer, the priests are clothed in salvation and the people rejoice (6:40–42).

2 CHRONICLES 7:1–22

TEMPLE DEDICATION CONTINUES

Solomon Dedicates the Temple	7:1–11
God Appears Again	7:12–22

Setting Up the Section

The Chronicler parallels 1 Kings 8:54, 62–66 in this section, but he changes the focus. Here, he emphasizes the glory of God rather than the people's blessing (the focus of the 1 Kings passage).

📖 **7:1–11**

SOLOMON DEDICATES THE TEMPLE

In chapter 7, the glory of God fills the temple for a second time. The first time it is in response to worship, and this time it is in response to prayer (7:1–3). When God consumes the sacrifices, it is a sign of acceptance of those offerings. There are other examples in the Bible where this occurs. For instance, the same thing happened when the priests began their work in the tabernacle (Leviticus 9:23–24). Also, after David's unauthorized census described in 1 Chronicles, he offers sacrifices that are miraculously consumed (1 Chronicles 21:26).

The influence of David is clear in this passage. He invested heavily in the worship life of ancient Israel. He organized the worship leaders and the worship times, both day and night. He made the instruments used in worship and even wrote songs and psalms of praise to the Lord (2 Chronicles 7:6).

The bronze altar is the altar of sacrifice, which stands fifteen feet high by thirty feet long by thirty feet wide. Even so, it isn't big enough for all the sacrifices that are being offered. So Solomon sanctifies the entire outer court in order to offer all the sacrifices. The priests are in attendance for all the sacrifices and the work that needs to be done (7:7).

The feast lasts fifteen days, and as Solomon dismisses the people to their homes, they leave with joyful hearts. Even though the lessons have been difficult, God's children rejoice that God is working in them and among them (7:8–11).

📖 **7:12–22**

GOD APPEARS AGAIN

Solomon's prayer is answered with a tremendous promise: God will hear His children's cry for repentance, forgive the people's sins, and heal their land (7:14). This promise is especially powerful considering that the original audience for whom the Chronicler was writing was the remnant of Jews who had returned home from their Babylonian exile. A promise of restoration would have given them great hope (7:12–14).

Demystifying 2 Chronicles

Why had these people, the original audience of the Chronicles, been exiled? Basically because of the very warning recorded here from Solomon—they had forsaken the God of their fathers and worshiped idols. In light of that, the city of Jerusalem and their temple, the very temple whose dedication this section describes, had been destroyed. Just as described in verse 20, the Israelites as a nation and a culture had become a byword to many of their neighbors. The journey of this ragtag group to reassemble as a nation is filled with hardships. In some cases, however, it is only because of these trials that God's people will turn to Him. When they do, He will protect and heal them (7:15–20).

The reason for the captivity is simple: The Israelites turned from the Lord. Solomon is warned against precisely that rebellion, and yet he and future kings do not heed this warning. May modern believers learn from their mistakes and heed the warnings of God. Solomon was praying for this very thing, and he still becomes distracted—and his fall is mighty and hard (7:21–22).

Setting Up the Section

Following God's conditional blessing of the work Solomon had accomplished, Solomon continues to build Israel's infrastructure, even receiving praise from the Queen of Sheba. And yet in the final analysis, despite his tremendous achievement and wealth, Solomon is destined to join his father in the grave.

📖 8:1–18

SOLOMON'S ADDITIONAL ACHIEVEMENTS

Solomon spends seven years building the temple and thirteen years building his own house and administrative buildings. There is nothing wrong with building projects unless they become the focus of one's life, as with Solomon. Remember that when Solomon became king, he was just fourteen years old and dependent upon the Lord to guide him and give him wisdom to lead his people. Now twenty years have passed, and Solomon has become more self-reliant. He has placed his faith in himself instead of the Lord (8:1–8).

Critical Observation

The cities Solomon built up were located on the trade routes. Solomon used his God-given wisdom for his own personal and financial gain. Hamath Zobah was located 300 miles north of Jerusalem. Tadmor was a desert oasis located on the main highway from Mesopotamia, about 150 miles northeast of Damascus. Beth Horon was located about ten miles northwest of Jerusalem, on the border between Judah and the northern tribes. Baalath was located in the territory of Dan. These cities serve as places of prosperity and protection for the growing kingdom of Israel under Solomon's reign. Unfortunately, in many instances, the natives of the conquered cities remained and established a foothold within Israel. God had warned His people against not driving out the enemy—they posed a threat to Israel's faithfulness. But Solomon's heart was by this point focused on satisfying himself instead of obeying the Lord.

Verses 9–10 describe Solomon only using foreigners—and not his own brethren—as a forced labor force, as slaves. The children of Israel are placed in a higher position, overseeing the work (8:9–10). Later however, when the Israelites look back on Solomon's reign, they describe him as a harsh master (10:4).

Solomon recognizes that his marriage to Pharaoh's daughter is not pleasing to God. Although he is moving away from God and is aware of it, he continues going through the motions (offering sacrifices) without truly turning from his ways (8:11–15; see also 1 Samuel 15:22–23).

Take It Home

Many times God speaks to our hearts and warns us that what we are doing is wrong, and it is clear that He is not pleased with our actions. But instead of turning from what we are doing, we try to justify our actions and maybe make minor changes, as Solomon does, so that we can make ourselves look better and ease the conviction that God has placed upon our hearts. But that does not change how God feels about what we are doing. Be sensitive to His leading and then follow His direction.

The Israelites aren't a seafaring people, even though they sail and fish on the Sea of Galilee. So Solomon again hires Hiram, king of Tyre, to assist him in obtaining riches from other nations by his ships. The Phoenicians are truly a great seafaring people. These ships returned every three years full of riches and possessions from various nations. Solomon acquired 450 talents of gold from Ophir, which is quite small compared to the 3,000 talents of gold David acquired from Ophir during the same amount of time. Solomon is trying to do this by the works of his own hands rather than by the direction of the Lord. Solomon's focus is on obtaining wealth, but spiritually he is bankrupt (8:17–18; see Solomon's reflection on gold and silver in Ecclesiastes 5:10).

9:1–12

THE QUEEN OF SHEBA'S PRAISE

The Queen of Sheba travels some twelve hundred miles from Arabia to test Solomon's wisdom by asking him some tough questions. Tradition tells us that Solomon is tested with riddles. (This happens in the life of Samson as well [Judges 14].) Tradition also suggests that one of the riddles that the Queen of Sheba gives to Solomon has to do with two bouquets of flowers. One is real and the other fake. As she stands at a distance that makes it impossible to tell with the naked eye which is which, Solomon has bees released and they fly into the real flowers. Solomon solves the riddle (2 Chronicles 9:1–3).

The Queen of Sheba can't believe all she sees. Although she had been skeptical at first, the queen is now amazed at Solomon's wisdom and grandeur—so much so that she believes in God (9:4–8; Matthew 12:42).

When algum wood (or, as some translations say, juniper wood) is cut, it releases a sweet fragrance, which does not decrease in its intensity. Also, it does not rot like some wood. It is a marvelous gift (9:9–12).

SOLOMON'S GREAT WEALTH

Solomon places a heavy tax burden upon the people, but he does not need it any longer. The temple and the buildings are all completed, and he could have eased up on the taxation. His son, Rehoboam, is going to be asked to bring tax reform to the nation, but he refuses, and as a result, the nation is divided. Solomon's yearly income of 666 talents of gold is an interesting symbol of how wealth is often a tool used by the devil himself to corrupt even God's own servants (see Revelation 13:16–18). God is saying to Solomon and his future servants, "don't let the things of this world draw you away from serving me" (2 Chronicles 9:13–14).

The House of the Forest of Lebanon (9:16, 20) is one of Solomon's homes. This structure is 150 feet long by 75 feet wide and 45 feet tall. It is surrounded by forty-five cedar pillars, so as you look at the building, it looks like a forest. The richer the person, the more extravagant they are; they don't know what to do with their money. Solomon has his throne made of ivory, and then he goes and covers the ivory with gold. What a waste of God's money (9:15–17). Solomon's kingdom outshines any other. The people are hurting from the heavy burden of taxes, but even so Solomon is living a life of luxury (9:18–20).

Every three years ships returned from their voyages and brought back with them a huge cargo of merchandise. The common goods are no longer satisfying, and it is taking more to satisfy Solomon. The things he acquires seem to be getting more and more bizarre. This is true for anyone who turns from the Lord and tries to fill that void with other things (9:21).

Solomon is charging people to share this gift that God has given to him. God gave him this wisdom, and now he is making a profit off it. How sad when people prostitute the things that God has given to them. Greed is a terrible enemy to a relationship with God, and we see evidence of this within the church today (9:22–24). Solomon is doing everything that God told him *not* to do (Deuteronomy 17). Maybe Solomon thinks he is above the common people and that, because of his great wisdom, God no longer needs to speak to him. But he soon finds out how wrong he is and how prideful his attitude has become (2 Chronicles 9:25–28).

Critical Observation

The camel was domesticated and used for transportation by traders and merchants. They were perfectly suited to the region, because they could travel long distances through the desert without the need for water. Jerusalem was the hub between Egypt and Mesopotamia.

SOLOMON'S DEATH

Solomon's death marks a transition. Now his son Rehoboam is on the throne, and instead of following the spiritual influence of King David, Rehoboam continues riding the materialistic wave that began with his father, Solomon. The downward spiral that this creates in Israel will continue until their captivity.

2 CHRONICLES 10:1–11:23

POWER SHIFT

Revolt against Rehoboam	10:1–11:4
Fortifying Israel	11:5–23

Setting Up the Section

Solomon has died, and his son Rehoboam reigns in his place. But the people are overburdened by taxes and stand ready to challenge their new leadership. The events described in this section propel Israel into a permanent state as a divided kingdom.

REVOLT AGAINST REHOBOAM

Note that Rehoboam travels to Shechem to be approved by the people as king, rather than Jerusalem where his father Solomon was anointed. Shechem was a significant place to several Jewish fathers. It was a strategic battle site as well as religious site. Abraham and Jacob built altars there (Genesis 12:6–7; 33:18–20). After the final conquest of Canaan, Joshua's covenant renewal happened there (Joshua 24).

Rehoboam, Israel's next king and the son of Solomon, reigns for seventeen years. In that amount of time, Israel deteriorates into a second-class nation. At one time, people from near and far came to see the glory of this kingdom, but that is going to change very quickly (10:1–2).

Jeroboam is a young and industrious man of whom Solomon had taken notice. Solomon placed him in charge of the labor force over the house of Joseph. It is after this that Ahijah the Shilonite, a prophet of God, meets with him in a field. Ahijah takes the garment of Jeroboam, tears it into twelve pieces, and tells him to take ten of those pieces (1 Kings 11:31–40). Solomon heard about this situation and tried to stop it by killing Jeroboam, who then fled to Egypt for safety. Now that Solomon is dead, Jeroboam returns from Egypt to Jerusalem (2 Chronicles 10:2).

Now that Rehoboam is king, the people want him to ease up on the taxation, for it is becoming a tremendous burden for them (10:3–4). Rehoboam, after hearing the requests of the people, takes three days to come to a decision—which shows his desire to make the right one. Rehoboam brings this matter first to the wise men, Solomon's counselors.

They tell the king to ease up on them and be kind to them—serve the people and they will serve the king. Often titles breed power and pride, and God is reminding His leadership to be humble and serve the people (10:5–7).

Rehoboam now consults young men to hear their counsel, for he rejects the counsel of the wise men. Although the text refers to these advisors as young men, they are no teenagers. Rehoboam has grown up with these men, and he is over forty years old himself. Nevertheless, due to inexperience, if not youth, their counsel is truly foolish (10:5–7). They tell Rehoboam to assert his authority and let the people know who is in charge (10:9–11).

The all-knowing God ordains what happens next (10:15). Rehoboam, in his pride and arrogance, thinks he is in total control, but he is completely unaware that he is going to fulfill what God had said would happen (10:12–15). The nation divides—the ten northern tribes separate from Judah and Benjamin in the south. This is a truly tragic chapter in Israel's history (10:12–16). Up to this point, both the northern and southern tribes are referred to as Israel. Here the conflicting groups are identified as the house of David and the house of Israel. Eventually, however, the northern tribes come to be known as Israel and the southern tribes come to be known as Judah, the largest of the territories there (10:16–17).

Hadoram (10:18) is sent to do the king's dirty work. But instead of paying their taxes, the northern tribes kill the messenger. Finally Rehoboam recognizes the trouble Israel is in and flees from Shechem, traveling about twenty-five miles south to Jerusalem (10:17–19).

Critical Observation

In verse 19, the term *Israel* refers to the northern tribes. The term *rebellion* is more than a description of the civil conflict. Here the northern tribes have rebelled against the covenant God had made with David, that his house would rule all of Israel.

God speaks to Rehoboam through the prophet Shemaiah and tells him to stay at home and not to fight (11:2–4). Rehoboam has developed a plan, but it is not God's plan, and he has to be redirected (Proverbs 16:9). Amazingly, he listens and obeys.

The division grieves God, and yet He allows it. The northern kingdom of Israel begins and ends in idolatry. They have no king who truly leads them in the ways of the Lord.

On the other hand, the southern kingdom of Judah is not perfect but at least has its share of godly kings who bring reform to the land. Thus, this division is healthy, in a sense, for the southern kingdom of Judah (2 Chronicles 11:1–4).

The references to Judah and Benjamin in verses 1 and 3 refer to tribes as well as locations.

11:5–23

FORTIFYING ISRAEL

In this section, Rehoboam is ready to buckle down and focus. He fortifies Judah's cities with military strength because he has legitimate concerns about his kingdom being overthrown (11:5–12).

Verses 13–17 describe the religious fallout of the civil rebellion. The Levites, who are spread throughout the land, side with Rehoboam. Jeroboam has cut them off from being priests anyway, and he sets up his own priesthood. Jeroboam is concerned that all the people might go to Jerusalem to worship God in the temple, and many won't return. So he makes two golden calves for them to worship. The priests—relieved of their duties by Jeroboam—head to Jerusalem to continue the work they are called to do. Not only do the priests begin to leave but some of the people do as well, in light of the idolatry that Jeroboam is bringing into the land (11:6–17).

The calf idols mentioned in verse 15 are reminiscent of the earlier act of rebellion in which the Israelites created and worshiped a golden calf after they left Egypt but were still on the way to Canaan (Exodus 32:1–10; Deuteronomy 9:16).

Rehoboam prepares his son Abijah to be the next king in the southern kingdom of Judah. But the king is also concerned that his sons might be murdered, so he spreads them out throughout the land to prevent them from being wiped out. Whereas Solomon's rule represents a time of great peace, the king is now afraid of rebellion from within and attack from outside. Israel has very little stability in her rebellion (2 Chronicles 11:18–22).

2 CHRONICLES 12:1–16

FURTHER TROUBLE

Setting Up the Section

In the first three years of his reign, Rehoboam walks in the way of David and Solomon, and the southern kingdom is strengthened.

12:1–12

EGYPT ATTACKS JUDAH

Rehoboam starts his regime looking to the Lord for help. He isn't a godly man, but as he takes over the kingdom, the nation is divided and he needs help. But he allows his success to deteriorate because of pride and self-reliance. The southern kingdom follows after their king, who forsakes the Lord. God brings judgment upon Rehoboam and the southern kingdom of Judah because they turned away from Him. When they looked to the Lord, the kingdom was strengthened, but now, because they have forsaken Him, the kingdom will be weak (12:1–4).

It is clear from verses 1 and 2 that Egypt's attack under Shishak is considered a judgment on the fall of Rehoboam and his people from faith. The reference to "all" of Israel in verse 1 is a reference to the southern kingdom. At this point, many of the faithful from the northern kingdom have immigrated southward. So this is a reference to all of Israel that remain in the southern kingdom of Judah.

Critical Observation

Keep in mind that the writer of Chronicles is not making a record at the time these events are happening. His audience, instead, is the last remnant of Jews who have experienced the complete fall of Judah, not just the division of the earlier kingdom. Here, as the writer recounts the beginnings of that fall, he is reminding the people of the price of disobedience.

God's prophet Shemaiah helps the king and his leaders recognize their failure and see the righteousness of God (12:5–6). God is waiting with His forgiveness, and as soon as they humble themselves before Him and repent of their sin, He forgives them (12:7). God is not going to allow Egypt to wipe Judah out, but He is going to allow them to oppress Judah. The contrast that is placed before Judah is clear: Serving a holy and merciful God is far more rewarding than serving a wicked and cruel earthly king (12:8).

Take It Home

When Shishak takes the gold shields, which may have been more a tribute paid by Rehoboam to Shishak than an actual theft, Rehoboam makes bronze shields to replace them. Bronze is worthless, but it can be polished so that from a distance it gives the appearance of gold. The king goes through all the motions, making it look like nothing has happened, and yet it is worthless. Our cover-ups cannot replace the reality of our faith lives (12:9–11).

📄 **12:13–16**

THE END OF AN ERA

Rehoboam does not make it a priority to seek the Lord (12:14). God always sees the heart. Rehoboam's heart is not fixed on the Lord, and thus the fruit of his life is evil (12:12–14; see Matthew 6:21; 16:26). Moses prepared his heart before the Lord (Hebrews 11:24–26), because that was the only way to lead the nation in the right way. Rehoboam is preparing Abijah for the throne (1 Kings 15:1–8). Now he has replaced his father as king (2 Chronicles 12:15–16).

This account of Rehoboam's reign is much longer than the parallel account in 1 Kings. The extrabiblical documents listed in verse 15 may have supplied additional information. The mention of these documents reminds us that these writers were real-life people with records to keep and an interest in historical documentation.

2 CHRONICLES 13:1–14:15

CHANGING TIMES

Setting up the Section

Even as Israel experiences turmoil, power shifts, and civil war, God still works with them to restore the nation. This chapter tracks history in both the southern and the northern kingdoms of Israel.

📄 13:1–14:1

THE REIGN OF ABIJAH

War breaks out between the northern and southern kingdoms of Israel. Abijah, king of the southern kingdom of Judah, is outnumbered two to one. Abijah tries to talk his way out of this battle, explaining that David and his descendants have the right to the throne and Jeroboam doesn't. He speaks boldly, because he knows that what he says is what God has already promised (13:1–3).

God has established the house of David to rule over the nation, and no other dynasty can rule. The covenant of salt speaks of preservation—the dynasty of David is not to end (13:4–5). Abijah blasts Jeroboam and his men for taking advantage of Rehoboam when he was young and inexperienced and leading the people into idolatry (13:6–8). The whole scene is a tragic moment for Israel as they struggle against their brothers from the northern kingdom in what is essentially a civil war.

Jeroboam has been defiant of God. He fires all the priests and makes for himself his own priesthood. To become a priest under Jeroboam, all one needs is a young bull and seven rams—Jeroboam treats it like an auction. Yet serving God is not for sale; it is a calling from God (13:9). Abijah declares that Judah has not forsaken God; their priests are of the Levite lineage, and they are doing what God has told them to do (13:10).

Abijah accused the northern kingdom of not serving God (13:10–12). As Abijah is giving this rebuke, the enemy encircles his men. They are outnumbered and surrounded. So they cry out to the Lord for help (13:13–14).

Critical Observation

Verse 12 provides a line drawn in the sand between the kingdoms as Abijah declares that God is on his side. To fight against Abijah's kingdom is to fight against God's purposes. This highlights the important of the covenant God made with David, that his house would rule forever. This covenant is Abijah's claim and his judgment against Jeroboam.

The smaller army of Judah kills over half of Jeroboam's men. God gives the southern kingdom of Judah the victory (13:15–17) and strengthens them (13:19–22). Verse 18 reveals the key to Judah's victory—they trusted God, the God of their ancestors. They were not relying on their own strength but on God's power. This statement would serve as a reminder to the original hearers of this document to return to the faith of their ancestors if they were to have any hope of reestablishing themselves as a nation.

In many ways, this period of turmoil and war with the north strengthens Judah, and when Abijah dies, his son Asa will reign over some of the most peaceful years during this era of Israel's history (14:1).

14:2–15

THE REIGN OF ASA

Asa is one of the few godly kings to rule the southern kingdom of Judah. He does what is good and right, meaning that he is not only going through the motions of serving the Lord, but his heart is in the right place as well (14:1–2). Asa brings spiritual reform to the southern kingdom of Judah, destroys the worship of foreign gods, and follows after the Lord. But, like many spiritual revivals, it does not go far enough (14:3–5).

Asa fortifies the cities of Judah and builds up Judah's army during this time of peace. When the enemy comes against them, they are prepared (14:6–7). Indeed, when Zerah the Ethiopian (or Cushite) comes, he brings an army of a million men. This far outnumbers Judah's forces (14:8–9), so Asa cries out to God for help—the key turn of events in this situation. He realizes that God does not need a whole army to win. Asa is at peace, because he trusts God (14:10–11).

Asa and the southern kingdom of Judah come home victorious in this battle against the Ethiopians. They must have been on a spiritual high. But sometimes this is when we need to be on guard, for after the victory we can easily take our eyes off the Lord. Judah has no more battles with Egypt until Josiah meets Pharaoh Neco in 609 BC (14:12–15).

Take It Home

Just as Judah, under Asa's godly leadership, prepares to meet the challenge of more invaders during a time of peace, we must practice daily the spiritual disciplines that strengthen us so that we can be ready when times of trial come. And when trials arrive, we must turn to the Lord for strength and trust that He will prevail—we will share in His victory if we are on His side.

Asa's prayer stands as a model still for us today. He acknowledges God's power, acknowledges his own helplessness and need, and then requests God's help, not on behalf of the convenience of the people but on behalf of God's glory and reputation.

2 CHRONICLES 15:1–17:19

JUDAH'S GODLY KINGS

Setting Up the Section

Asa, too, eventually becomes prideful and pursues his own desires. This does not go unnoticed by God. As the seer declares, "The eyes of the LORD run to and fro throughout the whole earth, to give strong support to those whose heart is blameless toward him" (16:9 ESV). Jehoshaphat picks up his father Asa's legacy and reigns in the fear of the Lord (17:3).

📄 **15:1–19**

GODLY REFORMS

The prophet Azariah comes to Asa after this great victory and reminds him to continue walking with the Lord—warning that if he forgets to rely on the Lord for strength, God will forsake him (15:1–2).

Azariah is recounting Israel's history. Before there were priests, before there was the law, God was the one who was still faithful even though His people were not. It is as Jeremiah said, "It is of the LORD's mercies that we are not consumed, because his compassions fail not. They are new every morning: great is thy faithfulness" (Lamentations 3:22–23 KJV).

The *distress* referred to in verses 3–5 is not identified as a specific era or event in the history of Israel. Throughout the history, however, there were cycles of a falling away from the faith, the consequences that falling away incurred, and then God's deliverance of His people from the destruction faced in light of those consequences.

Azariah encourages Asa to continue in the work and to not give up. Even though the work may be difficult and seem unrewarding, the labor is not in vain, even though immediate results may not always be evident (2 Chronicles 15:3–7).

As word spreads to the northern kingdom about the spiritual reform in the southern kingdom of Judah, and how God is blessing Asa, many come down to Judah to reap some of those blessings (15:8–9). The nation comes together and they make a covenant to seek the Lord wholeheartedly. How awesome it would be if the nation did so (15:10–12).

The Israelites have good intentions, but they go too far when they put to death those who refuse to turn to God. You can't force love for God (15:13). The people come before the Lord in prayer and worship, not because they have to but because they have the desire to; it flows from their lives (15:14–15).

Asa removes Maacah, who is either his mother or his grandmother, from office because of her idolatry. His first loyalty is with the Lord; no one is given special treatment (15:16). The Asherah pole was a symbol of a Canaanite fertility god named Asherah. Moses clearly forbade the Israelites to set up any worship centers to Asherah (Deuteronomy 16:21).

Asa and the nation again enjoy a time of peace, a time to rebuild, to grow, and prepare for the coming battles. But just because he does right the first time doesn't mean he is going to continue down that path. But God is still working, molding, and shaping His servant into the leader He wants him to be (15:17–19).

16:1–14

THE EYES OF THE LORD

Baasha, king of the northern kingdom of Israel, builds up Ramah, which is located about five miles north of Jerusalem on the border between the two kingdoms and on an important trade route linking Egypt and Mesopotamia. This is to stop the migration of his people to Judah. In the process, Baasha brings his men and supplies to likely prepare for war against Judah (16:1).

Note the contrast in what Asa does here versus what he did when the Ethiopians had him outnumbered at the beginning of chapter 12. He is in trouble again, but instead of turning to God, he turns to a man. Asa takes the treasuries of God and gives them to Ben-hadad, king of Syria, to help him with his problems (16:2).

Ben-hadad has a treaty with Baasha, but he is bought out and comes to the aid of Asa. Now Baasha is down in Ramah, in the southern part of his kingdom, so Ben-hadad strikes Israel at its northern borders. The plan works. Asa is free of Baasha, but this success does not mean God is pleased (16:3–6).

God rebukes Asa through the prophet Hanani, a seer about whom we know nothing more than what is recorded here (except for a mention of his son, Jehu, in 2 Chronicles 19:2). Hanani reminds Asa that when the Ethiopians came upon him, he turned to the Lord for help. He did not place his faith in the arm of flesh (16:7–8).

Take It Home

God wants to use His people. There are three types of givers: the reluctant kind, the willing kind, and the proactive kind described in verse 9. God is not a reluctant giver—He is looking for people in whom He can invest. God is an aggressive giver. He gives to us abundantly for the work of the kingdom. But to know where He is leading means we must be in tune with Him, and we must be directed by His Spirit.

It is important to remember that 2 Chronicles 15:17 describes Asa as a person whose heart was fully committed to God. Perhaps his legacy can not be determined by any one downfall or disappointment (as is described in chapter 16). At his best moments, after all, his hope was in God's strength, not his own.

After Asa is told how God feels about what he has done, he angrily puts God's messenger in prison and oppresses those who oppose him. Let us never be so proud and arrogant that we never think we need correction (16:10).

God illustrates how trusting in the Lord as a last resort has become a pattern in Asa's life. Asa's walk with the Lord has been hampered. He no longer has an intimate relationship with the Lord, and his spiritual walk is hindered by his disease (16:11–12). Asa's life, like Solomon's, looks promising, and yet it has such low points of disappointment. At significant times he trusts more in mankind than he trusts in the Lord, particularly in the latter part of his life (16:13–14).

<hr>

📖 17:1–19

REIGNING IN GOD'S STRENGTH

Jehoshaphat does not seek Baals, (the nature gods) to make the land fertile, but instead he seeks the Lord. The Lord had told His people to not make graven images or idols for themselves (Leviticus 19:4). God is the only true God. The other gods are nothing more than demons (2 Chronicles 17:1–3).

At this time, the northern kingdom of Israel is ruled by wicked king Ahab and his wife, Jezebel. Ahab and Jezebel introduce Baal worship to the Israelites and even set up altars to worship this false god. Meanwhile, Jehoshaphat and the southern kingdom of Judah follow the Lord (17:4). Here is the difference between Solomon and Jehoshaphat: Solomon focused on riches and prosperity, while Jehoshaphat focuses on the Lord. He finds joy and peace in the ways of the Lord (17:5–6; see Genesis 15:1; Psalm 62:10; Matthew 6:33).

Critical Observation

The description of Jehoshaphat in verse 5 contains echoes of David's prayer as he dedicated the temple. He claimed God's kingdom all around with wealth (or riches) and honor. This may have been a way to affirm an answer to the prayer of David through the life of Jehoshaphat.

Jehoshaphat not only removes the idolatry from the land but he also recognizes that to successfully remove something from a person's life, you have to replace it with something else so that the person will not return to their old ways. So as he removes the false worship, he replaces it with the true worship of God. Jehoshaphat does not just condemn people for being wrong; he leads them in the ways they should go (17:7–9). Jehoshaphat enjoys times of peace and prosperity as a result of his faithfulness to God. Even the Philistines, who are a constant thorn in the side of Israel, are subdued during this time (17:10–11).

Jehoshaphat, like his father, brings spiritual reform to the southern kingdom of Judah. This brings the fear of the Lord to the kingdoms around Judah so that they do not seek war against Jehoshaphat (17:12–19).

Critical Observation

Asa's life parallels his great-grandfather Solomon's. Solomon started out young and inexperienced and asked God for wisdom to lead his people. He looked to the Lord for strength until he grew strong and wealthy. He then took his focus off the Lord as he grew confident in his own strength. Asa also takes his eyes off the Lord and places his confidence in his own strength toward the end of his life. His son, Jehoshaphat, manages to honor and seek God throughout his reign and enjoys God's blessing as a result—Judah experiences tremendous peace and prosperity once again. The eyes of the Lord are always searching for people whose hearts are loyal to use in His service, and He blesses them accordingly (16:9).

2 CHRONICLES 18:1–19:11

SEEK GOD

A Warning to the Wicked	18:1–27
Death of a King	18:28–19:3
Reforms of Jehoshaphat	19:4–11

Setting Up the Section

Jehoshaphat allows his son Jehoram to marry the daughter of Ahab and Jezebel, the famously wicked duo of the Old Testament. As we read about the consequences of this and other choices made by Israel's leaders, we are reminded of how important it is to seek God in all our decisions.

📖 18:1–27

A WARNING TO THE WICKED

Perhaps Jehoshaphat is trying to heal the wounds between the two kingdoms, but just as oil and water don't mix, neither do good and evil. An alliance between the two kingdoms, and between Jehoshaphat and Ahab, would be strange and unworkable (18:1).

As Jehoshaphat goes to visit Ahab, the king of Israel requests the help of Jehoshaphat in regaining Ramoth-gilead back from the Syrians (18:2). Jehoshaphat has only one request: Instead of rushing ahead, he wants to seek the Lord's will (18:3–4).

The false prophets described here are not the prophets of Baal, destroyed by Elijah at Mount Carmel prior to this time (1 Kings 18). These prophets are likely the false prophets of the calf worship that Jeroboam had established. Ahab has prophets, but not prophets of God. These men speak to please the king and use the name of God even though it is meaningless to them (2 Chronicles 18:5). Jehoshaphat recognizes that something is not right, for God has given him discernment as he looks for a true prophet of God (18:6).

Ahab is not interested in the truth. But Jehoshaphat rebukes Ahab for his harsh words against this man of God (18:7).

As both of these kings sit before the four hundred prophets, one of them, Zedekiah, grabs some horns, places them on his head, and starts charging all around the room. This is meant to show them that Ahab and his men are going to push back and defeat the Syrians. But these are not the words of God (18:8–10).

Take It Home

It is interesting that these false prophets know of Jehovah, but they do not follow after His commands (18:11; Matthew 7:23). Everyone knows that Micaiah speaks the truth of God, but they are not interested in the truth—they only want a positive message (2 Chronicles18:12). It is not always easy to speak the truth, but the heart of a true man or woman of God will always speak the truth. Our first responsibility must be to the Lord. We should not water down what we say or try to placate people. We must speak the truth in love (18:13).

The prophet says what the king wants to hear, but the king is not convinced the prophet is speaking the truth (18:14). The king picks up on the prophet's sarcasm. Ahab only wants Micaiah to speak in a convincing way (18:15). Eventually the prophet tells the king that he will be killed in the battle and that his men will be scattered. Clearly Ahab doesn't want to hear the truth, for once it is spoken, he shuns the words of the prophet and says to Jehoshaphat that he is a negative person (18:16–17).

Take It Home

Many theologians have difficulty with this passage—questioning how a holy and righteous God can send forth a lying spirit. Satan is not bound nor is his domain in hell alone (see Job 1:6). Satan and his demons will be cast from heaven, but that has not taken place yet (Revelation 12:7–9). God gives all of us a choice: If we reject the truth, then we open ourselves up to receive a lie, just as Ahab does. Ahab hears the truth, but he rejects it, and because of this he opens himself up to be deceived by the enemy (2 Chronicles 18:18–22). In this is a lesson for us all.

Zedekiah is a false prophet, and he contradicts what God has said (18:23). If someone is speaking for God, they will always speak according to His Word. And for those who speak of future events, time will tell if they speak the truth or not (18:24–27).

DEATH OF A KING

After hearing these words of Micaiah, Jehoshaphat follows after Ahab anyway, even though God tells him not to go (18:28). In this way, Jehoshaphat actually fulfills Micaiah's prophecy that he will be lured into destruction (18:20–22). Ahab, concerned that the prophecy of his death may come true, disguises himself as a regular soldier (18:29).

The king of Syria knows that if the king is killed, his army will be scattered. So he tells his men to focus on the king and destroy him. So Ahab is wise in disguising himself. Jehoshaphat works so hard to relate to Ahab, to unite the kingdom, that the enemy mistakes him for Ahab (18:30–32).

We know that nothing happens by chance, but all is ordained by God. As the archer releases his arrow, not trying for any particular target, it strikes Ahab between his armor with a mortal wound. You simply cannot escape the judgment of God no matter how hard you try (18:33–34).

As Jehoshaphat returns home, the prophet Jehu rebukes him for his actions. Jehu is the son of Hanani who rebuked King Asa of Judah when he entered into an alliance with a foreign king (16:1–9). In this case, Jehoshaphat was fellowshipping with Ahab, and it put him in a position to be led astray. But Jehu mentions the good that Jehoshaphat has done and the fact that he seeks after God, which tends to be a theme in Chronicles (19:1–3).

REFORMS OF JEHOSHAPHAT

During the king's absence, the people of Judah stray from the Lord. Jehoshaphat tries to get the people back on track, for without a shepherd the sheep are scattered (19:4).

As opposed to being merely representatives of the king, the judges appointed in this section represent God and His justice in the social order of Israel (19:5–7). It is crucial to have judges in office who are guided by God to deal with civil matters. Jehoshaphat seeks to restore godliness to the system in Israel since it is a nation guided by God. Note that he appoints two "attorney generals" of sorts, Amariah for religious matters and Zebadiah for civil matters (19:8–11).

2 CHRONICLES 20:1–37
THE BATTLE IS THE LORD'S

Enemies Defeated   20:1–30
The End of an Era   20:31–37

Setting Up the Section

This chapter describes how three nations rise up against the southern kingdom of Judah. This battle is not described in Kings, which parallels the same period of Israel's history. It is a powerful story distinctive to the Chronicles.

📖 20:1–30

ENEMIES DEFEATED

Verse 1 mentions three people groups who come to make war. The third group, after the Moabites and Ammonites, is associated with the Edomites in this passage, but it is sometimes translated Menuites. While the Menuite territory was associated with Mt. Seir, a mountain range in Edom, they are a separate nation. In 2 Chronicles 26, this same people group brings a tribute to Hezekiah (26:7).

The Moabites and the Ammonites are all blood relatives of Israel. Both people groups descended from the daughters of Lot, Abraham's nephew. Their ancestors were the children of an incestuous relationship between Lot and his two daughters after the destruction of Sodom and Gomorrah (Genesis 19).

Verse 2 does mention specifically the Edomites. This nation was also related to Israel. Esau, the son of Isaac and the brother of Jacob (from whom the nation of Israel descended), is the ancestor of the Edomites (Genesis 36).

Jehoshaphat is fearful and seeks the Lord. Fear causes him to refocus on the Lord and look to Him for strength. Jehoshaphat sets out to seek the Lord and calls for a national fast (2 Chronicles 20:1–5).

Jehoshaphat brings his concerns before the Lord in a kind of prayer/speech. It is important to have a proper perspective on God, especially in the midst of battle. He is in total control; nothing happens without His knowledge and without His permission. Looking to God's history of faithfulness reminds us what He is capable of doing in our lives and gives us confidence for the situations we find ourselves in now (20:6–8).

When Solomon dedicated the temple, his prayer was that God would answer the cry of His people when they were in trouble. Jehoshaphat is echoing the prayer of Solomon here (20:9). When the Israelites had come out of Egypt, Ammon, Moab, and the Edomites had refused Israel passage through their land, and God had forbidden Israel from destroying them. Now this is how they are repaying them: They are joining forces to destroy Judah. (Edom: Numbers 20:18–20; Ammon: Deuteronomy 23:3–4; Moab: Judges 11:17–18).

Take It Home

Jehoshaphat recognizes that he cannot win on his own, and so his eyes are upon the Lord (see Psalm 46). It is when we lose the consciousness of God in our life that things get out of focus and we become anxious and terrified. Just like the Israelites, we often find ourselves surrounded by the enemy. We must remember what David said in Psalm 31:24. Cry out to God and He will remain faithful to answer your prayer (2 Chronicles 20:10–13).

God puts things in proper perspective: Through a man named Jahaziel, He reminds Israel that it's His battle (20:14–15). The battle plan is simple: Go into battle with praise and worship, and see the salvation that the Lord will bring. It seems like a foolish military plan, but God uses it to bring about a great victory (20:16–21).

Demystifying 2 Chronicles

Tekoa is located approximately twelve miles south of Jerusalem and about six miles southeast of Bethlehem. It is located on high ground between two watersheds. The area around it is referred to as the Desert of Tekoa.

As instructed, Jehoshaphat's army enters singing God's praises. The enemy, confused by the people's spirit of praise in the midst of difficulty, ends up killing one another (20:22–24). What was once the valley of the shadow of death God has now made the Valley of Beracah, or the valley of blessing (20:25–26).

When the other nations see what the Lord has done, how He fought for Judah, the fear of the Lord comes upon them. Now God gives the southern kingdom of Judah rest (20:27–30).

📄 20:31–37

THE END OF AN ERA

Jehoshaphat is a godly king. Still he continues to make alliances with the ungodly kings of the northern kingdom in a misguided effort to bring unity between the two nations. Here he makes an alliance with Ahaziah, the son of Ahab. Treaties, however, are not going to smooth over the real differences that exist between the split nation (20:31–35).

Verse 33 reveals the continuing problem with the nation of Israel—they are still not wholehearted in their faith. Even after seeing God's provision, they had not set their hearts on God, clearing away the debris of idolatry around them (1 Kings 22:43).

God is not going to bless an endeavor with those who are rebelling against His law. Here Jehoshaphat makes an alliance with Ahaziah to gather some merchant ships, but before it even gets off the ground, God puts an end to it, refusing to bless the venture (20:36–37).

2 CHRONICLES 21:1–28:27

TURNING FROM GOD

Setting Up the Section

This section marks the end of two generations of spiritual reform in the southern kingdom of Judah under Asa and his son, Jehoshaphat, and the beginning of a period of turning from God.

📖 21:1–20

JEHORAM'S WICKED LEGACY

The people and things you surround yourself with always affect your own walk of faith. Such was the case with Jehoram, the next king of Judah. In this section, the wickedness that flows from Ahab and Jezebel, rulers of Israel, not only affects their daughter, Athaliah, who becomes Jehoram's wife, but also the king himself.

Though Jehoram was preceded by a father and grandfather who led Judah to faith and prosperity, he instead begins his reign with the murder of his brothers (to remove competition for the throne) and leads the people of Judah into idolatry (21:1–6).

God could choose to destroy Jehoram, and thus the reign of a descendant of David, because of Jehoram's wickedness. Instead He honors His promise to David to establish his throne forever (2 Samuel 7:13; 1 Kings 15:4–5; 2 Kings 8:19; 1 Chronicles 17:4–14). Nevertheless, judgment does come upon the nation by various nations rising up against them (2 Chronicles 21:7–11).

Some have called into question the authorship of the letter attributed to Elijah in verses 12–15, since Elijah's death had been recorded in 2 Kings during Jehoshaphat's reign. Others point out, however, that Jehoram and Jehoshaphat ruled together for a time. Elijah would have been elderly but could have been alive long enough to be aware of Jehoram. The text does not say what affliction Jehoram is struck with, but it is serious enough to cause him a slow death (21:12–15).

Critical Observation

Just as Jehoram experienced God's judgment in the form of a physical ailment, so did Asa, the king of Judah who suffered from a foot disease but refused to ask for God's help (16:12–14), and Uzziah, the king of Judah who was cursed with a skin rash (26:16–19).

The reference in verse 13 to the people of Judah prostituting themselves is a reference to their idolatry. They were spiritually unfaithful to God because they mingled their religion with the Canaanite religions around them.

Jehoram only reigns for eight short years, and in his death there is no great burning of incense like they do for the other kings, the ones they loved. In fact, the scriptures say the people didn't care that he died, and they had no sorrow. A person living in sin is affected emotionally, spiritually, and even physically (21:16–20).

📄 22:1–9

AHAZIAH'S FAMILY OF STRIFE

Families can be forces for good and supportive environments, or they can be sources of great strife, bad influences, and true tragedy. Athaliah greatly influences her son to rule wickedly. Ahaziah saturates himself with evil counselors, including his mother, and that is what flows from his life (22:3–4).

Demystifying 2 Chronicles

In 2 Kings 8:26, we are told that Ahaziah is twenty-two years old when he becomes king (not forty-two years old, as is stated here in 2 Chronicles). Scholars agree that it seems likely the copyediting error is here in 2 Chronicles (22:1–2).

This minor discrepancy is often cited as evidence that the Bible, especially the Old Testament, is unreliable. The earliest manuscripts of the Old Testament still in existence today are from the Dead Sea Scrolls, which date around 125 BC. In comparing those scrolls with a scroll of Isaiah from 900 AD, scholars find only 5 percent variation, consisting chiefly of spelling differences. No significant change in meaning is found. The scriptures have been one of the most highly analyzed books of antiquity and are found to be one of the most reliably and carefully transmitted works available today.

The relationships in the intermarriages between the rulers of Israel in the north and the rulers of Judah in the south are becoming increasingly messy. Acting to fulfill a prophecy that predicts he will become king, Jehu goes on a killing spree—he kills Joram, king of Israel; then he kills forty-two of Ahaziah's brothers; and finally he kills Ahaziah. This places Jehu on the throne in the northern kingdom of Israel, and in the southern kingdom of Judah the throne is vacant (22:6–9).

ATHALIAH'S LEGENDARY WICKEDNESS

Once Athaliah gets word that her son is dead, instead of mourning, she kills all the royal heirs and is now going to assume the role as king. This is a direct attack on God's promise to David that his descendants will rule forever. Note that with the other rulers, the Chronicler bookends their accounts with a kind of "stats" report. In Athaliah's case, however, no such stats appear. This provides a statement of a lack of credibility for her reign.

By God's grace, Athaliah has not been entirely successful in her campaign to wipe out the heirs to the throne, and the Davidic dynasty barely survives once again. This time the only surviving heir is one-year-old Joash. Joash is hidden by his aunt for six years in one of the chambers that surrounds the temple (22:10–12).

The Zodakite priest Jehoiada resists Athaliah even as he is raising the hidden heir to the throne. He raises support for reform both in the temple and politically, but it is still risky business to restore the throne to someone from the line of David. Extreme measures are taken to protect the young heir, who is the final link to the Messiah that God had promised (23:1–8).

Jehoiada influences Joash in a positive manner. As he is proclaimed king, he is given a copy of the Law of God, the first five books of Moses, so that he can read and apply them to his life. Joash is only seven years old at the time he takes the throne from Athaliah. Note the irony in verse 13 as Athaliah cries treason—she who usurped the throne and committed murder to attempt to ensure her power. While Jehoiada is credited with Joash's rise to the throne, it seems clear that the coup had both religious and political roots (23:9–15).

JOASH: YOUNG AND IMPRESSIONABLE

Jehoiada makes a covenant that Judah will once again be the Lord's people. The sacrificial system is brought back, as God is truly worshiped once again. Jehoiada is a positive influence on young King Joash and the entire kingdom of Judah (23:16–18).

The gatekeepers are needed not only to prevent anything that is unclean from entering and defiling the temple but also to allow those who belonged in the temple to freely enter (these people had not succeeded in protecting Israel from Athaliah). Now that the proper king, Joash, a descendant of David, is in place, peace returns to the land for a brief period (23:16–21).

At this point, high priest Jehoiada is truly the power behind the throne. He is a good role model for Joash, and the people of Judah are blessed by his actions (24:1–3). Joash wants to rebuild and repair the temple of God, and he sets the Levites in charge of this project. But they don't do it quickly and are dragging their feet, moving at a snail's pace. They have no heart to restore the worship of God (24:5–6). Athaliah and her sons plundered the house of God, and now it is time to restore and rebuild what she destroyed (24:6–7).

Verse 7 refers to Athaliah's sons, yet part of the history recorded is that Athaliah murdered any possible rivals to the throne. We don't know the exact use of this expression. It could be that her sons had a part in the plans for destroying the temple, or it could be that the term *sons* is used of Athaliah's followers.

Joash has a box placed outside the temple so that the people can give extra money to God for this restoration project. A half-shekel is already given each year, by every male over twenty years old, for the upkeep of the tabernacle and later the temple (Exodus 30). Now the people have a way to give more if they desire, and the people respond with a willing spirit by rejoicing in the opportunity to participate in the Lord's work (2 Chronicles 24:8–14).

Jehoiada dies once he has completed the work he was called to do (24:15–16). The description of his old age in verse 15 signifies honor and respect. He was a positive influence in the life of Joash, and the nation was blessed by God as a result. His burial is in sharp contrast to that of Jehoram. Jehoiada is buried with the kings because the people loved him for bringing spiritual reform to the nation and for putting God back on the throne (24:15–16).

Joash is like a spiritual chameleon, changing his behavior to fit those who are around him. Joash never really had a heart for the Lord—he is more influenced by others. God's desire is not to bring judgment and destroy Joash but to see him turn from his evil ways and live. In light of this, God sends prophets to warn him, but Joash refuses to heed their warnings (24:17–19).

Asherah, the false god mentioned in verse 18, is a fertility goddess of the Canaanite religions and mythologies. Often associated with Baal, her shrines took the form of upright wooden poles. The tree was a symbol associated with Asherah worship.

Zechariah must have been like a brother to Joash, because they grew up together. Joash has a choice to heed the warnings from this close confidant, but instead he orders the death of Zechariah to be carried out at the very place he was anointed king by Jehoiada. It is a terrible sign of how quickly our hearts can forget. Oftentimes—even when we speak the truth in love—the truth is the opposite of what people want to hear (24:20–22).

Chronicles again equates the military defeat of Judah—at the hands of the Syrians—with the judgment of God against Joash's sin. This is meant to both remind and warn the remnant of Israel, who is the audience for the book. Just like with the other evil kings, no fanfare is given in Joash's death, which transpired at the hands of his own servants. He is not even buried with the other kings—a stark contrast to how his mentor was celebrated in his death (24:23–24).

📖 **25:1–28**

AMAZIAH'S HARD HEART

Amaziah is not wholeheartedly devoted to the Lord, although he responds to the prophetic warning properly. This is an idea Jesus returns to when He speaks of those who honor God with their lips and yet their hearts are far from Him (Matthew 7:21–23). Amaziah executes those who murdered his father, which is considered a relatively mild reaction when compared to the customs of other kings at the time. He honors the laws of Moses by sparing the children, and in fact the Chronicler quotes the Mosaic Law in verse 4 (Deuteronomy 24:16; 2 Chronicles 25:1–5).

Amaziah hires 100,000 mercenaries from Israel to assist him in battle. But a prophet of God warns him not to receive help from Israel, for God is not with them. If he uses Israel to help him, they will be defeated. Amaziah is torn—he wants God's help, but he also wants the money (25:6–9).

God gives Amaziah and the children of Judah a great victory over the Edomites, even without the help of the dismissed mercenaries. These soldiers-for-hire lose the chance to add to their fee by taking spoils from the battle. On their way home to Israel, the mercenaries attack some of the cities and villages in Judah, getting back some of the spoil that they would have gained if they had been able to fight against the Edomites (25:10–13).

In response to Judah's God-granted victory, Amaziah immediately strays, gathers the gods of the people he has just defeated, and brings them home with him. In doing this, he is now worshiping these gods. God is gracious and sends a prophet to warn the king of his destructive ways. However, Amaziah has hardened himself so much to God that he is unwilling to heed the prophet's warning. Instead, he prepares to avenge what the mercenaries have done to his people by fighting the northern kingdom (25:14–17).

Demystifying 2 Chronicles

Amaziah's looting of the temple idols in verse 14 is not uncommon. At the time, these were considered war trophies. First Samuel, in fact, describes a time when the Israelite's ark of the covenant was captured and held on display by the Philistines (1 Samuel 5:1–2). Amaziah's worship of these gods, however, clearly disregarded God's commands and set him on a path of destruction.

The king of the northern kingdom of Israel is a different Joash than Amaziah's predecessor. The king of Israel cautions Amaziah against attacking them, reminding him that his victory against the Edomites was God's doing. As we watch yet another rebellious and wicked king lead the Israelites into trouble, we are struck by the Chronicler's explanation that Amaziah's hardness of heart is from God. As a result, Judah is defeated because of its sin (25:18–22). Not only is the house of God plundered, but so, too, is the king's house, and many are taken away captive as slaves (25:23–24).

Take It Home

Sin destroys your defenses, just as Israel destroyed six hundred feet of the wall of Jerusalem (25:23). The suffering of Judah reminds us of the consequences of sin—it affects our worship of God, destroys and robs us of our witness, and eventually enslaves us completely. Amaziah has led the people astray, and their anger burns into a murderous rage. His sin has pushed them over the edge and bred their own sinfulness (25:25–28).

26:1–23

UZZIAH: THE PROUD KING

People recognize that Amaziah's heart is far from the Lord, and during his reign, after only six years, his son Uzziah begins to co-reign with him. For twenty-three years they reign together. Then after his father's death, Uzziah is the sole king in the kingdom of Judah, reigning for another twenty-nine years. Uzziah is a good king and a strong leader, which is the reason the people place him on the throne at the age of sixteen (26:1).

After the death of his father, Uzziah begins to recapture cities that were lost to the enemy and restore them or build them up. The nation enjoys a time of prosperity, not because Uzziah is doing good works but because he places God before everything else in his life (26:2–5). God has begun to once again bless the southern kingdom of Judah with victory over their enemies. The Chronicler emphasizes this again and again: When the Israelites seek God, they become mighty (26:6–8). Under Uzziah's leadership, the people begin to honor God and also return to cultivating the land. As a result, it truly blossoms once again (26:9–10).

Uzziah is able to achieve success in three areas: victory in war, massive building projects, and making the land fruitful again. The strength of his army and his ability to develop weapons of war also help to put down the enemy (26:11–15). In fact, Uzziah becomes too self-important for his own good. He is a king, not a priest, and thus not allowed in the temple to offer incense to the Lord. But, because of his pride, he approaches God without humility. As a result, God strikes him with leprosy, and he is banished from the city, forced to co-reign with his son, Jotham (26:16–23).

Take It Home

Many today try and do what Uzziah did—approach God any way they desire. The story follows Uzziah from power to pride to his downfall. His strength is his weakness (Proverbs 16:18–19; 18:12). When we become proud, God always has a way to humble us and give us the right perspective again. We are strong when we look to the Lord for our strength in humility (2 Corinthians 12:10).

📖 27:1–9

JOTHAM: A FORCE FOR GOOD

In contrast to the mixed records of his predecessors, Jotham is a good king. The Chronicler is almost completely positive about his reign. His only flaw is that he avoids the temple, most likely because he witnessed what happened to his father, Uzziah. Tragically, this kind of reluctance is common even today; children see what has happened to their parents in church and retreat or isolate themselves from any kind of Christian fellowship (27:1–2; see Hebrews 10:24–25).

Ophel is where the old city of David was located, farther down the slope of Mount Moriah (2 Chronicles 27:3). Jotham looks to the Lord for guidance, but he never really has a true heart of worship. Still, his victory over the Ammonites highlights God's approval of him (27:4–6).

As Ahaz, Jotham's son, takes the throne, Judah is at a relatively good place. Unfortunately, whatever strides were made toward the Lord are going to be pushed back by the new king. The kingdom of Judah will never fully recover from the influences of King Ahaz (27:7–9).

📖 28:1–27

AHAZ: INFIDELITY AND DEFEAT

When God associates a king with the kings of Israel, it is a rebuke. Ahaz is just as wicked as the northern kings were. He is not at all like David, the standard for all kings to be judged by. Ahaz goes crazy and sets up places of false worship, offering sacrifices to pagan gods, and even offering his own children in the fire as a sacrifice to them (28:1–4).

Demystifying 2 Chronicles

The sacrifice of unwanted children was a pagan ritual mentioned elsewhere in scripture (Leviticus 18:21; Deuteronomy 12:31; 2 Kings 16:3). The place where they offer these children to the god Molech, by passing them through the fire, is located in the valley of Hinnom, which is just south and west of Jerusalem. In the New Testament, this area is used as a garbage dump, which continued to burn day and night. Jesus uses the valley of Hinnom as an illustration of hell, Gehenna (Matthew 10:28).

God now brings judgment upon Ahaz and Judah for their wickedness. He uses the Syrians and the northern kingdom of Israel to carry out His judgment. But Israel goes overboard and takes back home with them many slaves, which God forbids (28:5–8).

The prophet Oded rebukes Israel for thinking that they are better than Judah. The people in Samaria actually obey the prophet's warning (28:9–10). These leaders are wise in what they say. They recognize that they are not perfect, that the nation has many problems, and by continuing to disobey God's commands, they are fearful that they will just add to their sin and judgment (28:11–13).

It was a common practice to humiliate captives, and many times they took them away naked. But now they are given clothes and food, and the weak are even given donkeys to ride on so they can make their way home. The Israelites do the right thing in releasing their captives (28:14–15). Ahaz and the kingdom of Judah are being attacked from every side. You would think this would at least get Ahaz's attention, but the king's heart is so hard that he refuses to listen to the warnings. He shuts his eyes to the truth (28:16–21).

As the pressure from God increases, Ahaz hardens his heart even more and refuses to look to God. Ahaz is sincere in his walk with these other gods, just as many people are today (28:22–23). Because the king doesn't hear from the true and living God, he makes sure that no one else hears either, and he blocks the house of God so no one can enter.

In Ahaz's death, Hezekiah will now reign in Judah. Although he is truly a great king, he will not be able to overcome the spiritual darkness that was blanketed by his father, king Ahaz. The kingdom of Judah is only about 110 years away from the Babylonian invasion. Even one bad leader can affect the course of a nation for hundreds of years and generations to come (28:24–27).

2 CHRONICLES 29:1–32:33

HEZEKIAH: A GOOD KING

Setting Up the Section

Judah never fully recovers from Ahaz's negative influence, and judgment in the form of the Babylonian captivity is looming a mere 110 years down the road. Even a good king, like Hezekiah, cannot reverse their path away from the Lord.

📖 29:1–36

THE TEMPLE RESTORED

Hezekiah is probably the best king since the time of David. He brings spiritual reform to the nation, and he is also able to remove the idols that had crept into the people's practice of worship, including the bronze serpent that Moses had used to challenge the people to stop grumbling in the desert following their deliverance from captivity in Egypt (Numbers 21:4–8; 2 Kings 18:1–4). It's been about eight hundred years since their ancestors wandered in the wilderness, and the people are now worshiping this bronze serpent on a pole (2 Kings 18:4).

Hezekiah is sandwiched between his father, Ahaz, who was Judah's worst king up to that point, and his son, Manasseh, who also followed evil ways. Yet clearly God is the focus of Hezekiah's life. Isaiah the prophet influences his life in a positive manner

(Isaiah 36–39). Hezekiah wastes no time in bringing forth spiritual reform to the nation, beginning with the reopening of the house of worship, the temple. He begins immediately to cleanse, repair, and restore it to usher in an era of spiritual revival (2 Chronicles 29:3). Under his father, the temple had become a place to store junk—an appropriate metaphor for the clutter in the hearts of the people. Hezekiah is ready to de-clutter (29:4–5).

Hezekiah asserts that Judah is under judgment for its neglect of the temple—including the rituals that God had given the people to remember His faithfulness, such as lighting the menorah (29:6–9). Hezekiah is going to gather the religious leaders to see that they get right with God and to consecrate their hearts before the Lord (29:10–11; Hosea 4:6).

It takes sixteen days to clean the temple proper and to restore the house of God to a place of worship. Imagine the amount of garbage that needed to be hauled out. This is a major project of restoration (29:18–19). The ceremony of restoring the temple consists of three crucial parts: atonement sacrifices brought by the leaders, arrangement of music, and sacrifices of thanksgiving from the people. Hezekiah orders sacrifices to be offered for *all of Israel*—an expression that, from here on, the Chronicler uses to refer to Judah together with the refugees from the northern tribes. The entire process—propelled by God's Spirit and blessing—takes less than three weeks (29:20–36).

📖 30:1–27

PASSOVER OBSERVED

The northern kingdom of Israel has been carried away captive by the Assyrians for their idolatry. Only a few people remain in the land, and Hezekiah reaches out to them and urges them to get right with God. Hezekiah began his reign the first month of the ecclesiastical (or religious) year, which was the month of Nisan, or March/April. Now the Passover was also celebrated in the month of Nisan. The problem was that the temple was not cleaned until the sixteenth of the month, and Passover began on the fourteenth of the month, followed by the Feast of Unleavened Bread. God made a provision to the people, through Moses, that if they could not celebrate Passover in the first month, they could celebrate it on the fourteenth day of the second month, so this is precisely what Hezekiah begins to institute (Numbers 9:9–11). The king also invites those who have escaped from the hands of the Assyrians in the northern kingdom, not only to join in the Passover celebration but to return to the Lord and restore unity to the kingdom (2 Chronicles 30:1–9).

Even after many have been carried away captive, some Israelites in the north still refuse to repent of their sin. They laugh in the face of God. Some do respond and go to Jerusalem to celebrate the Passover. In Judah, they experience unity in the Lord, which unites them as one nation (30:10–12).

Demystifying 2 Chronicles

During the feast of Passover you were to take your own lamb, without spot or blemish, and sacrifice it yourself (Deuteronomy 16:16–17). The problem was that many of the people had not ceremonially cleansed themselves, and so the Levites sacrificed the lambs for those who were unclean. These people were seeking God, and thus, they just came as they were. Hezekiah understood that it is not the religious ritual that makes one acceptable to God; it is a matter of the heart (2 Chronicles 30:13–20).

When true revival breaks out, God often gives new songs, as happens here. Studying the Word of God also becomes a focus again. The energy is so amazing that they extend their celebration, and Hezekiah gives out of his own possessions unto the Lord (30:21–24).

When your eyes are focused on the Lord, you can't help but rejoice. You have the right perspective on life (30:25–27).

31:1–21

THE REFORMS OF HEZEKIAH

The spiritual revival is leading now to social changes, as the false worship places are destroyed—and along with them all the sexual perversion and carnality that accompanies them. This is not only affecting the southern kingdom of Judah but has also spread northward, into Israel. Hezekiah is following the example that David laid out regarding temple service for the priests. Each division serves for two weeks out of the year in the temple, and the rest of the time they minister to those in their hometown. Remember that during the time of David, the priests were spread out throughout the land of Israel in forty-eight Levitical cities so that no one was more than a day's journey from a priest. Hezekiah leads by example. He gives to the work of God, and he is encouraging the people to do the same (31:1–4).

When people's hearts are touched by God, they willfully and joyfully give. For four months, the people keep bringing gifts to help support the priests and their families, so much so that it is in heaps. The priests and Levites are blessed beyond measure—they have more than they need (31:5–15; Ephesians 3:20).

Hezekiah makes sure everyone gets what is rightfully his or hers. Throughout the land, anyone who works in the temple receives a portion for every family member over three years old (31:16–19). (Children younger than three were still nursing, but once they were weaned from breast milk, they received their portion). Hezekiah and the nation prosper, because his heart is set on doing what is right before the Lord. His eyes are properly focused on God, and his priorities are right. He puts God first in his life (31:20–21).

HUMILITY REWARDED

King Ahaz, Hezekiah's father, had made a treaty with Tiglath-pileser, king of Assyria, for protection (2 Kings 16:7). Now that Hezekiah is on the throne, he breaks any treaties that his father had made (2 Kings 18:7). Jerusalem has two main sources of water, the spring of Gihon in the Kidron Valley and the spring of En-Rogel, which was two miles to the south. Hezekiah has two groups of workers—one group working from the spring of Gihon, digging a tunnel through solid rock toward the city, and another group digging from the pool of Siloam out of the city. His goal is to bring the water supply into the city. And this tunnel, which is some 1,777 feet long, is a constant source of fresh water. This tunnel Hezekiah builds exists in Israel to this day (32:1–4).

Hezekiah fortifies the city, builds what was broken, builds towers on the walls, and prepares weapons for war. Hezekiah does all that he can do, and then he commits the rest to God. Hezekiah not only strengthens himself but his people as well—by sharing with them the Word of God (32:5–8).

Lachish is about thirty miles southwest of Jerusalem. It's from this nearby location that Sennacherib, the king of Assyria, sends his representatives to Jerusalem to give the Israelites an ultimatum to surrender or die fighting. Intimidation plays a big role in what the Assyrians are doing. Rabshakeh, the field commander—not understanding why Hezekiah had removed the places of false worship—tells them that their God is not going to spare them when their own king has destroyed all the high places. Rabshakeh is comparing the God of Israel with other gods. However, this only reveals his ignorance of the God of Israel (32:9–15). As Rabshakeh speaks his threats in their native tongue, Hebrew (2 Kings 18:26), he is trying to also intimidate the crowd (2 Chronicles 32:16–19).

Hezekiah and Isaiah are prayer partners, lifting their concerns up to the Lord, the only one who can truly help them and give them peace in the middle of this storm. One angel wipes out 185,000 Assyrians in one night, so that when Israel wakes that morning, they see all the dead bodies of their enemy. Not bad for one night's work. Sennacherib, king of Assyria, heads home in retreat and goes into his temple to worship his god, and while he is there his two sons kill him (32:20–23).

With the southern kingdom of Judah victorious, Hezekiah is exalted, and this may be the spark that sends him on a downward trend. The account in Chronicles of Hezekiah's pride is fleshed out in more detail in 2 Kings 20 and Isaiah 38. First his pride begins to build, but Hezekiah recognizes it and repents of it. Because of that, God says judgment will not come in his days but in future generations. Again Hezekiah greatly prospers, which again leads to pride in his life. As these ambassadors from Babylon come, he opens all the storehouses and shows off his wealth. Isaiah tells him he acts foolishly and warns of the coming captivity (Isaiah 39:6–7). Hezekiah is truly a great king and comparable to king David in his actions. However, even his godly reforms are not enough to rescue the future of a rebellious people (2 Chronicles 32:24–33).

2 CHRONICLES 33:1–36:23

RAPID DECLINE

Setting Up the Section

The account of Manasseh in 2 Kings 21:1–18 is harsher than this one. The writer of Chronicles wants to emphasize to his audience that even the worst sinner can be forgiven and restored through repentance and faith. However, we also witness Israel's rapid decline before their eventual defeat at the hands of the Babylonians.

📖 33:1–20

MANASSEH'S SINFUL REIGN

Manasseh was arguably the most wicked king in Judah's troubled history. Manasseh destroys the reforms of his father with remarkable speed. He even goes as far as setting up an idol in the Holy of Holies, sacrificing his children to the god Molech, and going after all the abominations that the nations who were driven from the land practiced (33:1–9).

God's mercy is unbelievable. Manasseh should have been wiped out, and yet God is calling to him, trying to get him to listen and gain the attention of the nation, but he refuses. Tradition tells us that during Manasseh's reign, he takes Isaiah the prophet captive, places him in a hollowed out log, and saws him in two pieces. He does not want to hear what the prophets have to say, for they go against what he is doing. Since he refuses to listen to the prophets, God tries to get his attention by taking him captive by the Assyrians. They place hooks in his nose and fetters on him, and carry him away to Babylon. This is exactly what Manasseh needs to turn to God. Manasseh's conversion is very similar to that of Nebuchadnezzar, king of Babylon. Nebuchadnezzar's pride brings him to a state of madness until he finally looks up to the true and living God (33:10–20).

📖 33:21–35:27

FAITH IN THE FACE OF NEARING JUDGMENT

Amon, Manasseh's son, is also a wicked king, and he is spinning out of control. Amon does not repent of his sin but remains lost, moving in the opposite direction of God. The die is cast, and the nation sinks lower and lower, drowning in its wickedness. Amon is only king for two years before his own men assassinate him (33:21–25).

With Amon's death, Josiah becomes king and brings about the last revival before the southern kingdom of Judah is taken into captivity by the Babylonians. It is thirty-four years before Babylon's first invasion of Judah. Israel has already been in Assyrian captivity for eighty years. God brings judgment upon the northern kingdom of Israel via military defeat and enslavement, and Judah still does not repent. Since the split, Judah has had five good kings who try to steer the nation back toward God—Asa, Jehoshaphat, Joash, Hezekiah, and now Josiah.

Critical Observation

Josiah takes the throne in Judah when he is only eight years old. Then, when he turns sixteen, he begins to seek the Lord with all his heart. By the time he is twenty years old, he is purging the land of all the false worship that his grandfather, Manasseh, had started. Jeremiah's ministry begins in Josiah's thirteenth year as king, when Josiah is twenty-one years old, and continues some forty-one years—into the Babylonian captivity. Josiah is the fulfillment of a prophecy from three hundred years earlier (1 Kings 13:1–2), when God calls Josiah by name (2 Chronicles 34:1–7).

Shaphan goes throughout all Judah and Israel collecting money for the restoration of the temple, and when he is finished, he brings the offering to Hilkiah, the high priest. Now the massive temple restoration project begins. As they purge the temple of garbage, Hilkiah finds a copy of the books of Moses (34:8–15). Josiah tears his clothes because the Word of God pierces his heart. He understands why judgment has come upon God's people. Josiah rightly recognizes that not only he stands guilty before God but so does the entire nation (34:16–19).

Josiah wants Hilkiah and his men to go to Huldah, the prophetess, to inquire of God in what they should do next. Their sin is exposed and they need wisdom (34:20–22). Huldah tells them God will spare Josiah; however, judgment is still coming for the nation—God is not convinced that their hearts are sincere. Jeremiah describes Judah's reform as pretense rather than wholehearted repentance (Jeremiah 3:10). God rebukes Judah for her false loyalty (Jeremiah 7:8). The temple and the rituals of faith have become a false mask for the people's true convictions (2 Chronicles 34:23–28). Instead of giving up in the face of coming judgment, Josiah leads the people by giving them the Word of God and being an example to them (34:29–33). Just as his great-grandfather Hezekiah had done, Josiah reinstitutes the Passover celebration. Josiah also follows in his forefather's footsteps by properly organizing the priests (1 Chronicles 24; 2 Chronicles 8:14). He is generous with his own resources and models the heart of a shepherd caring for his flock (35:1–9).

The people celebrate the Passover with urgency, just as they did in Egypt during the first Passover (Exodus 12:11). The priests serve everyone, just as Christ will one day offer Himself for the salvation of the world (Mark 10:45). This Passover celebration is even bigger than Hezekiah's (35:10–19).

It is 610 BC, and the Assyrian Empire is on the decline. Nineveh has fallen to the Babylonians in 612 BC, forcing the Assyrians to concentrate their forces around Haran and Carchemish, in the area of the upper Euphrates River. Egypt also is weak and ineffective. So Pharaoh Neco is coming to Carchemish to make an alliance with Assyria to fight off the Babylonians. Pharaoh Neco warns Josiah not to get involved in this battle, but Josiah does not listen. It costs him his life. Josiah was truly a godly king, but he had his weaknesses as well (35:20–27).

📖 36:1–23

INEVITABLE EXILE

The Chronicler quickly traces the reign and disobedience of Josiah's three sons (Jehoahaz, Johoiakim, and Zedekiah) and his grandson (Jehoiachin). The account is expanded on in Kings (2 Kings 23:31–24:20), but here it underscores how the Israelites are tumbling ever nearer to the inevitable exile from the promised land (36:1–14).

Critical Observation

The southern kingdom of Judah was in captivity for seventy years because of their idolatry and failure to follow God. God had lead them into the promised land and commanded them to work there for six years, allowing the land rest every seventh year—a year of sabbatical that was meant to purge and restore, and during which time all debts were forgiven. But the Israelites neglected to obey God's command for 490 years. Scholars note that God gave the land its seventy years of rest and taught His people about trusting in Him during their time in captivity.

The events of this chapter coincide with Jeremiah's prophecy. Often nicknamed "the wailing prophet," Jeremiah is crying out that it is all over and to not fight against the Babylonians, for this is of God (Jeremiah 21:3–10). The nation is sinking deeper and deeper into idolatry, becoming more wicked, even after the judgment of God has begun. God tries to warn them over and over again by sending them prophets, but they refuse to listen and mock the messengers of God. God's long-suffering has come to an end, and the people and the nation have come to the point of no return (Jeremiah 32:1–5). The time is now 586 BC, and the Babylonians make their final invasion into Jerusalem, destroying the city, the temple, and taking with them the rest of the people, killing many. Zedekiah and his sons are captured. Then the Babylonians put out the eyes of Zedekiah— the last thing he sees before being led away captive to Babylon is the death of his sons, who are executed before his eyes (2 Chronicles 36:15–21).

The Chronicler is careful to emphasize one final time the main theme of his account— the faithfulness of God. This passage is very similar to the opening of Ezra (Ezra 1:1–4), and Cyrus's release of Israel is intended to allow them to reenter the land that God has given them and rebuild the temple (2 Chronicles 36:22–23).

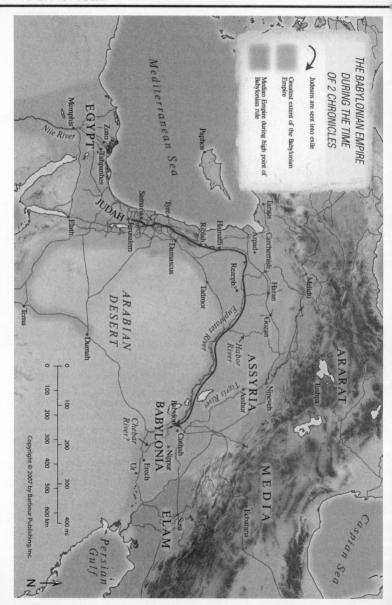

THE BABYLONIAN EMPIRE
DURING THE TIME
OF 2 CHRONICLES

Judeans are sent into exile

Greatest extent of the Babylonian Empire

Median Empire during high point of Babylonian rule

Mediterranean Sea

EGYPT
Memphis
Nile River
Zoan
Tahpanhes

JUDAH
Samaria
Jerusalem
Elath
Damascus

Paphos

Tyre
Ribiah
Hamath
Arpad
Carchemish
Melidi
Haran
Gozan

Targus

ARARAT
Tushpa

Rezeph?
Tadmor

Euphrates River

Habor River

ASSYRIA
Nineveh
Asshur

Tigris River

MEDIA

Echatana

Tema

ARABIAN
DESERT

Dumah

BABYLONIA
Babylon
Cuthah
Chebar River?
Nippur
Erech
Ur

ELAM
Susa

Caspian Sea

Persian
Gulf

N

0   100   200   300   400   500   600 km
0   100   200   300   400 mi

Copyright © 2007 by Barbour Publishing, Inc.

EZRA

INTRODUCTION TO EZRA

The book of Ezra is a chronicle of hope and restoration. Originally, Ezra and Nehemiah were together as one book, recording the stories about a remnant of God's chosen people who had been taken captive by the Babylonians after the destruction of Jerusalem and who were returning to the promised land to rebuild their nation.

The dramatic narrative starts in 538 BC and revolves around three epic tales. First is the struggle to rebuild the temple in Jerusalem under Zerubbabel (chapters 1–6). Next is the second expedition from Babylon sixty years later, led by Ezra, a scribe and scholar, whose task it is to reestablish the Law of Moses (chapters 7–10). Third is the work of Nehemiah, the appointed governor leading the rebuilding of Jerusalem until around 433 BC.

AUTHOR

Bible experts have long suggested that the author of Ezra also wrote 1 and 2 Chronicles and Nehemiah, referring to the writer as "the Chronicler." But recent scholars question this assumption and conclude both Ezra and Nehemiah were not written by the Chronicler. As to who wrote Ezra and Nehemiah, there is support for the Jewish tradition that teaches Ezra was the writer of both books. It's interesting to note that the narration switches from third person to first person after Ezra appears in the story (chapter 7).

The book was likely written between 460 and 440 BC, but there are competing views regarding the date.

PURPOSE

Ezra, with Nehemiah, tells the story of God's faithfulness to His promises regarding His chosen people, restoring them to their land after seventy years of captivity.

OCCASION

Three views dominate regarding the date of Ezra's return to Jerusalem. If the Artaxerxes mentioned is Artaxerxes I, Ezra returned in 458 BC, in the seventh year of the king's reign. About thirteen years later, Nehemiah begins rebuilding the walls of Jerusalem. During the dozen years Nehemiah is building, Ezra returns again, and the two work together in shaping the nation. This view is the most plausible, but there are a few issues with it. For one, Nehemiah is not mentioned in Ezra. Also, Ezra is only mentioned once in Nehemiah, with nothing said of his reforms earlier in 458 BC.

Another view suggests Ezra actually returns to Jerusalem under Artaxerxes II, in 398 BC, after Nehemiah. This would fit better, for example, with the issue of marrying foreign wives. (Ezra battles the trend, so why would it still be a pervasive problem thirteen years later when Nehemiah arrives?) Yet Nehemiah 8:2 suggests Nehemiah and Ezra are contemporaries.

Third, Ezra may have returned in the thirty-seventh year of Artaxerxes I, during Nehemiah's second term (428 BC). This view is willing to say the text has been corrupted, with the seventh year actually meaning thirty-seventh. There is no evidence to support this position.

THEMES

Ezra, with Nehemiah, relates historical events that communicate the love and power of a God active in the world. Some themes include: God's sovereignty, God's covenant with His people, and God's grace.

HISTORICAL CONTEXT

Ezra covers the period following 539 BC, well into the time in biblical history called the post-exilic period. The exile of Judah occurred under Nebuchadnezzar, who deported the remnant of Israel to Babylon in 587 and 586 BC. But on October 29, 539 BC, Babylon surrendered to the Persians, and the policies of a new emperor, Cyrus II, came into place. This was good news for the Jews because Persians were known for being temperate in their treatment of captors. In general, they did not deport and relocate captive peoples. They also were ecumenical in their religious policy. They encouraged subject peoples to worship their own gods and goddesses. And, perhaps most importantly, they encouraged exiles to return to their homelands.

Demystifying Ezra

Here is a list of Persia's most prominent leaders, most of whom you'll meet in Ezra and its companion book, Nehemiah.

- Cyrus II, also known as Cyrus the Great (539–530 BC)
- Cambyses II (530–522 BC), son of Cyrus
- Darius I (521–486 BC)
- Xerxes I, also known in the Bible as Ahasuerus (486–464 BC), the king in the book of Esther
- Artaxerxes I (464–423 BC)
- Darius II (423–404 BC)
- Artaxerxes II (404–359 BC)

OUTLINE

GOD MOVES HISTORY

WHAT YOU CAN DISCOVER ON THE CHURCH ROLL

GOD'S PEOPLE IN GRAY TIMES

LET THE TROUBLES BEGIN

GOD IS THE RULER YET

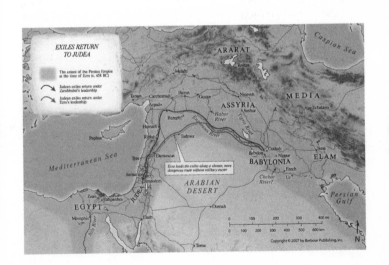

EZRA 1:1–11

GOD MOVES HISTORY

Setting Up the Section

Israel was not a major player in the days of Ezra and Nehemiah. The big powers were first Babylon, then Persia. No one cared about the postage-stamp size kingdom in the political backwater of the Ancient Near East or about the people who used to live there. But God did indeed still care about the Israelites. He had made promises to them and will see to it they are fulfilled.

📖 **1:1–4**

THE WORD THAT DRIVES HISTORY

In this passage, *the word* is more central than the event. In Cyrus's edict, quoted in Ezra 1:2–4, the Jews are allowed to return to Judah and rebuild the temple. But behind this event is the word that Yahweh had spoken years previously to Jeremiah (see Jeremiah 25:12; 29:10–11).

Jeremiah had said there were seventy years for Babylon. The numeral is approximate. It was seventy-three years from the fall of Nineveh (612 BC) to the fall of Babylon (539 BC). From the accession of Nebuchadnezzar and the taking of the first crop of Judean exiles (605 BC) to the fall of Babylon, it was sixty-six years.

Critical Observation

The Jews' freedom came through Cyrus, the Persian conqueror. Note the prophecies about him in Isaiah 41:2–3; 44:24–28; and 45:1–6, especially verse 4. This text reveals the secret: It is the Lord who stirs the heart of Cyrus, king of Persia (Ezra 1:1), thus Cyrus's edict in Ezra 1:2–4.

Cyrus's permission for the Jews to return home and to rebuild Yahweh's house is consistent with his practices in Babylon toward conquered people. They are reflected in the famous Cyrus Cylinder, the cuneiform-covered clay cylinder that recounts his rule after the conquest of Babylon.

THE SECRET THAT EXPLAINS OBEDIENCE

God works not only in Cyrus's heart, but He also stirs the leaders of the Jewish remnant to leave what they have known and go home to rebuild the temple in Jerusalem (1:5).

Note the central focus: rebuilding the house of Yahweh (1:2–5, 7). Rebuilding the temple has to do with the restoration of public worship. Seeking God in public worship is the heart of the Jews' existence, and yet they have to be stirred up by God to do it.

Take It Home

This is the same thing that Paul teaches in Philippians 2:12–13. Why do Christians obey? Because "God is working in you, giving you the desire to obey him and the power to do what pleases him" (Philippians 2:13 NLT). We obey—we work out our salvation—because God enables us to do so.

SIGNS THAT ENCOURAGE BELIEVERS

Nebuchadnezzar originally takes the vessels mentioned in these passages to Babylon in 605 BC and places them in the "treasury of his god." Since Yahweh's furniture is pilfered, Yahweh is considered "weaker" than Babylon's gods (compare Ezra 1:7–8 to Daniel 1:1–2; 5:2–4, 22–23).

In Babylon they toast one another as they use the defeated god's table service (Daniel 5:4). (They don't know that in Daniel 1:2 we are told that the Lord gave these vessels to the Babylonians.)

But we see here in Ezra that the utensils that had been taken from Yahweh's house are being inventoried to Sheshbazzar, the leader of Judah (Ezra 1:8). The Jewish believer who saw this must have savored each vessel counted, each article tallied; each one was a token that defeat had been turned to victory.

Demystifying Ezra

The mundane inventory of this passage actually constitutes, item by item, signs that Yahweh is removing the stigma and taking away the shame. These are not dramatic signs. They are low-key signs that Yahweh is restoring His people and His worship. Although the Lord sometimes gives His people dramatic signs, those tend to be exceptional. He usually offers modest signs, like the bread and the wine at the Lord's Table.

EZRA 2:1–69

WHAT YOU CAN DISCOVER ON THE CHURCH ROLL

Setting Up the Section

Most of Ezra 2 is instructional more than entertaining. It shows what is—or should be—characteristic of the people of God.

Ezra 2 includes a list of returnees in 538 BC, the first group led by Zerubbabel—years before Ezra comes on the scene. There's a parallel passage in Nehemiah 7.

📄 2:1–35

THE PILGRIMAGE THAT CALLS

In Ezra 2:1, we're reminded that this historical book is about *people*: the remnant of God's chosen ones, descendants of Nebuchadnezzar's captives who had not forgotten the promised land or God's promises—and who had not been forgotten by God.

The leaders are listed in 2:2. Zerubbabel is the grandson of King Jehoachin. There are ten others, eleven if Nahamani, listed in Nehemiah 7:7, is included

The lay people in Ezra 2:3–35 are listed either by a recognized family or clan, or by hometown. The totals do not exactly match Nehemiah 7, probably a result of copying errors as ancient manuscripts were copied by hand through the years.

📄 2:36–42

THE PASSION THAT RULES

In verses 2–35 we have the tallies of the lay people; in verses 36–39 we have the tallies of four clans of priests. The total of almost 4,300 (actually 4,289) priests constitutes approximately 10 percent of the total found in Ezra 2:64.

One in ten of the returnees is a priest. Why so many? Because they long to serve at the altar in a restored temple and participate in public worship of God, serving where they are meant to serve.

Those mentioned in 2:40–42 probably are Levites, 341 in all. But some scholars think that only the seventy-four mentioned in verse 40 directly assisted the priests. That's one Levite to every fifty-eight priests: precious few to do the chores and the tasks connected with temple worship—a lot of work and little recognition. Not a big incentive for a Levite to move home, but nonetheless seventy-four of them do.

A good bit of Christian work is plain and basic, with not much flair involved. We are not called to gain recognition. Yet, an assisting role does not always appeal to our pride. These seventy-four Levites stand as an example of devoted assistants unscathed by pride.

📖 2:43–58

THE PROVIDENCE THAT LEADS

This passage contains two sections of names: the temple servants (2:43–54) and the sons of Solomon's servants (2:55–57), totaling 392 people.

According to Ezra 8:20, David had given these temple servants to the Levites to assist them. Their work, therefore, consists of the most menial tasks around the temple complex.

Three quarters of the temple servants' names and more than a third of Solomon's servants' names are foreign, according to scholars. The speculation is that these people are descendants of prisoners of war (during David's time) or of the pagans that Solomon pressed into slavery (see 1 Kings 9:20–21). If so, now the descendants of these pagan ancestors are listed among the covenant people of God as they are restored to their land.

It seems a chance occurrence: an ancestor captured in war and taken to Israel to do grunt work around the first temple. But it places him or her in the very sanctuary of truth. Somewhere in the passing of generations, the truth takes hold so that these foreigners are later numbered among God's people.

Can you identify something similar in your life, or in the life of someone you know? A change of fortune, a circumstance altered—turning out to be a setting where God reveals Himself? That's the providence that leads us.

▤ 2:59–63

THE UNCERTAINTY THAT SHADOWS

This passage tells about three lay families and three priestly families that are unable to prove their ancestry. This is not to say they are not Israelites or priests, but they cannot *prove* it.

However, it does not keep them from coming up from Babylon, joining the pilgrim people, and returning to Jerusalem. They remain among the people of God even though this uncertainty hangs over them.

▤ 2:64–69

THE GENEROSITY THAT SHOWS

The gift of the heads of households consists of 61,000 darics (about 1,133 pounds of gold) and 5,000 minas (about 6,300 pounds of silver). The numbers in the Nehemiah 7 account differ somewhat. Note the number of slaves in light of the overall number (2:64–65), showing there to be about one slave to every six freemen. Therefore, some of the returnees must have substantial wealth, and though there is reason to hold it back in view of the uncertain times, they instead give generously.

EZRA 3:1–13

GOD'S PEOPLE IN GRAY TIMES

The Circumstances We Will Face	3:1–6
The Restoration We Can Expect	3:7–11
The Disappointment We Must Control	3:12–13

Setting Up the Section

A less-than-enthusiastic attitude toward life typifies the Jewish remnant around 538 BC. Life is hard and times are tough. But Ezra 3 shows that God's people can live through bleak times.

▤ 3:1–6

THE CIRCUMSTANCES WE WILL FACE

The focus in this passage is not on the temple but the altar. Observe how the text describes Israel and, by implication, all God's people.

1) *They are fearful.* In verse 3, we are told that the exiles set up the altar, for (note the causal connection) it is on account of dread upon them because of the peoples of the lands. The NIV obscures the connection (see the NASB). The *peoples* apparently mean not only the Samarians but also those of the surrounding territories.

2) *They are faithful.* In verses 2 and 4, Joshua and company join Zerubbabel and the others in building the altar to offer burnt offerings. Then they celebrate the Feast of Tabernacles (3:4). Their worship is inaugurated and carried out in accordance with what God requires of them (as it is written). Indeed, they establish a program of regular, ongoing worship (3:5–6).

Critical Observation

Verse 3 implies that fear drives the people to seek God and worship. Should we have higher motives than fear? Perhaps. But in our fears, what better recourse can we have than God? Together these two sub-points make a crucial point: You can be fearful and faithful at the same time.

3) *They are fragile.* Note the reference in verse 4 to observing the Feast of Booths, also known as the Feast of Tabernacles (see Leviticus 23:39–40, 42–43; Numbers 29:12–38). The seventh month indicates the time for this festival. The Feast of Tabernacles is meant to remind Israel of their wilderness experience post-Egypt. During this week, they live in huts (booths), which conjure up their precarious existence during the wilderness years. It is as though God is saying to Israel, "Don't forget that your life hangs by a mere thread."

📄 3:7–11

THE RESTORATION WE CAN EXPECT

Now Israel looks beyond restoring the altar. The exiles start to plan to rebuild the temple. There is much preparation involved, including gathering materials, organization (3:8–9), and celebration (3:10–11).

Critical Observation

Verses 10–11 bring to mind the promise of Jeremiah 33:7, 10–11. Think what it must have been like when the Babylonians finally destroyed Jerusalem and the temple (the situation Jeremiah's word presupposes). In that heap of rubble and smoking destruction, who would have thought this day (Ezra 3:10–11) would come? Against all human likelihood, God's people see God's goodness again.

📖 3:12–13

THE DISAPPOINTMENT WE MUST CONTROL

From the second part of verse 12, it seems as if the memory of the first temple clouds the day for some. The older individuals can still recall the magnificence of the original temple (see 1 Kings 5–7), and this projected temple will have none of the pizzazz of Solomon's. There is no problem here with the candor of their weeping, but there is a danger in the negativity of these people.

Take It Home

In our culture of materialism and immediate gratification, we tend to think that what is plain, simple, and quiet to be of less worth—even among God's people. Sometimes we can be so caught up in desiring revival and restoration that we forget it's possible, even preferable, to be faithful even when God has yet to send revival and restoration.

Ezra's account reminds us not to despise the little things (also see Zechariah 4:10). What matters is not whether the church is grand, but whether it is genuine.

EZRA 4:1–24

LET THE TROUBLES BEGIN

The World's Subtle Hostility   4:1–3
The World's Obvious Hostility   4:4–5
The World's Persistent Hostility   4:6–24

Setting Up the Section

The returnees from exile proceed to work on the rebuilding of the temple. But not everyone is excited about the project.

📖 4:1–3

THE WORLD'S SUBTLE HOSTILITY

In this passage we see hatred under the guise of friendship. People in the area approach Zerubbabel to offer assistance in the rebuilding project (4:2). They seem trustworthy because they say they seek God.

But the Word of God has already labeled them for what they are: enemies of Judah and Benjamin. And Zerubbabel, Jeshua, and the leaders of Israel have the discernment to see them for what they really are (4:3).

The people described in Ezra 4:1–2 refer to the Assyrian king Esarhaddon, which raises suspicions as to their intentions. This reference to the Assyrian kings reveals these people to be, to a large degree, pagan imports who probably have a religion that combines various deities (see 2 Kings 17:24–41, especially 17:33, 41).

The discoveries of fourth-century papyri at Wadi Daliyeh (located some distance above Jericho) seem to support this. A great number of skeletons were also found here, the remains of families of Samaria who had fled the advance of Alexander the Great in 331 BC. Their names include references to such false deities as the Canaanite Baal and the Babylonian Nebo.

The point? Sometimes the choice to stand separate, as the people do here, is crucial (Ezra 4:3). While we live in a world that values tolerance and inclusion, there are times when the task before us requires us to stand alone on behalf of our values.

📖 **4:4–5**

THE WORLD'S OBVIOUS HOSTILITY

Now the enemies launch a withering campaign of hostility against the people of Judah. The Hebrew text stresses the ongoing, wearing effect of this opposition in that it has three participles, which indicates continuing action: They *kept on making* their hands drop; *kept frightening* them; *kept hiring* counselors against them.

Ezra 4:4 indicates that the intimidation must have occurred on site, with the hired professionals working the halls of power back in Persia (4:5). Apparently all this proves effective, as we will see in Ezra 4:24.

📖 **4:6–24**

THE WORLD'S PERSISTENT HOSTILITY

To understand the flow of the intimidation, you need to know that 4:6–23 constitutes a sort of big bracket piece, breaking up the chronology of the entire chapter.

We've just seen, in verses 1–5, opposition in the time of Cyrus and into the beginning of the reign of Darius (522 BC). Then in verses 6–23, we read an ongoing description of opposition to Judah down through the years. But in verse 24, we are wrenched back to the early reign of Darius. If read in chronological order, one would read verses 1–5, then verse 24, then verses 6–23.

The opposition in 4:8–23, under Artaxerxes, is effective in bringing the project to a stop, as noted in verse 24.

It is as though the writer, who is relating the earlier days after the return from exile, begins telling about the opposition Judah experienced from the beginning and then decides that he will simply go on and pile up all the opposition that Judah has experienced through the years. But at 4:24, it is as if he says, "Now we need to go back to the time period that my record here in Ezra 4 really concerns; let's get back to about 520 BC, early in Darius's reign, when the work on the temple stopped because Judah seemed under so much duress."

The specific objects of construction help us detect the different situations. Note especially 4:12–13, where the people of Judah draw fire for rebuilding the city and its walls, not the temple, as in verses 1–5 and 24.

Demystifying Ezra

Ezra 4:6 contains an accusation against Judah in the reign of Xerxes (Ahasuerus). Scholars point out that when the emperor Darius dies at the end of 486 BC, Egypt rebels. His successor, Xerxes, has to march west to suppress the revolt. The Persians gain control by the end of 483 BC. If the accusation in verse 6 has to do with an innuendo alleging revolt by Judah during this time, one can imagine the Persians would be concerned, with Egypt already on their hands.

Verse 7 apparently deals with a second accusation (later than that of verse 6), this one leveled during the reign of Artaxerxes. Then verse 8 indicates a third accusation, also under Artaxerxes, of which we have a copy preserved in Ezra 4:11–16.

EZRA 5:1–6:22
GOD IS THE RULER YET

The Stirring of the Word	5:1–5
The Surrounding Providence	5:6–6:5
An Extravagant Providence	6:6–12
An Encouraging Providence	6:13–15
The Seizing Joy	6:16–22

Setting Up the Section

At the end of Ezra 4, the work on the temple had stopped. About fifteen years have passed. Chapters 5–6 consist of the inquiry of Tattenai and the favorable response of the Persian court.

📖 5:1–5

THE STIRRING OF THE WORD

Note how verse 1 speaks of Haggai and Zechariah prophesying "in the name of the God of Israel, who was over them" (NIV). Ultimately, neither the king of Persia nor any other ruler is master. Only the God of Israel rules over the people.

Take It Home

In verse 1, we are told that Haggai and Zechariah prophesied, and in verse 2, Zerubbabel and Jeshua began to rebuild the temple. God's Word enables God's servants to do His will. The Word packs power that moves and sustains obedience. This is especially necessary in light of the fear and intimidation that the community had endured (4:24).

We see the same theology in 1 Thessalonians 2:13, where Paul alludes to the Word of God that is at work in believers.

No sooner do Judah's leaders obey God's Word than they run into renewed opposition (5:3–5). Tattenai, the governor, and Shethar-bozenai, his assistant, ask Judah for authorization for this project, but apparently theirs is not the blatant opposition related in Ezra 4.

Demystifying Ezra

In verse 5, the Aramaic verb *betel* is used (meaning "stop"; 4:21, 23–24). This is an example of negative providence: something God does not allow to happen (compare Psalms 124 and 129). Judah may be under investigation, and there is another potential frustration pending, but Judah is allowed to keep building in the meantime.

5:6–6:5

THE SURROUNDING PROVIDENCE

Ezra 5:6–17 records the letter written to King Darius by Tattenai and Shethar-bozenai. In it they lay out the background to their inquiry and ask Darius to verify the people of Judah's claims.

Note that in verses 11–16, Tattenai and Shethar-bozenai quote the response that the exiles gave them when they challenged them about their authority for rebuilding. In one sense these words are a response of praise. And yet they are also words of confession, as verse 12 makes clear. Judah admits that they are a people who have been under Yahweh's wrath, and He had taken the temple and land from them.

Critical Observation

The Persian Royal Road was a kingdom-wide communication network. Every fifteen miles or so sat a postal station where couriers could replace exhausted horses with fresh mounts. Scholars estimate that a courier could average 240 miles a day, in contrast with a caravan, which would average 19 miles. If Darius's road system was fully operational early in his reign, the correspondence noted in Ezra 5–6 could have been completed in a month or two at most.

6:6–12

AN EXTRAVAGANT PROVIDENCE

Darius finds a copy of Cyrus's original decree in the archives (see 6:1–5), confirming what the people of Judah had said. And not only is Judah granted freedom from interference from Tattenai and company (6:6–7), but the elders of Judah receive provision for the maintenance of the temple worship as well. Darius will underwrite the functioning of the temple with state funds and punish anyone who stands in his way (6:8–11).

Demystifying Ezra

The dimensions of the temple in Ezra 6:3 are sixty cubits high and broad, possibly indicating the limits of what the Persians would underwrite.

Take It Home

This occasion in Ezra 6 is very much like that in Exodus 2:1–10, where Moses' mother not only gets her baby back but raises him under state protection, and with a salary to boot. God delights to go far beyond all that we ask or think (Ephesians 3:20). Here also the Jews receive far more than mere permission to build. Providence strikes again.

AN ENCOURAGING PROVIDENCE

After Tattenai and Shethar-bozenai carry out Darius's decree, the elders of the Jews finish building according to God's decree.

The writer lets the timeline run down from Darius to Artaxerxes, omitting mention of Xerxes (Ahasuerus). Artaxerxes is king in Ezra's time (see 7:1). If Ezra is the one writing the historical account in chapters 5–6 (see 6:14), then he may have included Artaxerxes' name in his summary note because in his own time Artaxerxes had also supported the worship and life of the people of God (indeed, he did; see 7:11–26). It may be Ezra's little hint of acknowledgement that God is showing the same providence in Ezra's own time as He had shown to the previous generation about whom Ezra writes.

Demystifying Ezra

Adar, the last Babylonian month, is equivalent to our February–March. The temple is finished on March 12, 515 BC, a little over seventy years from the destruction of the first temple. Renewed work had begun on September 21, 520 BC (see Haggai 1:4–15), so a sustained effort continued for over four years to complete it.

THE SEIZING JOY

In Ezra 6:16–18, we see the people worshiping. The number of sacrifices on this occasion may be paltry compared to what Solomon had offered (see 1 Kings 8:63), but the sin offering is for all Israel, the entire twelve-tribe nation, even though most of those present are from Judah, Benjamin, and Levi.

The people in Ezra 6:19–20 are celebrating Passover. There is a diligence and eagerness about the ceremonial preparation of the priests and Levites. Would this post-exilic community have looked upon this Passover as commemorating a second Exodus, that is, from Babylon?

Verse 21 shows that the attitude of Ezra 4:3 is not narrow-minded nationalism. Here is a community open to others. Yet there is a price to pay: They must separate themselves from the impurity of the nations.

The last half of verse 22 explains the joy of their celebration: "Everyone was happy because the Lord God of Israel had made sure that the king of Assyria would be kind to them and help them build the temple" (CEV).

Demystifying Ezra

The king mentioned in 6:22 is Darius, king of Persia. Why is he called the king of Assyria here? Scholars note that there is evidence from the Ancient Near East that new rulers or foreign rulers were incorporated into the king lists of a particular country. Because Darius was also the sovereign of Assyria, he could easily have been called the king of Assyria.

EZRA 7:1–8:36
THE STRONG HAND OF GOD

Setting Up the Section

Ezra 7 introduces the scribe Ezra himself into the narrative. It's now 458 BC, decades after the first group of returnees returned from Babylonian captivity under Zerubbabel. Ezra 7 summarizes that King Artaxerxes authorizes Ezra to lead another, smaller group to Judea. Ezra 8 gives the details. A thematic element that binds these chapters together is the repeated reference to the hand of God.

📖 **7:1–10**

EZRA ARRIVES IN JERUSALEM

The phrase *after these things* is a clue that what follows occurs a while later (7:1). In fact, Ezra 7 is set almost sixty years after the events narrated in Ezra 6. The writer is very selective as to what is included in the section. Not every detail is given, only what is significant for the people of God.

At this point the book is placing focus on different concerns: not only on restored worship (Ezra 1–6) but also on reformed life according to the law and the Word of God (Ezra 7–10).

In 7:1–5 we're shown Ezra's credentials by virtue of his ancestry (see 1 Chronicles 6:1–15). (See Ezra 2:59–63 on the importance of the documentation [see also Exodus 6:14–27]. Note the gaps in the genealogy.)

Demystifying Ezra

The date described in verses 7–9 can be interpreted several ways. Some scholars teach that Ezra departs April 8 and arrives August 4, 458 BC. Another proposal is based on amending the text of Ezra 7:7 to the thirty-seventh year (428 BC) as opposed to the seventh. Others have construed the seventh year as that of Artaxerxes II (which puts the date at 398 BC). Keep in mind, however, that the significance of the events is the same no matter the exact date.

In 7:6, Ezra is described with the term *mahir*, which means quick, speedy, and hence skilled. According to verse 6, the Law of Moses is a divine gift and apparently complete. Here is also the first "hand of God" clause. So here we have an assembly of realities: a completed revelation (the Torah of Moses) and an ongoing providence (the hand of God)—the latter operating in conjunction with human ingenuity and initiative.

Critical Observation

In Ezra 7:10 we're given a clue as to why the hand of God is on Ezra. The Hebrew text includes the initial *ki* ("because"). God prospers the venture because of Ezra's purpose. Ezra has set his heart to study the law, practice it, and teach it.

📖 7:11–28

THE DECREE OF THE KING

This decree of Artaxerxes gives more people permission to return to Judah, but there are several other concerns and purposes. It is, in part, a fact-finding mission, as implied in verse 14.

The decree includes instructions having to do with the worship of the house of God, whether it is silver and gold—from royalty, from others in Babylon, or from the exiles themselves (7:15–16)—or the delivery of utensils to be used in the temple (7:19). Needs were to be met from the royal treasury (7:20–22), up to 3.75 tons of silver, 650 bushels of wheat, 600 gallons of wine, and 600 gallons of oil.

Note the royal concern in verse 23. Maybe the king is trying to cover all his religious bases. Still, according to Jeremiah 29:4–9, the exiles are to seek to benefit their captors and seek the welfare of the regime under which they exist.

Ezra 7:24 includes a cautionary note to Artaxerxes' regional IRS agents. The clergy (priests, Levites, singers, doorkeepers, and servants) are to be kept tax-free.

The people in Trans-Euphrates ("beyond the river"), mentioned in 7:26, are probably the Jews living there. Also note in verse 26 the law of Ezra's God is also the law of the king. Remember, Ezra's mission is to teach the people of God afresh the law and to discipline them to live according to it. Hence, the focus of Ezra 1–6 is the temple while that of Ezra 7–10 will be the Torah.

Ezra ends the account with a doxology in praise of Yahweh's covenant fidelity, sovereignty, goodness, and encouragement (7:27–28).

Take It Home

King Artaxerxes may make the decree and grant the permission, but why does he do so? Because there is another King behind Artaxerxes, one who turns the king's heart whichever way He desires (Ezra 7:27; Proverbs 21:1). Yet Yahweh's sovereignty is not always blatant—frequently it is hidden and subtle. Yahweh chooses to carry out His decrees through the decrees and decisions of the lesser kings and rulers of the earth.

Note in verse 28 the juxtaposition of the power heads of the Persian Empire (the king, his counselors, all the king's mighty princes) and Ezra's position. There is something astounding in how this miniscule Judean could command such favor from the bureaucracy of Persia! Ezra revels in the thought. Clearly God placed Ezra in a position of authority in Babylon for His purposes.

In verse 28, Ezra says he takes courage or strengthens himself. But he doesn't neglect to give credit to the hand of God, who is the anchor of his story.

8:1–20

THE CONGREGATION OF ISRAEL

The list of households in this section may provide a flicker of hope for the nation of Israel. In it is a descendant of the royal line of David, Hattush (8:2).

Those who came back under Ezra tend to be from families whose members also returned in 538 BC. Compare the list in Ezra 8:1–14 to that in Ezra 2.

Parosh	(2:3; 8:3)
Pahath-moab	(2:6; 8:4)
Zattu	(2:8; 8:5)
Adin	(2:15; 8:6)
Elam	(2:7; 8:7)
Shephatiah	(2:4; 8:8)
Bani	(2:10; 8:10)
Bebai	(2:11; 8:11)
Azgad	(2:12; 8:12)
Adonikam	(2:13; 8:13)
Bigvai	(2:14; 8:14)

Demystifying Ezra

See the listing of Davidic descendants in 1 Chronicles 3:17–24. If you scrutinize that list carefully, it seems that the main thread of the list goes from Jehoiachin, Pedaiah, Zerubbabel, Hananiah, Shecaniah, Shemaiah, to Hattush. Hattush is then the fourth generation after Zerubbabel. If Zerubbabel was born around 560 BC, and if one allots approximately twenty-five years per generation, then Hattush appears here about 458 BC, which fits the traditional date of Ezra's arrival in Jerusalem.

Ezra discovers a lack of Levites (8:15). So he sends ambassadors to a place called Casiphia (8:16–17). It's unclear where or what Casiphia is, but apparently it is a site near Babylon, perhaps a Judean study center. Note the acknowledgement of Yahweh's goodness in verse 18. The appeal nets a total of 38 Levites (8:18–19) and 220 temple servants (8:20).

There is likely a level of comfort, even prosperity, for the exiles in Babylon. If the Levites are to go with Ezra back to Judea, they will leave a life where they may have a good bit of autonomy from the strict routines of the temple. In Judea, life would be perhaps more about hardship and obedience, like the life the apostle Paul called Timothy to in 2 Timothy 2:3—to suffer hardship as a Christian.

📄 8:21–23

THE ADVENTURE OF FAITH

In Ezra 8:21–23, we're reminded that the exiles are undertaking a nine hundred-mile journey. That is quite a peril to face. How fragile they seem. One can imagine the interest they might have kindled when word got out that a caravan was about to leave with goods (8:25–30). Could they afford to go without state-provided protection?

But Ezra's statement of faith sets the tone, especially in verse 22. There are times when faith must take priority over reason or fear, when what is professed must be expressed in concrete situations. So Ezra calls for fasting and a time of prayer (8:21, 23) to humble themselves before God (see Leviticus 16:29, 31). This pleading and confession does not contradict their professed confidence but is the expression of it.

📄 8:24–36

THE VINDICATION OF FAITH

For a defenseless group of Jews exposed to daily danger for months, arriving safely in Jerusalem is proof of the strong protection of God. Their arrival is for them one of the outstanding miracle stories of life.

The inventory of Ezra 8:26–27 will come out a bit differently depending on the commentator. But the amounts on any scheme are substantial: 650 talents of silver equal 49,000 pounds, or about 25 tons of silver. One hundred gold talents equal 7,500 pounds, or 3.75 tons.

The twelve leading priests Ezra entrusts with oversight of this wealth (8:24) are called holy in verse 28, as are the utensils they guard. In the latter case, *holy* means, in part, "off limits." Note the vigilance that Ezra requires of these priests (8:29).

EZRA 9:1–15

TROUBLE IN COVENANT CITY

A Report of Faithlessness   9:1–4

A Prayer of Confession   9:5–15

Setting Up the Section

Ezra and his group of exiles have been in Jerusalem about four and a half months when the problem of intermarrying, and therefore rejection of the law and its demand for spiritual purity, is brought to his attention.

📖 **9:1–4**

A REPORT OF FAITHLESSNESS

The old problem of intermarriage with pagans, in violation of the Torah (Exodus 34:11–16; Deuteronomy 7:1–5) is a problem of sanctification. The people would be hard-pressed to stay true to their religious faith if they are mingling that faith with the idolatry of the cultures around them. Since the spiritual leaders such as the priests and the Levites are implicated as well, this is an extensive and serious issue.

Ezra visibly reacts by tearing his clothes, hair, and beard, and sitting down appalled (desolated, devastated). He seems simply beside himself in helpless frustration. Others share Ezra's essential reaction, even if theirs does not duplicate his exactly (Ezra 9:4).

Why is the news of intermingling with the people of the land such a shock? A possible answer comes from Ezra 8:36, namely that upon arrival Ezra did not stay in Jerusalem. He was taking his credentials from the Persian king to the high officials of the empire in the region.

Note two corollaries of this report of faithlessness in verses 1–4: 1) The professing people of God are disappointing. Never be surprised at how sinful covenant people can be. 2) We usually cannot understand a genuinely holy reaction to sin, as for example the violence and intensity of Ezra's response in verse 3. Don't demean the external as of no consequence (see Joel 2:12–13, where both the external and the internal are held together).

Critical Observation

Ezra says in 9:4, "Then everyone who trembled at the words of the God of Israel gathered around me" (NIV). This trembling is precisely what God wants in His people: "This is the one I esteem: he who is humble and contrite in spirit, and trembles at my word" (Isaiah 66:2 NIV). That is the paradigm for the church.

A PRAYER OF CONFESSION

Ezra's prayer of confession covers the immensity of guilt and the majesty of God's grace. Note how Ezra switches to the plural pronoun *our* in verse 6, in identification with the sins of his people.

The immensity of the guilt (9:6–7) involves quantity: Ezra tries to express the huge mass of guilt in these pictures. It also involves history: It goes back to their fathers, is longstanding, and has been experienced in judgments, the effects of which continue to the present time.

The majesty of God's grace (9:8–9) starts with a significant (brief) moment. It is the grace of survival (God left a remnant), security, encouragement, and consistency. Lastly, it is the grace of providence and protection. The wall (*gader*) is metaphorical for protection (9:9). It is not a literal city wall since it is in Judah and in Jerusalem.

Demystifying Ezra

The *peg* or *firm place* in Ezra 9:8 (NASB) could refer to a tent peg, driven into the ground as secure anchorage for a tent; or it could refer to, as in Isaiah 22:23, a peg or nail securely fastened in a wall so that items can be hung on it. Some theologians have taken the peg to refer to the rebuilt temple, as the following phrase "in his holy place" might suggest. In any case, the idea is that Israel has been given some degree of security in her otherwise tenuous post-exilic experience.

In 9:10–12, Ezra highlights the folly of such unfaithfulness and acknowledges that God's people have confronted the problem before. Hence, they are without excuse.

He goes on to note that God has punished the remnant of His rebellious people less than they deserve. How could they break His commandments? Will it mean God washes His hands of them?

Critical Observation

In Ezra 9:10–15 we see both suspense (in that there is no definite, particular plea that Ezra makes) and frustration (on Ezra's part, for what can he ask? He can only throw Israel upon the mercy of Yahweh).

The word *peletah* ("escaped remnant" NASB) occurs in verses 8, 13, 14, and 15. As we look back on the book of Ezra, we must say that it is a wonder there is an escaped remnant in light of their enemies (chapters 1–6) and sin (chapters 9–10).

EZRA 10:1–44

MAKING CONFESSION

Setting Up the Section

Ezra and his leaders respond to a large outpouring of exiles motivated by Ezra's lamentations to repent of their sin of intermarriage and make things right with God.

📖 **10:1–4**

A WORD OF HOPE

Ezra may have been a highly respected leader, but he is willing to throw sophistication to the wind in his grief (10:1). The effect is to motivate his people to repent. Not just men, but women and children gather to weep and lament.

In verses 2–4 we see a minor character with a major role in the story. Shecaniah puts Israel's corporate unfaithfulness into words. The hope he refers to in verse 2 is based on a call to covenant with God, in which there is fruit that shows repentance. It is a repentance that takes the hard road: to send away the women and children.

Shecaniah also lays out a plan of repentance (10:3–4). He calls Ezra and the other leaders to courageous action and offers him the support of the people.

📖 **10:5–15**

A PROCESS OF DISCIPLINE

In verse 5, Ezra succeeds first in getting the priests, Levites, and laity to enter into the covenantal proposal. He continues in his repentance in Jehohanan's private room (apparently in the temple; we are not told who Jehohanan is), refusing to eat food or drink water (10:6).

Critical Observation

Ezra's fasting has been called a reflection of Moses' fasting (see Exodus 34:28; Deuteronomy 9:18) after the golden bull-calf episode of Exodus 32. It would not be unreasonable to see Ezra as a kind of "second Moses."

In Ezra 10:7–14, the leaders call the assembly. The people generally live within fifty miles from Jerusalem. Non-participation means excommunication (10:8).

The leaders recognize that logistically it will be virtually impossible to have the entire assembly make confession out in the open because it's cold and it will take more than a few days (10:12–14). So they make a proposal that offenders appear to representatives by appointment. They should be accompanied by the elders and judges of their towns—an important element, supporting a fair investigation.

Demystifying Ezra

The date given in verse 9 (ninth month, twentieth day) is December 19, 458 BC. It is the rainy season, in which temperatures are in the forties.

The few who resist likely oppose the whole process, perhaps thinking it too harsh or wanting to protect relatives. The *Meshullam* of verse 15 may well be the same person named as son of Bani in verse 29, who himself had married a foreign wife.

📖 10:16–44

CAREFUL INVESTIGATION

The hearings last from the first day of the tenth month until the first day of the first month (10:16–17). That's three months of work, finishing on March 27, 457 BC.

Offenders come from all levels: priests, Levites, and laity. According to the lists in 10:18–43, the offenders included seventeen priests, six Levites, one singer, three gate-keepers, and eighty-four laity. That makes a total of 111 (depending on the specific text). This indicates careful work. Assuming they take the Sabbath off, it takes abut seventy-five days to complete the investigations of 111 cases.

We're not told what happens to the divorced women and children. They probably went back to their extended families, but that is not the concern of this text.

Critical Observation

The marriage crisis here is on a par with the crisis faced by the earlier community (4:2), in which adversaries seek to help and then oppose the exiles' obedience.

The 536 BC community repulses the direct attack and avoids being diluted. The 458 BC community begins to succumb to a more subtle assault.

Yet, if the 111 names recorded in Ezra 10 is the total number of men who had taken a foreign wife, it's a very small percentage of the entire community. Estimates of its size at this point total 30,000 or maybe 50,000. Yet the purging must be done.

Take It Home

Is Ezra 9–10 a model for the Christian church to follow? There is debate about the matter, but most likely Ezra 9 and 10 are descriptive of a specific time, not prescriptive for all times.

What we see in Ezra 9–10 is Exodus 34:11–16 and Deuteronomy 7:1–5 applied in a new post-exile situation. Do those texts not still apply to the church? Do they incorporate Paul's stricture in 1 Corinthians 7:39, teaching that a Christian widow is free to marry only in the Lord? Ezra's action in these chapters could be viewed as a corporate application of Matthew 5:29–30.

But the situation Paul faces in 1 Corinthians 7:12 and following is different from that of Ezra 9–10. Paul is speaking of marriages that were originally between pagans but became mixed because one of the spouses was converted to Christ. In that situation, if the unbeliever is willing to continue the marriage, the Christian should not try to end the marriage.

The problem in Ezra involves covenant people contracting marriages with pagans. If this occurs in a new covenant context, such Christians should be—in accord with Matthew 18:15–20—admonished to repent of such deliberate sin.

Yet if there is repentance, would that require divorce? Wouldn't Ezra 9–10 point that way? Not necessarily. Ezra 9–10 was a unique situation. Remember what was at stake: the survival of a definable people of God in this world. Hence the drastic measures.

NEHEMIAH

INTRODUCTION TO NEHEMIAH

The book of Nehemiah is one of the Old Testament's historical books. Until the fifteenth century AD, Ezra and Nehemiah were considered to be one book, and we see evidence of this with Ezra's abrupt ending. The events of Nehemiah pick up naturally where Ezra leaves off, with the continual rebuilding of Jerusalem and the return of the final group of exiles from Babylon in 445 BC.

AUTHOR

Nehemiah is believed by some scholars to have written the majority of the text—much of the book of Nehemiah is written in the first person, and Nehemiah 1:1 identifies the speaker as Nehemiah, son of Hacaliah, an exiled Jew who served as the cupbearer to the Persian king, Artaxerxes I. Yet Jewish tradition holds that Ezra authored the books of Ezra and Nehemiah. Because Ezra and Nehemiah were one book, Nehemiah may have been edited by Ezra, or the two may have been combined by a historical chronicler. No one knows for certain.

PURPOSE

The book of Nehemiah has two primary purposes—to provide a historical account of the rebuilding of the wall of Jerusalem and to document the reformation of the post-exilic Israelites who returned to the city and renewed their covenant with Yahweh. Through these two main purposes, God's continuous provision for His chosen people is revealed.

OCCASION

The events recorded in the book of Nehemiah are dated from circa 445 to 431–432 BC. It begins with Nehemiah returning to Jerusalem in the twentieth year of the reign of King Artaxerxes I of Persia (1:1), approximately thirteen years after Ezra returned with the second group of exiled Jews. Nehemiah leaves Jerusalem for a brief period of time in the thirty-second year of the reign of Artaxerxes I and returns shortly thereafter (13:6–7), dating the events at the end of the book around 432 BC.

THEMES

Revival is one of the main themes of the book of Nehemiah. Nehemiah leads in the rebuilding of the wall, and he also makes sure the Jewish practices are reestablished so that temple worship is also revived.

This book also focuses heavily on the importance of godly leadership. Nehemiah seeks wisdom from the Lord.

Adversity is another theme evident throughout the book, as Nehemiah faces opposition to his rebuilding plan, conflict among the people working on the wall, and specific instances of the covenantal law being broken by the people. Despite the various adversities Nehemiah and the Israelites face, the wall is rebuilt and temple worship resumes, at least for a time.

HISTORICAL CONTEXT

While there were surely other groups of Jews returning from Babylon, those who return with Nehemiah to rebuild the wall mark the third group described specifically in the Old Testament. Of the specific accounts offered in Ezra and Nehemiah, Zerubbabel led the first group home in 538 BC (Ezra 1:1–6:22), and Ezra returns with the second group in 458 BC (Ezra 7:1–10:44). The first group is tasked with the rebuilding of the temple, a work that couldn't truly be celebrated until the wall that protected the city and the temple was also complete. Nehemiah brings closure to the events recorded in Ezra and the aftermath of the Babylonian exile.

CONTRIBUTION TO THE BIBLE

Nehemiah's memoir provides a genealogy of a third specific group of Israelites to return to Jerusalem. More than a history of the people and the rebuilding of the wall, Nehemiah also provides a historical account of the rejuvenation of the holy city. With the rebuilding of Jerusalem and its wall complete, it is once again the holy city of God.

OUTLINE

NEHEMIAH 1:1-11

PRAYER IN THE PALACE

Background   1:1–4
Nehemiah's Prayer   1:5–11

Setting Up the Section

Nehemiah introduces himself and his times in Nehemiah 1:1–3. The reference to the twentieth year (1:1) is to the year of Artaxerxes I, or 445 BC. Comparing Ezra 7:7, we note that this is thirteen years after Ezra's coming. The month of Chislev is November–December. Susa was in what is now southwest Iran, in the alluvial plain 150 miles north of the Persian Gulf. It serves as a winter palace for the Persian kings.

📄 1:1-4

BACKGROUND

Although Nehemiah lived most of his life in Babylon, his home was Jerusalem. Verse 2 reveals the concern and affection Nehemiah still has for his homeland and its people. His brother Hanani's news that the walls of Jerusalem remain in ruins causes Nehemiah much grief. Verse 4 indicates that Nehemiah's grief and distress are a continuing affair and that his fasts and prayers have been ongoing for some time. The prayer of verses 5–11, then, is a sample of what his prayers are like during this time.

Critical Observation

Ezra 6:6–12 includes an edict banning the reconstruction of Jerusalem's walls. The fact that the walls remained untouched reflected the oppression that crippled the Jewish people. Jerusalem was the holy city of the Jews, and a wall in ruin was a visible reminder of the city's prior destruction, the Jewish exile, and an overall loss of national identity and pride.

📄 1:5-11

NEHEMIAH'S PRAYER

Nehemiah begins his prayer by identifying God as both awe-inspiring and faithful. Note how these two aspects of God's character complement one another: God is both frightening and dependable. Nehemiah goes on to state that God is approachable as well (1:6).

In verses 6–7, Nehemiah doesn't point an accusing finger at others but rather identifies with his people. The offenses, as noted in verse 7, are committed in violation of the revelation of God's law received through Moses. Verses 8–9 correspond with Deuteronomy 30:1–10, particularly verses 3–5. The language of Nehemiah 1:9 links up with the promise of help and restoration from judgment in Deuteronomy 30:3–5.

Nehemiah pleads to God on the basis of the identity Israel has because of redemption (Nehemiah 1:10). When Nehemiah uses the verb *redeemed*, he is likely referring to redemption from Egypt and the resulting covenant, not to redemption from Babylon after the exile. It's as if Nehemiah says, "Look at what you have made them. Look at what you have done for them. Do you mean all of that to go for nothing?"

Demystifying Nehemiah

Nehemiah's prayer is in reference to the contemporary need—the grave crisis of the people of Judah—as well as to the suspense over what the king's reaction might be. Nehemiah refers not merely to his own prayer but to the prayers of others (1:11). Nehemiah does not stand alone in prayer; there is a fellowship of intercession.

The text brings us up to the edge of when Nehemiah will broach the subject with the king. While most people do not have access to the king, Nehemiah reveals in verse 11 that he was the king's cupbearer, thus giving him access to approach the throne.

Critical Observation

The position of cupbearer was one of great responsibility and influence. Kings wanted a cupbearer they could trust. When Nehemiah makes his cupbearer remark, he is recognizing that Yahweh's providence has been at work long before this moment. He was high up in the civil service with access to the king, and therefore, in a favorable position to seek good for the people of Judah.

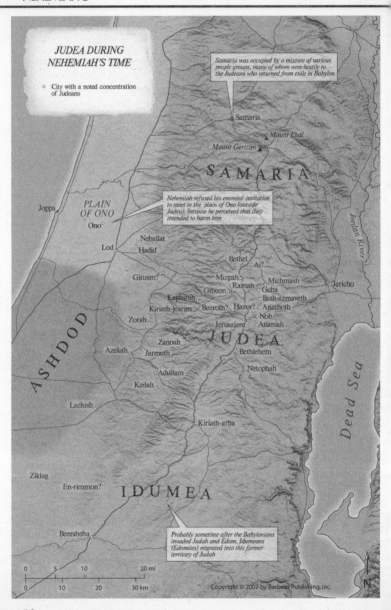

JUDEA DURING NEHEMIAH'S TIME

○ City with a noted concentration of Judeans

Samaria was occupied by a mixture of various people groups, many of whom were hostile to the Judeans who returned from exile in Babylon

Samaria

Mount Ebal

Mount Gerizim

SAMARIA

Joppa

PLAIN OF ONO

Nehemiah refused his enemies' invitation to meet in the plain of Ono (outside Judea), because he perceived that they intended to harm him

Ono

Neballat

Lod   Hadid

Bethel   Ai?

Gittaim?   Mizpah   Michmash
          Gibeon   Ramah   Geba
    Kephirah   Beth-azmaveth
    Kiriath-jearim   Beeroth? Hazor? Anathoth
Zorah   Nob
          Jerusalem   Ananiah

JUDEA

Zanoah
Azekah   Jarmuth   Bethlehem

    Adullam   Netophah

Keilah

Lachish

ASHDOD

Kiriath-arba

Dead Sea

Ziklag

En-rimmon?   IDUMEA

Jordan River

Jericho

Beersheba

Probably sometime after the Babylonians invaded Judah and Edom, Idumeans (Edomites) migrated into this former territory of Judah

| 0 | 5 | 10 | | 20 mi |
| 0 | 10 | 20 | 30 km | |

Copyright © 2007 by Barbour Publishing, Inc.

N

NEHEMIAH 2:1–20
FROM COURT TO CITY

Setting Up the Section

Nehemiah doesn't act hastily on his desire to return to Jerusalem and lead in the rebuilding of the walls. Following his prayer in chapter 1, he waits four months before taking the first step toward returning—asking King Artaxerxes' permission to leave.

📄 2:1–8

A DAY AT COURT

Nehemiah cannot keep his depression about the state of his homeland from showing—and this may have been a breach of royal court etiquette. Nehemiah's fear in verse 2 likely arises in light of the accurate diagnosis and the knowledge that this king has nullified precisely what Nehemiah seeks to do (see Ezra 4:7–23). Note that at this point Nehemiah does not explicitly mention Jerusalem.

Nehemiah 2:4 is the moment of opportunity—and of uncertainty—hence Nehemiah's resort to impromptu prayer. This is a reflection of Nehemiah's piety, but this prayer is also a balance between dependence and boldness (2:4–5). His request is presented and royal permission is given (2:5–6).

The care and planning and thought Nehemiah has given to this matter are reflected in his request for official letters and for obtaining materials (2:7–8). The explanation of Nehemiah's success comes not merely as information but as praise. The king gives provision, but it is by Yahweh's hand that he does so.

📄 2:9–16

A NIGHT AT THE WALLS

Where Ezra rejects an armed escort as a matter of faith in Ezra 8:21–23, here we have Nehemiah's acceptance of an escort as a matter of wisdom (Nehemiah 2:9). It will add authority and support to his position and work.

Demystifying Nehemiah

Verse 10 introduces the opposition. They simply cannot endure a man who seeks good for the sons of Israel (2:10). This is not mere human animosity; this is the serpent's seed hating the seed of the woman. There is far more theology in this text and situation than is immediately apparent.

Nehemiah conducts a nighttime (2:12–13, 15) survey of the conditions of the wall. Nehemiah doesn't tell (2:12, 16) about his plans or his preliminary investigation. He needs direct knowledge of the condition of the wall, so if there are any objections, he will know on what basis to answer. Also, some of the Jews were in contact with neighboring peoples and may have leaked Nehemiah's plan.

If there is any incensed opposition, there is also a sense of divine calling on Nehemiah's part, as he points out in verse 12. This is not just Nehemiah's desire, but one spurred by God-given motivation.

📖 2:17–20

AN HOUR OF DECISION

Nehemiah identifies with the people of Judah. His appeal is based on their current shame—they should rebuild so they will no longer be a mockery. He also intends for them to be moved by seeing how God has been at work in His providence as had been shown in the king's authorization for the project (2:18). In response to Nehemiah's motivation, the people agree to his plan to rebuild, and they begin the work. But the dissenters—Sanballat, Tobiah, and Geshem—make their voices heard. Notice that the enmity in verse 19 is expressed by both ridicule and innuendo. Nehemiah's response is typically abrupt and pointed (2:20):

God will give us success.

We, His servants, will build.

You have no part with us.

Take It Home

Chapter 2 marks the beginning of Nehemiah's leadership of the Jerusalem project, and already he has established himself as an effective leader, capable of both motivating the people in their rebuilding effort and handling the adversity that has already started to arise. Nehemiah's leadership will only be strengthened as the book continues. He is arguably one of the strongest examples of godly leadership in the Old Testament.

NEHEMIAH 3:1–32

BLESSED BUILDERS

The Gate Workers	3:1–16
The Eastern Wall and the Final Gates	3:17–32

Setting Up the Section

Chapter 3 is Nehemiah's detailed account of the rebuilding of Jerusalem's walls. The description starts at the Sheep Gate in the northeast corner and works its way counterclockwise.

📖 3:1–16

THE GATE WORKERS

The account begins with an illustration of leadership by example (3:1). The high priest and other priests are the first people named as helpers in the rebuilding effort. They apparently do not have the idea that such work is for peons. Rather, those with sacred office take the lead in the restoring work. Many names are mentioned in this chapter as those who helped rebuild, evidencing that this was a task that demanded all hands on deck.

Because it is such a large city, Jerusalem is a necessary stop on many trade routes. Its size also requires many gates by which to enter the city, as mentioned in this chapter. The Fish Gate (3:3) is the entrance for one of the main roads, and it likely received its name because of the fish market that was just outside the gate (2 Chronicles 33:14).

Nehemiah 3:5 is puzzling, but it seems that there are some from the town of Tekoa, the nobles, who refuse to assist in the work. Perhaps they think it is beneath them to do this kind of work. By contrast, however, the chapter is full of others with social and political clout who avidly contribute their share to the work (3:9, 12, 15, 19). The men from Tekoa who do help evidently work on more than one section of the wall (3:5, 27). Meremoth, the son of Uriah, is mentioned in verse 4, and he, too, is named later as working on a second part (3:21). This taking on more than one's share speaks well for these workers.

The Jeshanah Gate (3:6) is also translated Old Gate, and it is repaired by a group of Jebusites, whose descendents were the original owners of the land on which the temple was built. The stretch of wall from the Old Gate to Broad Wall includes a wide range of people, from Jebusites to those from the Trans-Euphrates, to goldsmiths and perfume-makers (3:6–8). From the Broad Wall, the building continues around to the Tower of the Ovens, or Furnaces (3:11), which is located on the western wall of the city.

Critical Observation

There are some who seem marked by special zeal for the work. Shallum's zeal leads to making the rebuilding a family affair—even his daughters help in his section of repair (3:12).

The Valley Gate (3:13) is likely located near the southwest corner of the city. The Dung Gate, which received its name because it was the gate that led to Jerusalem's landfill, is next along the wall's repair route (3:14). The Fountain Gate and the Pool of Siloam (3:15) mark the southernmost point of Jerusalem. From there the wall route Nehemiah is tracing turns northeasterly along the valley of the Kidron.

3:17–32

THE EASTERN WALL AND THE FINAL GATES

Verses 17–27 continue with repetitious "next to him" statements, cataloguing the list of those who worked on the eastern portion of the wall between the Fountain Gate and the Horse Gate. The Horse Gate (3:28) is at the easternmost part of the wall. The Inspection Gate (3:31) is the last gate before returning back to the Sheep Gate, where Nehemiah begins his record. It marks the northern part of the eastern wall.

Take It Home

The names here constitute a roll of honor of Yahweh's workers, recorded for lasting remembrance. This is typical scriptural and divine practice, for Matthew 10:42 tells us that Christ sees and remembers all puny acts of love and devotion offered to and for Him (see also Mark 14:9; Hebrews 6:10).

NEHEMIAH 4:1-23

THREATS AGAINST GOD'S WORK

Ridicule	4:1–6
Intimidation	4:7–12
Organized Perseverance	4:13–23

Setting Up the Section

Having chronicled the building efforts in chapter 3, here, in chapter 4, we return to Nehemiah's memoirs. The last verse of chapter 2 reflects on the success God will grant to those in the rebuilding efforts (2:20), so it is not surprising that shortly thereafter an enemy's voice speaks out.

RIDICULE

Verse 1 suggests that ridicule proceeds out of helplessness. Note the presence of the army of Samaria (4:2), which indicates Sanballat has armed help at hand. And yet he can hardly benefit from it because Nehemiah has official permission from the king, which surely frustrates Sanballat to no end.

Not being able to use military force against God's people, Sanballat turns to mockery. Tobiah's fox remark is said in reference to walls that are undoubtedly thick and capable of withstanding strong military force (4:3). Note that Nehemiah does not let go with a retort to the mockers but has recourse to God (4:4–5).

Critical Observation

How are we to view Nehemiah's prayer? It is a prayer for justice against sin. As such, it is a prayer for God to act. Nehemiah is not presuming to take vengeance into his own hands; he commits that to God. These are not personal enemies but enemies of God's kingdom. There is no indication that Sanballat, Tobiah, and their men seek repentance. There is a high cost to mocking the people of God (implicit in Nehemiah's prayer in verses 4–5).

INTIMIDATION

Despite the resistance to their work, Nehemiah and the wall builders are persistent.

Verses 7–9 reveal that from all four directions the builders are surrounded. Sanballat has been angry, but now he and his cohorts are furious (4:7), so much so that there is a possibility of an armed assault (4:8).

Critical Observation

Since the time of the Assyrian conquest of Palestine, the Philistine territory had been a separate province called Ashdod. With Samaria to the north, Arabs to the south, Ammon to the east, and Ashdod to the west—Judah was surrounded.

The discouragement of the builders is evident in verses 10–12. Perhaps this is in light of the fresh threat in verses 7–9, and this is their despairing response. Not only does Judah speak but the enemy's threat and intimidation is also announced (4:11). It also sounds as though the Jews living in neighboring villages pick up the threats and propaganda from the enemies and repeat it to the workers (4:12). Perhaps the enemies leak word of the plans that are being made, then those Jews come to Jerusalem and repeat the rumors among the workers. It is all intended to demoralize.

📖 4:13–23

ORGANIZED PERSEVERANCE

Nehemiah admits that people are placed in vulnerable positions to stand guard at the wall (4:13), but he charges them to remember the Lord (4:14). Note the effectiveness this immediate defense has on their attackers (4:15).

Demystifying Nehemiah

Nehemiah's speech in verses 14–15 is very much like Deuteronomy 20:1–4, and it serves to assuage the people's fear and remind them that they fight both in the name of God and in defense of their families. God's sovereignty is stirring (see Nehemiah 4:9) and moving the people.

In the revised building scheme there seems to be several groups. Some are permanent guards (4:16). Some serve as load haulers (4:17), who carry loads and their weapons at the same time. Then there are the builders (4:18), each with his sword strapped on. Finally, there is an alarm system in place (4:18–20).

Take It Home

In verse 20, Nehemiah says, "Our God [emphatic in Hebrew] will fight for us" (NIV), revealing the confidence that undergirds their toil. And with that reminder, the wall continues to go up. Commuting is done away with, and the people are constantly on guard. The unusually perilous circumstances call for uncommon measures for the immediate future.

NEHEMIAH 5:1–19

FOLLY AMONG GOD'S PEOPLE

Setting Up the Section

While the threat of external assault is the fear in chapter 4, here in chapter 5, internal dissension begins to take place.

📖 5:1–11

NEHEMIAH'S CONFRONTATION

Notice the outcry in verses 1–5. It seems there are three groups raising dissension in the midst of the building efforts. The first group consists of families who may have owned no land for food, and thus taking time to work on the wall diminished their ability to earn wages (5:2). The second group consists of those who are mortgaging their land, farms, and homes in order to get food, and these people will lose this security completely if they cannot pay their debts from the annual harvest (5:3). The third group consists of those having to borrow, with fields and vineyards as collateral, in order to pay the king's taxes (5:4–5). Some of their family members are in debt-slavery because of this hardship.

The crying shame in Nehemiah 5, however, is that the profiteers are fellow Jews (5:1, 7). The problem is probably not interest/usury but debt-slavery, with loan sharks possessing the pledge or the collateral that is put up. So Nehemiah turns prosecutor (5:8–9). Apparently, some Jews have been sold to surrounding peoples and redeemed, meaning that some of the loan sharks (5:8) must have sold their fellow Jews obtained by debt default to surrounding peoples.

Critical Observation

Nehemiah admits that he and his associates have also made loans of money and grain for collateral, but there is no reason to suppose that Nehemiah had pressed the claims and profiteered from the loans he'd made. In fact, he says that all claims are not to be pressed; they are to be abandoned. Hard-pressed people must be cut some slack.

📄 **5:12–19**

THE RESPONSE

Nehemiah's order in verse 11 is for the profiteers to restore collateral they have sucked up as well as surcharges they have demanded. The moneylenders give their consent (5:12) to Nehemiah's directive. However, Nehemiah presses for even more clout and calls the priests to administer an oath, after which Nehemiah depicts the curse (5:13) that will overtake those who renege on their obligation.

Demystifying Nehemiah

Nehemiah 5:14–19 is something of an extract out of Nehemiah's diary. It interrupts the chronological flow of the matter at hand but is likely placed here to set forth a positive sample of Nehemiah's walking in the fear of God (5:15) over against the heartlessness of the profiteering Jews in verses 1–13.

Nehemiah has certain rights by virtue of his position as appointed governor—a food allowance, or a stipend—but he voluntarily relinquishes them. He also doesn't allow his staff to lord their stipends over the people as the underlings of past governors had (5:14–15). Apparently, Nehemiah pays for his stock and food supply (5:17–18). What motivates this kind of self-sacrificing, non-oppressive leadership? Why is Nehemiah different from his predecessors? Because he fears God (5:15). This is what should have—according to Nehemiah—motivated the wheelers and dealers in verse 9.

Take It Home

Here is the true basis for biblical ethics: the fear of God. The awe of God controls your treatment of others. The fear of God leads to compassion for people. Nehemiah not only demands the scoundrels of verses 1–13 change, but he himself has consistently set an example of proper servant leadership.

NEHEMIAH 6:1–19

STRATAGEMS AGAINST GOD'S SERVANT

God Gives Strength	6:1–9
God Gives Clarity	6:10–14
God Gives Tenacity	6:15–19

Setting Up the Section

The schemes recorded in this chapter are directed toward Nehemiah, either to eliminate him or at least to discredit him. Undoubtedly his enemies want to bring trouble to his exemplary leadership. Note the emphasis on fear throughout the chapter (6:9, 13–14, 19).

6:1–9

GOD GIVES STRENGTH

At this point there has been substantial progress on the wall. Now Sanballat and company want a consultation with Nehemiah (6:2). Verse 2 relates Nehemiah's perception, which is likely an accurate one: They intend to harm or do evil to him. Their persistence (6:4) shows their helplessness or weakness, since they can't think of any other approach except to repeat the last ploy. The fifth time (6:5–7) Sanballat sends an open letter. Note the interjected prayer in verse 9.

Critical Observation

There is an emphasis on fear throughout the chapter (6:9, 13–14, 19). However, Nehemiah remains perceptive (6:2), tenacious (6:4), and clear-headed (6:8), yet also weak. Otherwise, why pray this way? Here in the thick of it all he casts himself upon God's strength.

GOD GIVES CLARITY

Apparently Shemaiah wants an interview, so Nehemiah calls on him. Shemaiah's being behind closed doors could be a prophetic action reinforcing his word of seclusion for Nehemiah (6:10). The first part of Nehemiah's answer in verse 11 seems to mean, "I have more guts than that!" The second part of his answer seems to mean, "And it's wrong!" When he asks if one like himself (a layman and not a priest) can go into the temple, the expected answer is no. (He is referring to the temple itself, not merely its courtyards.) This is a privilege and right that is off limits to laymen (see Numbers 18:7; 2 Chronicles 26:16–20).

Shemaiah's intent is to get Nehemiah to commit a ritual transgression and thereby be discredited. But Nehemiah discerns (Nehemiah 6:12) that God has not sent Shemaiah, but that Tobiah and Sanballat have paid him off. It is all a plot to lead Nehemiah into sin (6:13). And Shemaiah is only a *part* of the problem; the prophetess Noadiah and other prophets are conspiring together (6:14), seeking to magnify Nehemiah's danger and send him into paranoia.

Demystifying Nehemiah

Verse 14 is a prayer for vengeance, a plea for God to remember and deal with the dastardly deeds and designs of the likes of Shemaiah. There is nothing wrong with such a prayer. What can be more wicked than placing one's office as bearer of God's Word up for hire, using the Lord's Word as a tool to manipulate people and gain power over them? This situation highlights the discernment God's servants need. This sort of ploy is so tricky because it involves a revelation claim, an alleged word from the Lord—and not just from one person but a plurality of people (6:14).

GOD GIVES TENACITY

The rebuilding of Jerusalem's wall is completed in just fifty-two days, on the twenty-fifth of Elul, which would've been late August or early September (6:15). All of the Jews' enemies are overcome with awe because there is no question that this building has been accomplished by the hand of God.

Verse 17 begins with the particle *gam*, translated *also*, as if to say, "This, too, is going on at that time." This is all taking place during the time Tobiah has steady correspondence with the more powerful people among the Jews. Likely, some of the important citizens of Jerusalem are against the isolation of Judah, perhaps for commercial reasons. Tobiah has many connections with the Jews, as many of them are under oath to him (6:18). Tobiah is also linked by marriage; his son is married into one of the families of the wall builders (3:4, 30).

Verse 19 highlights two items: intimidating letters from Tobiah and a constant stream of gossip, part of which is propaganda about the good deeds of Tobiah. This is continuous (as the Hebrew participles suggest). Some want to wear Nehemiah down to a reasonable solution of reconciliation and compromise.

Take It Home

There is no doubt that Tobiah is powerful, and his power combined with his desire to see Nehemiah's plans fail make for an intimidating combination. Whether Nehemiah is intimidated or not, Tobiah's threats don't stop him, and the wall is still completed in an extraordinary amount of time.

NEHEMIAH 7:1–73

THE EXILES WHO RETURNED

The Registration	7:1–5
The Listing	7:6–73

Setting Up the Section

The rebuilding of the wall, Nehemiah's original task, is now complete. But his work in rebuilding Jerusalem and the morale of the Israelites is far from over. This chapter begins the shift in focus from the wall to the securing and populating of the city.

7:1–5

THE REGISTRATION

In Nehemiah 7:1–5, Nehemiah makes a series of necessary arrangements after the completion of the wall. First Nehemiah appoints guards to the city's gates in order to ensure the city's safety (7:1). In charge of the guards, he appoints his brother, Hanani, and another man, Hananiah, based on their integrity (7:2). Second, he also establishes new security regulations that include the gates to the city only being open during the busiest parts of the day, and various people throughout the town stand guard over their neighborhoods (7:3). Third, Nehemiah notices the town's vacancy and the need for people to fill it (7:4). A city the size of Jerusalem is safer with more inhabitants.

Upon noticing the low number of inhabitants in the city, Nehemiah has all of the families in Jerusalem register (7:5). The list that follows is not a list compiled of the people who returned with Nehemiah to build the wall but rather is the genealogical record of those in the first post-exilic return in 537 BC. Nehemiah later uses this list of Israelite families as part of his plan in chapter 11.

THE LISTING

Nehemiah uses the same language following the genealogical parallel in 8:1 that Ezra uses following his in 3:1. But the gathering Nehemiah 8 describes is a wholly different gathering than that of Ezra 3:1. It occurs in the same month (seventh month), yet some ninety years later. Nevertheless, the editor of Nehemiah wants us to view the two assemblies side by side. He wants to draw a distinct parallel between the watershed beginning in Ezra 3 (when the returned exiles began to build the temple) and the contemporary gathering in Nehemiah's day after the temple had been rebuilt and the city restored. In this way, the editor emphasizes that the occasion of Nehemiah 8–10 is as central and seminal as its earlier counterpart, namely the initial restoration under Zerubbabel. That had been the critical commencement, and Nehemiah 8–10, in turn, is a kind of consummation.

Critical Observation

This list in Nehemiah 7:5–73 reproduces the record found in Ezra 2. The figure of 42,360 (in Ezra 2:64) appears as the total also found in Nehemiah 7:66, yet the individual items add up to three different totals. There is general agreement that the divergences are copying errors, arising from the special difficulty of understanding or reproducing numerical lists.

More than anything, the list shows God's faithfulness in preserving His chosen people. Genealogies are also important because Jews used them to prove their bloodline as descendents of Abraham. For this reason, two of the three Synoptic Gospels include genealogies that trace Jesus back to David and Abraham as well.

Demystifying Nehemiah

The covenant renewal of Nehemiah 8–10 can be seen on a plane with the temple restoration of Ezra 3. Ezra 3 stresses the people and temple, while Nehemiah 8 stresses the people and Torah. Or, to say it another way, one depicts worship restored and the other depicts the Word restored.

NEHEMIAH 8:1–18

THE FOUNDATION OF REFORMATION

Ezra Reads	8:1–12
The Festival	8:13–18

Setting Up the Section

Now that the wall is rebuilt, Nehemiah moves on to the rebuilding of people's lives. The rest of the book of Nehemiah will deal with the reformation of the people, beginning with the reading of God's Law.

📄 8:1–12

EZRA READS

Although Ezra had been in Jerusalem since before Nehemiah (Ezra 7:6–9), this is the first mention of him in the book of Nehemiah (Nehemiah 8:1). In addition to being the scribe, Ezra also serves as a priest. Nehemiah governs the people, but Ezra is in charge of their spiritual well-being. The Book of the Law mentioned in verse 1 is probably the Jewish Torah, or Genesis–Deuteronomy of the full canon.

The audience consists of men, women, and all who can listen with understanding (8:2). This hearing of the Word is marked by patience, attention, reverence, and worship (8:3–6). The Levites circulate among the people, perhaps doing exposition of the Word in small groups.

Critical Observation

Much ink has been spilt over the participle *mephorash* in verse 8, which qualifies the verb *read*. Some hold that it means "translating" (from Hebrew into Aramaic). Others hold that it means "making distinct," or as an adverb, "clearly." Still others take it as "paragraph by paragraph," breaking it down into manageable chunks. Probably the second or third option is preferable: breaking it down and explaining the meaning. The intent, in any case, is to make the Word of God clear, to highlight the insight it holds, and to make its applications obvious.

This assembly takes place on the first day of the seventh month (8:2), which is the Feast of Trumpets (Leviticus 23:23–25; Numbers 29:1–6). The weeping of the people (Nehemiah 8:9) may be over sin exposed through the reading of the Torah. The weeping and sadness of verse 9 are balanced by the joy and gladness of verse 12. They celebrate because they understand. But they have to be ordered by Nehemiah and company to be joyful (8:9–11). Note that this is a social joy, not a selfish joy (8:10).

Demystifying Nehemiah

Three times the people are told that the day is holy (8:9–11), and they are commanded to be joyful. The last line of verse 10 contains the primary argument against sadness: "For the joy of the LORD is your strength" (NIV). Perhaps there is the suggestion that ongoing sorrow and grief, while proper at times, can leave the people of God vulnerable. The text implies that joy and delight in Yahweh fulfill a protective function in believers' lives, keeping them, perhaps, from being swallowed in despair.

8:13–18

THE FESTIVAL

The heads of households meet for ongoing Bible study (8:13). They find written in the Torah the regulations about the Feast of Tabernacles (or Booths; see Leviticus 23:33–43; Deuteronomy 16:13–15, with the emphasis on joy in the latter passage). Nehemiah 8:16 indicates the various locations of their booths, while verse 17 emphasizes the uniqueness of the celebration.

Take It Home

The "celebration" of Tabernacles was an appropriate activity to post-exilic Judah, as it should be to the Lord's people in all ages. Tabernacles was meant to force Israel to recall their tenuous post-Egyptian existence in the wilderness journey. In the midst of Israel's settled life in the promised land, they need to remember their former hand-to-mouth existence. In the midst of what is also a harvest festival, they remember that life can be a wilderness, and their only sustainer is Yahweh. They must never forget their humiliation in the wilderness (Deuteronomy 8) or the God who sustained them through it.

NEHEMIAH 9:1–38

THE PREPARATION FOR REFORMATION

Prelude to Prayer   9:1–5
The Prayer   9:6–38

Setting Up the Section

The reading of the Word of God is a catalyst for the Israelites' reformation. Having been away from the temple and the daily worship practices, the scripture they hear reminds them that a change on their part is necessary.

📖 9:1–5

PRELUDE TO PRAYER

After reading the Word of God, the people are now determined to get back to the business that had them so upset in Nehemiah 8:9. The term *seed* (*zara*) refers to the "seed of Israel" and implies the doctrine of the two humanities (in light of Genesis 3:15). Here Israel separates herself from amalgamating with the foreigners and from covenant compromise.

First comes the reading of the Torah and then confession and worship. The worship is built upon the Word (Nehemiah 9:3). The leaders on this occasion seem to be Levites. The Levites begin with a call to worship: "Arise, bless the LORD your God forever and ever!" (9:5 NASB).

📖 9:6–38

THE PRAYER

Observe the historical moments the prayer covers: creation (9:6); Abraham (9:7–8); Exodus (9:9–12); Sinai (9:13–14); wilderness (9:15–21); conquest (9:22–25); the judges and following (9:26–37). The prayer can be divided into three sections based around what they reveal about God:

1) *The gifts of God's grace (9:6–15)*

The majority of this section focuses on Yahweh as redeemer. However, verse 6 expresses homage to Yahweh as creator. Both verses 6 and 7 begin with the phrase *'attah hu,'* implying that the creator of verse 6 and the redeemer of verse 7 are one and the same. Verse 6 lauds Yahweh as not only creator of all things (heaven, earth, seas, and their contents), but as life-giver and sustainer as well. And for all this He receives worship from those conscious, invisible beings, the heavenly hosts. In the redemption section, the prayer highlights redemption and covenant (9:7–8). The root of covenant is election, as seen in the phrase "who chose Abram." The concern of covenant is place (the land) and people (his seed). The anchor of covenant is fidelity.

Though the note of compassion is not lacking (9:9), verses 10–11 stress the judgment aspect of Yahweh's deliverance. Yahweh does not grant redemption while withholding direction. Note how positively the Sinai gifts are described: upright ordinances, true laws, good statutes and commandments, holy Sabbath (9:13–14). Sinai is the assurance that Yahweh does not redeem a people from bondage only to abandon them to ambiguity.

Verse 15 reflects on the provision aspect of God's redemption. Episodes like those of Exodus 16–17 are in view here. This is not standard provision but the provision in extremity (hunger, thirst), provided in unpredictable ways: from heaven and from a rock.

2) *The tenacity of your goodness (Nehemiah 9:16–31)*

After the second-person perspective in verses 9–15, highlighting all that Yahweh has done, there comes a third-person comment: "But they, our fathers, acted arrogantly" (NASB). Verses 16–17 use strong language. This is no momentary lapse on Israel's part. Everything speaks of deliberate, open-eyed resistance to God's will. Rebellion is absurd in light of all the preceding acts of grace (9:7–15), and God does not withhold His forgiveness (9:17).

Critical Observation

Here is the phenomenal character of Yahweh. As if this were insufficient, we find the amazing words of verse 17: "You never turned away from them" (CEV). This passage tells us that our hope is not in denying or explaining away our rebellion but simply in the character of God.

Verse 18 alludes to the golden calf episode of Exodus 32. While they commit these grave acts of contempt toward God, they receive the same grace and guidance and provision as before, as verse 21 testifies. The following verses celebrate the conquest of the land east of the Jordan (9:22–23) and west of it (9:24–25).

Demystifying Nehemiah

One must remember that all this provision comes in the wake of their stubborn disobedience (9:16–18). Remembering this context leads to an important observation: God's gifts are no sign of our righteousness.

The prayer next rehearses the behavior of Israel when settled in the promised land, during the period of the judges. As in a previous generation (9:18), Israel again commits great sin (9:26). For this Yahweh brings them into distress, but the wonder is that there is deliverance (9:27). But nothing changes. Israel is in a cycle of repeated infidelity (9:28–31).

3) *The rightness of your justice (9:32–37)*

The Levites and the assembly are ceasing their historical review to make their contemporary request. They ask the Lord not to look on all this history of troubles ("hardship, weariness") as trivial. They confess, however, that Yahweh has acted rightly in all the distress that He has brought upon them. They clearly admit the rightness of Yahweh's action and the persisting sin of Israel (9:33–35).

Verse 36 reveals their condition at the current moment: slaves (stated twice) in distress. Even though they are back in the promised land, they recognize that this is not a state of blessing, because they are ruled over and taxed by others.

The prayer of chapter 9 ends descriptively, as if to say, "This is our situation." There is no directive, no particular petition here. That, however, is an implied petition in light of the whole prayer. They are asking, "Have your great compassions altogether ceased? You will not now forsake us, will you?"

NEHEMIAH 10:1–39

THE STRUCTURE FOR REFORMATION

The People Agree   10:1–29
The People Vow   10:30–39

Setting Up the Section

Here we find the response to the prayer of chapter 9, or perhaps better stated, the consequence of the prayer. In light of the ongoing history of apostasy and infidelity, what can Judah do but repent? Covenant is the vehicle of repentance.

10:1–29

THE PEOPLE AGREE

The names in verses 1–27 include both the leadership and the laity. Nehemiah and Zedekiah seem to be by themselves, then the priests, listed mostly according to family names (10:2–8), followed by the Levites, listed as individuals rather than families (10:9–13), and then the leaders (10:14–27; verses 14–19 follow Ezra 2; these are mostly lay families).

Nehemiah 10:28–29 reiterates that the people are entering under a curse, calling down judgment on themselves if they do not keep their oath (see Jeremiah 34). Covenant renewal cannot thrive on generalities and vague resolutions. The promises included here are precise. Nehemiah 10:30 is the promise that they will not intermarry with the pagan people around them.

Critical Observation

The covenantal promise to not intermarry with foreigners does not imply that God looks negatively on those who are not Israelites simply because of their nationality. Rather, this insures that the Israelites maintain households that honor and serve Yahweh. The nations around the Israelites were pagan nations with a variety of deities and religious practices. It was this religious intermingling that was the concern. The Old Testament accounts of intermarrying with pagan nations never produce positive results (see 1 Kings 11:1–11).

10:30–39

THE PEOPLE VOW

Nehemiah 10:31 prohibits trade in Jerusalem on the Sabbath, maintaining that Yahweh, and not money, is the God of the Israelites. The promise that every seventh year individuals will stop working the land and cancel all debts is a reiteration of the Sabbath law as recorded in Exodus 23:10–11 and Deuteronomy 15:1–2.

Then in Nehemiah 10:32–33, the people make a promise that they will participate in the giving of funds for worship maintenance. Because the temple is now rebuilt, the people promised temple taxes and offerings will also be restored. The law is even so specific as to include the provision of firewood to ensure the sacrifices can be burned on the altar. The people's covenant includes a lots system for calendaring when families are in charge of providing the wood (10:34).

The people also assume responsibility for bringing a number of offerings to the temple each year, as noted in verses 35–39. These provisions deal with the maintenance of the temple worship itself, particularly the temple staff—the Levites who receive the tithe (10:38–39). Provisions include the firstfruits of their crops, firstborn sons, first-born of all their animals, and a tithe of their crops.

Take It Home

The major concern in this chapter is found in verse 39: "We will not neglect the house of our God" (NIV). The people covenant, or promise, that they will keep worship priority in their lives.

The same matters here are still issues for Christians: marriage, Sabbath, and giving. While the cultural customs may work themselves out differently in modern culture, the call for God's people to prioritize their faith lives in practical ways is still the same.

NEHEMIAH 11:1–36

THE ORDER OF THE PEOPLE OF THE LORD

Anchoring the City   11:1–24
Possessing the Land   11:25–36

Setting Up the Section

Although Jerusalem had been a city with little structure and little to offer its residents, the completion of the wall and the city's increased morale make it a more appealing place to live. This section lays out Nehemiah's plan for encouraging the Jews to populate the city.

📖 11:1–24

ANCHORING THE CITY

Remember this is the holy city (11:1, 18), and yet the present situation is a far cry from all nations streaming to it as depicted in Isaiah 2. The leaders already live in the city. Then there is the lot-casting scheme, and those who volunteer (Nehemiah 11:2) are those who have been selected by lot.

Critical Observation

Nehemiah proposes that with the casting of lots, one out of ten families living in the territory of Judah should relocate and reside in Jerusalem (11:1). In this way, it is not Nehemiah who forces them to live in Jerusalem, but it is the will of God. They cannot bear a grudge against Nehemiah; they have been drafted by the Lord. And yet those selected willingly go. Here is sovereign direction willingly accepted.

The move into the city for those whose lots were chosen is a sacrifice. They do not prefer to live in Jerusalem or they already would have settled there. So they face the trouble of uprooting themselves from homes and means of livelihood, leaving everything for the city.

The listing for Jerusalem (11:3–24) is part of a list of the population of the whole province of Judah in the times of Ezra and Nehemiah. The population of Jerusalem in verses 3–19 tallies both the newcomers (verses 1–2) and all others who were already in Jerusalem. If the tallies are followed (11:6, 8, 12–14, 18–19), there is 3,044, so after including wives and children, one could estimate a population between 10,000–12,000 people.

11:25–36

POSSESSING THE LAND

The next verses (11:25–36) record a list of villages outside of the city walls where some of the Levites were living. As citizens of one empire, these people are free to settle where they want if they keep the peace (11:36).

Demystifying Nehemiah

Though it is a small, mustard-seed sort of beginning, can we not see in these mundane verses a renewing (even in dark, hard times) of the place-element (land) of the Abrahamic covenant? Hence, there is a hint of the fidelity of God in the geography of Judah here.

NEHEMIAH 12:1–43

THE CELEBRATION IN THE JOY OF THE LORD

Structuring the Worship	12:1–26
Dedicating the Wall	12:27–43

Setting Up the Section

This next section is the account of the dedication of the newly rebuilt wall of Jerusalem. We are not sure how long after the completion of the wall this dedication occurred. One has the impression that the dedication takes place after the events of Nehemiah 7–11. It is not something to be neglected, but there may have been other, more pressing concerns at the time when the wall was finished.

📄 12:1–26

STRUCTURING THE WORSHIP

The list of names continues in Nehemiah 12:1–26, now with the names of the priests and Levites who return from exile. These verses break down as follows:

Verses 1–9 list the priestly families and Levites at the time of Zerubbabel and Jeshua in 536 BC (see 1 Chronicles 24:7–19; Ezra 2:40–42). Verses 10–11 list the high priests from Jeshua's line (see 1 Chronicles 6:3–15). Continuing in verses 12–21 is a list of the heads of twenty-one priestly families during Joiakim's time, the second generation. The notes and records from the book of annals, mentioned in verses 22–23, include the list of Levites that follows.

📄 12:27–43

DEDICATING THE WALL

Now that the wall of Jerusalem is rebuilt, a celebration ensues for the people. Before the celebration began, verses 27–29 tell us that Levites, singers, and musicians from the region around Jerusalem were brought into the city to be a part of the dedication festivities.

The celebration begins with two large choirs circumnavigating the top of the wall, in opposite directions, singing songs of praise and thanksgiving (12:31–39). The choirs are accompanied by the Levites named in these verses. The first choir, which covers the wall from the Valley Gate counterclockwise, is led by Ezra (12:31–37), while the second group, covering the wall from the Valley Gate clockwise, is led by Nehemiah (12:38–39). The two groups meet at the temple where they continue to worship and offer sacrifices as they are joined by the women and children (12:40–43).

Take It Home

What is the significance of Nehemiah 12:1–26? Here are two historical generations of priests and Levites—people who are still serving in the worship of sacrifice and praise and vigilance as did an earlier generation. As God's people, we are part of a whole history of generations devoted to serving God. We cannot ignore the record of those who have served Yahweh before our own time.

NEHEMIAH 12:44–13:3

THE PERSEVERANCE IN THE WORSHIP OF THE LORD

Mundane Provisions   12:44–47
Essential Separation   13:1–3

Setting Up the Section

The dedication of the wall in Jerusalem marks a fully restored city, and as the holy city this means that the religious community is fully restored. Once again the temple functions as it once had, as the center of worship for a spiritually strong people. The Israelites have not had such a sense of security since before the exile, so to the very last detail they insure worship will resume as it once had.

📄 **11:44–47**

MUNDANE PROVISIONS

The joy and delight in those who lead in worship insures the proper continuity of worship. Among this action is the appointing of a staff to keep up with the tithes that were received. The aforementioned tithes of firstfruits, crops, and so on will be a large accumulation, therefore it requires a staff to collect the offerings and redistribute them to the temple workers who receive portions of the tithe (12:44–45). See Numbers 18:21–32 for the portions referred to in verse 47.

Critical Observation

The repeated mention of David in Nehemiah's account of the temple organization leads one to perceive Nehemiah as doing for the post-exilic temple what David did for the original one. Because music had been such an important part of David's design for worshiping the Lord, Nehemiah guarantees provisions be made for the singers and musicians (12:46–47).

📄 **13:1–3**

ESSENTIAL SEPARATION

The reference in 13:1 is to Deuteronomy 23:3–6. How do they interpret that passage? Do they infer from the mention of Ammonites and Moabites that the text intends the exclusion of all foreigners (13:3)? Observe how in 13:2 they recall not merely the threat of mankind but the protection of God.

There is a wonderful simplicity about this passage. There is something refreshing when the people of God order their lives out of the Word of God. Their practice simply flows out of what they had found.

Take It Home

Keep in mind Ezra 6:21 as you read this passage. The separation of Nehemiah 13:3 presupposes that such people clung to their paganism. After all, it was Israel's relationship with pagan nations that led to the exile that they were still recovering from. Converts to Yahweh were welcome. So, praise (12:44–47) and purity (13:1–3) must mark the ongoing life of God's people.

NEHEMIAH 13:4–31

THE ONGOING PERILS OF THE CHURCH

Compromise	13:4–9
Neglect/Indifference	13:10–14
Commercialism	13:15–22
Amalgamation	13:23–31

Setting Up the Section

The final chapter of the book of Nehemiah includes a closing series of reforms Nehemiah enacts among the people. Each reform covers an area of the covenantal law that the Israelites are guilty of breaking.

📄 **13:4–9**

COMPROMISE

To highlight the reform of verses 1–3, Nehemiah describes a problem that he dealt with regarding too much intermingling with foreigners. The Tobiah of verse 4 is the same Tobiah who made himself an enemy of Nehemiah by opposing the rebuilding of the wall. Not only that, but he is also an Ammonite, and as such is prohibited to enter the temple. There is a note of defiance in this. The ease of compromise is clear in verse 4: Eliashib is close to Tobiah. This may mean he is closely associated with him, or it could mean he is related to him. There may have been a marriage tie (see 6:17–19), and if so, his behavior simply shows that blood is thicker than covenant. Eliashib believes pleasing people matters more than fidelity to God.

The opportunity for compromise is the absence of Nehemiah (13:6), but the cure for compromise is the arrival of Nehemiah (13:7–9). Eviction is the answer, so Nehemiah throws all of Tobiah's belongings out of the storehouse (13:8). The compromise of Eliashib is in clear opposition to the Word of God (13:1–3), and therefore it had to be dealt with harshly instead of gently.

13:10–14

NEGLECT/INDIFFERENCE

The Levites are to live on tithes that are given (Numbers 18:21), but they had not received them—the procedures of Nehemiah 12:44–47 having gone into eclipse. So, the Levites flee to the towns and to their fields to gather what living they can. Hence, the house of God is forsaken (13:11).

Verse 12 reports that obedience is reactivated. And to attempt to ensure the system from breakdown, Nehemiah appoints reliable men over this business (13:13).

Demystifying Nehemiah

Note Nehemiah's prayer in verse 14. This is not a works-merit prayer. It is a prayer in the spirit of Matthew 10:40–42, Mark 14:9, and Hebrews 6:10. It is the prayer of one who knows that God does not ignore the earnest service of unworthy servants. Nehemiah asks that God not wipe out his *loyal deeds*, those done out of a covenant commitment.

13:15–22

COMMERCIALISM

The issue of work on the Sabbath arises (13:15). The offense is twofold: The people of Judah are working on the Sabbath, bringing loads of food into Jerusalem and (apparently) selling them. Secondly is the issue of the foreigners, the Tyrians, who do their fish selling on the Sabbath as well (13:16).

Nehemiah's rebuke is a theological one (13:17–18): These Sabbath-breakers are placing Israel under the anger of Yahweh again. See this same argument pressed by the prophet Jeremiah in the pre-exilic period (Jeremiah 17:19–27).

To prevent further offense, Nehemiah closes and guards the gates. He places his own men there to prevent traders from entering the city (Nehemiah 13:19). Then he makes threats against the lollygaggers in verses 20–21. Perhaps these people tried to hang around outside the walls hoping to draw people outside the city to buy. But Nehemiah shuts this off as well. Then in verse 22 he institutes a more lasting provision to insure compliance.

Critical Observation

Exodus 31:12–17, especially verses 13 and 17, indicates that the Sabbath is a kind of sign. It marks out Israel as unique, for other peoples do not have the blessing of the Sabbath. The Sabbath is a gift for the people because they are able to cease working (Exodus 20:8–11; 34:21). In Egypt they wouldn't dare stop work! But when Yahweh frees them from bondage, He enables them to cease from work—every week. The Sabbath is a sign of grace and freedom, not of bondage.

AMALGAMATION

In Nehemiah 13:23, the issue of intermarriage resurfaces. Note the drift seen in the second generation (13:23–24). Intermarriage with pagans occurs, and one discovers that the cultural ties of the children are closer to the mother's roots (13:23–24). Eventually, this will prove true for religious ties as well. Note the action taken in verse 25. Nehemiah's cursing of the people means that they reap the negative consequences of the covenant they established with God. Nehemiah calls God's judgment into effect.

Then Nehemiah makes the people take an oath to not give their daughters in marriage to pagans or to take pagan women in marriage for their sons (this is what they have already sworn to do in 10:28–30). Nehemiah presses an argument upon them—a biblical, theological, and historical argument, based on Solomon's drift toward paganism (13:26–27). He enjoyed vast privileges but came to ruin because of this very offense. Marriages to pagans had occurred among the priestly circles of the community (13:28–29). A grandson of the high priest became son-in-law to Sanballat. A priest should have been an exemplar of piety and covenant fidelity (see Numbers 25:13).

ESTHER

INTRODUCTION TO ESTHER

The book of Esther is a good complement to the books of Ezra and Nehemiah. While those books describe the trials and challenges of the Jewish exiles who were finally allowed to return to their homeland, Esther shows the plight of the Jewish people in Persia during the same period of time. Some people uphold Esther and Mordecai as heroic figures, yet others question whether they were actually godly individuals. God is not once mentioned by name in this book, yet it is a testament to divine providence.

AUTHOR

The author is unknown yet certainly appears to be a Jewish individual who had remained in Persia after other Jews had departed.

PURPOSE

Esther and Mordecai have become role models for their courage and perseverance. Yet their success requires the reader to acknowledge God's work in post-exilic Persia (though God is never *specifically* acknowledged).

OCCASION

The account of Esther is a magnificent work purely on the grounds of literature: character, plot, conflict, and so on. But it was probably written to provide the background and setting for the creation of the Jewish holiday of Purim.

THEMES

Much of the action of Esther takes place during banquets. Many significant meals are mentioned in this short book (1:3, 5, 9; 2:18; 3:15; 5:4, 8; 7:1; 8:17; 9:17–18). But perhaps more significant are the themes that *aren't* mentioned: God, prayer, Jerusalem/Judah, and worship (other than fasting).

HISTORICAL CONTEXT

Esther would be near the end of the Old Testament if the books were positioned chronologically. As God had forewarned, His disobedient people had been carried off into captivity, many to Babylon. But by the time Esther was written, the Persians had already conquered the Babylonians.

CONTRIBUTION TO THE BIBLE

Along with Ezra and Nehemiah, Esther offers a look into Jewish life under the rule of the Persians. Esther's distinction is an insider's look from within the Persian Empire. The book also provides the only mention of Purim, a Jewish feast, in the Bible. More than anything, this book shows how God's providence preserves His people.

ESTHER 1:1–2:18

A NEW QUEEN IN SUSA

Setting Up the Section

Due to their disobedience and pursuit of idols and other gods, the people of Israel and Judah have been carried into captivity by Assyria and Babylon. The Babylonians, in turn, are conquered by the Medes and Persians, so the group of Jews who originally went to Babylon is now under Persian rule. It is a trying time, but the story of Esther demonstrates how God's people obtain not only a voice but also an advocate in the king of Persia himself.

🖹 1:1–9

A LONG PARTY

The king in this passage is Xerxes, although many Bible translations use the Hebrew form of his name: *Ahasuerus*. He had been in power for three years after conflicts with Babylon and Egypt. His residence is in Susa, the capital of ancient Elam, which his father, Darius I, had rebuilt as a winter capital.

What had begun as an alliance between the Medes and the Persians (Daniel 5:28; 6:8, 12, 15) has by this time become the kingdom of Persia and Media (Esther 1:3, 14, 18–19), showing that Persia has become the dominant nation. Indeed, Ahasuerus is the great king of the Persians whom Daniel had prophesied would rise to power (Daniel 11:2).

The text does not provide the reason for Ahasuerus' elaborate six-month banquet, but history tells us that the following year he will (unwisely) wage war against the Greeks. This celebration may well have been an occasion for gathering support, rallying his group, and planning the military campaign. If so, Ahasuerus would have wanted everyone to see that he was richer and more powerful than anyone else.

After six months, the king's extravagance continues with a local weeklong banquet (Esther 1:5). Fine art is on display for the people of Susa—rich and poor—as they recline on expensive furniture, eat gourmet food, and drink fine wine. While the king entertains the men, the women have their own celebration, with Queen Vashti as their hostess.

🖹 1:10–22

THE FALL OF VASHTI

Much speculation is made about this section of the book of Esther. We know that at the end of the banquet, King Ahasuerus summons his wife, Vashti, to come wearing her crown to let everyone see how beautiful she is. But Vashti refuses to make an appearance. Was the king (who has indeed been enjoying wine) unreasonably asking his wife to appear before a crowd of drunken men, exposing her to potential embarrassment and shame? Or does Vashti coldly refuse a reasonable request to appear for the grand finale of the party? Opinions vary. But the result is clear: The king becomes furious (1:12).

Critical Observation

The Persian king had little regular interaction with his harem as a group. To ensure propriety, the women who associated with the king were attended to by eunuchs—men who had been castrated.

To his credit, Ahasuerus doesn't lose control and respond impulsively. He wisely calls his counselors and asks them how he should handle the situation. They know that as the most prominent woman in the Persian Empire, Vashti sets an example, and they fear that her actions will be influential on women throughout the kingdom. Consequently, they recommend that she be banned from ever again appearing with the king. Not only that, but they suggest she should be replaced by a woman more fit to be queen. Ahasuerus acts on their advice with an irreversible decree.

📖 2:1–18

THE RISE OF ESTHER

After a number of years pass (1:3; 2:16), King Ahasuerus is again ready for a queen. If he hadn't passed an official ban against Vashti, perhaps he would have relented and taken her back. But instead, his advisors recommend a national search for young virgins from whom the king can select his next queen. Not surprisingly, Ahasuerus gladly agrees with their suggestion.

One eunuch (Hegai) is designated to prepare the contestants for their interview with the king. The young women will spend an entire year getting ready, and then each will spend one night with King Ahasuerus. Afterward, they are placed in his harem of concubines under the supervision of another eunuch (Shaashgaz). Unless the king requests one of them by name, these women will never meet with him again (2:14).

One of the Jews living in Susa at the time is Mordecai. He is raising his cousin Esther (*Hadassah* in Hebrew) as a daughter because her parents have died. She is very beautiful, and she is chosen to be among those contending for queen. She soon impresses Hegai, who gives her special attention and instruction (2:9, 15).

Everyone who sees Esther is impressed by her (2:15), and the king is no exception. He chooses Esther over all the other young women in the kingdom to become his new queen. He not only throws another great banquet to celebrate but he even proclaims a holiday to commemorate the wedding (2:18). But throughout the year-long process, Esther keeps her Jewish identity secret (2:10).

Demystifying Esther

The actions and direction of God are evident throughout the story of Esther, even though the name of God is never mentioned in the book. However, some hold the perspective that the book of Esther even more so reflects the struggles of Jewish exiles who became too attached to the land of their captivity, and thus dishonored God by not returning to their homeland when they were able to. From this perspective, God's providential care for the Jews in Persia was accomplished not because of their faithfulness but in spite of their unfaithfulness.

Take It Home

Esther was born as a captive in a foreign land where she had neither social status nor power. Yet she became queen over one of the greatest empires in the world. If nothing else, her story seems to demonstrate how God places the right person in the right place at the right time. Those who willingly allow Him to use them—where they are—may be surprised at what can be accomplished.

ESTHER 2:19–4:17

THE INFLUENCE OF MORDECAI

Setting Up the Section

With Esther as queen, Mordecai has an ally at the highest level of government—and he will need it. He so alienates a villain named Haman that Haman determines to destroy not only Mordecai but all Jewish people. Because Esther has chosen not to reveal her ethnic identity, few people in Susa are aware that she is of Jewish descent. And that secret tends to complicate Esther's desire to help Mordecai.

📖 2:19–23

A FOILED PLOT

The second group of virgins (2:19) may have been a regrouping of the first group (2:8) or yet another selection of beauties (2:12). Either way, the king would most likely have been preoccupied with them, and it would not have been the best time for Esther to approach him.

Yet Mordecai had overheard a plot to assassinate King Ahasuerus. (Mordecai's position in the city gate suggests he had a respectable degree of status.) Mordecai sends word to Esther, and she passes the information on to the king. Persian justice is swift; the two conspirators are immediately executed, and the details of their arrest and judgment are recorded.

The record of the event will be important later in the story. Also essential to the account is the fact that Esther never got around to telling her new husband that she had been among the Jewish people exiled to Persia.

📖 3:1–15

MORDECAI MAKES AN ENEMY

The introduction of Haman to the story is sudden. Little is said about him or why Ahasuerus promotes him to second in command of the nation, but it soon becomes clear that Haman is a powerful and intolerant man. After he appears, we no longer read of the other princes who offered Ahasuerus wise counsel.

Critical Observation

One of the few things we are told about Haman is that he is the son of an Agagite (3:1). In contrast, Mordecai is a Benjamite (2:5)—the tribe of King Saul. By Persian times, the term *Agagite* might have been a reference to geographic area rather than a specific person, yet Israelites and Amalekites had long been bitter enemies, which might help explain Haman's widespread resentment toward the Jewish people.

Before the Israelites had even crossed from Egypt to Canaan, they contended with the Amalekites, and God promised Moses their eventual destruction. (Exodus 17:8–16; Deuteronomy 25:17–19). Later, King Saul had been instructed to kill King Agag of the Amalekites (1 Samuel 15).

Understanding this history sheds light on Mordecai's attitude. Ahasuerus has commanded that everyone is to bow in Haman's presence, but Mordecai regularly refuses to do so. The king's servants are first to notice Mordecai's defiance. When they confront Haman, he becomes furious, and his rage is directed not just toward Mordecai but toward *all* Jews.

It is the first month of the year (April or May)—the Persian new year. Haman plans to annihilate the Jewish people, and he casts a lot (*pur*) to determine when it should be done (3:7). The lot designates the thirteenth day of the twelfth month.

Haman's appeal to the king is calculated and intentionally vague in that it never mentions the Jews specifically, and he mixes truths with half-truths and lies (3:8–9). For example, as a captive people, the Jews had been instructed to cooperate with their host nations (Jeremiah 29:7). Haman's charge that they disobey the king's laws is unfounded.

Haman gives Ahasuerus two incentives to grant his request: (1) a promised reduction of rebellion in the kingdom, and (2) a generous contribution to the national treasury. Although Ahasuerus appears to decline the monetary offer (Esther 3:11), his initial disinterest may be a customary oriental bargaining exercise. Perhaps the king expected to benefit both from Haman's initial payment and from later portions of the spoils that would be confiscated. The deal is struck, and letters are sent out throughout the kingdom to order the utter destruction of the Jews eleven months later (3:12–14).

Demystifying Esther

Due to the "pious bias" of many readers (the tendency to assume Bible characters are more righteous than average people), Mordecai is often presented as a hero in this story. Yet nowhere in the book of Esther is the reader told that he is a godly person, nor is he ever seen praying or making a declaration of his faith. The argument can be made that Mordecai represents the rebellious Jewish people of his day. Perhaps his refusal to bow to Haman is a conscious stand for God, although bowing does not necessarily indicate an act of worship. For most, it merely demonstrates submission to authority, which is not unreasonable. Mordecai's refusal could also reflect the longstanding hostility between the Jews and the Amalekites, of which Haman was one.

📖 4:1–17

MORDECAI ENLISTS AN ALLY

The Persian king and his malevolent second-in-command have celebratory drinks after agreeing to the extinction of an entire people group (3:15), but the Jews across the Persian nation are soon fasting, weeping, and tearing their clothes. Although letters have gone out to all sections of the empire, the news still hasn't reached Esther. She finds out because she hears that Mordecai is just outside the city gate, mourning loudly and publicly. She sends new clothes to replace his sackcloth, but he will not be comforted. She then sends a messenger to see exactly why Mordecai is so distraught (4:4–5). Mordecai supplies all the details and sends the messenger back with a plea for Esther to intercede with the king.

Esther initially balks. She will be risking her life if she approaches Ahasuerus without being summoned, and she hasn't seen him in a month (4:11). But Mordecai presses her, appealing on both a personal and national level. Is it merely coincidence that she had been chosen as queen at just the time that her people are in dire danger? So Esther agrees to approach the king after a three-day fast of all the Jews in Susa.

Many people don't realize that Esther is certainly a reluctant heroine. Readers often presume that the fasting of her people also includes prayer and repentance, yet that is not necessarily the case. Fasting could be a ritual without real meaning (Isaiah 58:1–12). Even Esther's words, considered by some to be a statement of faith ("If I perish, I perish"), are actually a declaration of fatalism. Any nonbeliever can say as much, and often does when faced with similar circumstances.

Esther is certainly the heroine of the story, but she is not necessarily the godly heroine some people make her out to be. Otherwise, surely the writers would have included key observations such as prayer, repentance, and references to God. The absence of such things in the Esther account creates a deafening silence.

Take It Home

Many people find themselves in the position of Esther, to some degree. Life may be going quite smoothly for us even though we know of others who are fearful, endangered, or helpless. The need may arise to get outside of our comfort zones for the benefit of others, even if it involves a degree of risk. While Esther may have acted in response to Mordecai's coercion, our actions can be based on faith that God will see us through any situation. As a result, we might see God work in wonderful ways in our lives and in the lives of others.

ESTHER 5:1–7:10

TWO BANQUETS AND A HANGING

Esther's First Banquet	5:1–8
Haman's Humiliation	5:9–6:14
Esther's Second Banquet	7:1–10

Setting Up the Section

Esther has been chosen to be queen by Ahasuerus, the king of Persia, but he still is not aware of her Jewish ties. Meanwhile, her cousin/stepfather Mordecai has made a powerful enemy of Haman, the king's second-in-command. Haman has secured the king's permission to annihilate all the Jews. Mordecai has enlisted Esther's help, but by approaching Ahasuerus without being summoned, she places her life at risk.

📖 5:1–8

ESTHER'S FIRST BANQUET

After observing a three-day fast along with the other Jews in Susa, Esther approaches King Ahasuerus. Little is said about her state of mind, but she had numerous reasons to be fearful. To begin with, if she interrupts or interferes with the king at the wrong time, she might be put to death. And even if he welcomes her visit, she is going to have to confess to him that she is Jewish, convince him to reverse a law he has just instated (1:19; 3:10–11), and reveal that his closest companion (Haman) is a terrible villain. Most likely the king will feel deceived by Esther and/or Haman, and not many royal leaders like to admit to such poor judgment.

Still, Esther goes ahead with her plan. Dressed in her royal robes (5:1), she is graciously received by Ahasuerus. Yet when he asks what it is she wants, Esther only says she has prepared a banquet for him and Haman. The king sends for Haman right away, and as they are drinking after the meal, Ahasuerus again asks what Esther wants. She once more puts off her request by asking the two to attend yet another banquet the following day. At that time, she says, she will tell the king what she wants. The reasons for her delay are not explained, although during the interval God prepares the king to respond as He desires.

🔖 5:9–6:14

HAMAN'S HUMILIATION

Two special invitations for dinner—by the queen, no less—put Haman in a good mood, but it doesn't last long because Mordecai still shows him no respect. When he complains to his friends and family about Mordecai, they have a simple solution: Build a gallows and have him hanged. Haman need not wait for months until all the rest of the Jews are to be executed. Since he is so close to the king, he can get an edict to have Mordecai hanged right away. Haman is delighted with the idea and begins construction of the gallows immediately.

Critical Observation

In Persian culture, hanging was not the same as people today usually envision it. The execution was performed not with a rope around the neck, but by impaling the convicted person on a sharpened pole. The "hanging" is in reference to the impaled body displayed to public view.

While Haman plots with his kinfolk, the king is having trouble sleeping. To pass the sleepless hours, he has someone read to him from the chronicles of his reign, where he hears the account of how Mordecai had uncovered the plot on his life. He is disturbed that nothing has been done to reward Mordecai.

Enter Haman, rehearsing his request for Ahasuerus to grant him the right to kill Mordecai. But before he can even ask, the king has a question for him: "What should I do to honor a man who truly pleases me?" (6:6 NLT). Haman, of course, assumes the king is referring to him, so he gives a detailed and elaborate answer (6:7–9). What a bitter and shaming experience it must have been after Ahasuerus tells him to go out and do all those things for Mordecai. Haman rushes home in grief but receives no sympathy from his friends and family. They interpret it as a sign of bad things to come.

ESTHER'S SECOND BANQUET

Haman's dinner with the king will be no better this time. After the meal, when Ahasuerus asks Esther what her request is, she explains that her people are scheduled for annihilation. The king is incensed and wants to know who would do such a thing. She identifies the culprit as Haman (7:6).

After a big meal and plentiful wine, the enraged king goes into the palace garden. (Perhaps to get some fresh air or control his anger? To think of how to punish Haman? To give some thought to Esther's dilemma?) Haman senses that Ahasuerus has already passed judgment, and he wants to beg Esther for mercy. In approaching her, however, he falls onto the couch where she is reclining. At that moment the king returns and, in his anger, assumes the worst. He accuses Haman of molesting the queen and orders him to be led away.

Demystifying Esther

It was Persian tradition to recline while eating (7:8). The Greeks and Romans would do the same, and at some point the Jews adapted the habit. At the Last Supper, Jesus and His disciples reclined at the table (Luke 22:14), though some translations use the term *sat down*.

One of the king's servants was aware of the newly constructed gallows beside Haman's house. In a final irony, the king commands that Haman be executed on the gallows he had created for the murder of Mordecai.

Haman soon dies, but his dastardly plan is already set in motion. The order to kill all the Jews is still in effect. Addressing that threat is Esther and Mordecai's next priority.

Take It Home

Contemporary readers of the book of Esther should be encouraged by seeing what a difference a day can make. Life can appear to be desperate beyond all hope, yet God is able to turn things around in no time. He regularly saves and delivers those who turn to Him.

ESTHER 8:1–10:3

A NEW FEAST IS ESTABLISHED

Setting Up the Section

After discovering Haman's plot against all the Jews throughout the Persian Empire, Queen Esther has risked her life to approach the king for help. He is more than sympathetic to her request, to the point of having Haman immediately executed. Yet Haman's official message has already gone out, so Esther and Mordecai now turn their attention to preventing the potential damage that could be done.

📄 8:1–17

MORDECAI'S PROMOTION AND DECREE

After Haman's death, King Ahasuerus gives everything Haman had owned to Esther and rewards Mordecai with the position that Haman had held, made official by the gift of the king's signet ring (8:2). The ring's seal would also provide authenticity for any missive sent out from the capital, Susa. After Esther pleads with Ahasuerus to rescind the order that Haman sent out, the king sends for his scribes. Mordecai dictates a new letter that is recorded and translated into the languages of the various peoples. The letter is written in the king's name and sealed with the king's ring. And lest anyone doubt where the king stood on this issue, the couriers ride the king's own horses (8:10). The previous order as written by Haman was supposed to be irreversible, but Ahasuerus makes it known that he now supports the Jews.

Critical Observation

Rather than a request based on the Word of God, the Abrahamic covenant, or some other spiritual basis, Esther appeals to the king solely on the basis of his affection for her and on what the destruction of the Jews would do to her (8:5–6). As for Mordecai, the king's order doesn't just provide *protection* for the Jewish people and give them permission to defend themselves; it authorizes them to *avenge* themselves (8:11–13).

Mordecai clearly has the king's favor. He leaves the palace attired in royal clothes, a distinctive purple robe, and a golden crown. The Jews in Susa are celebrating and feasting, as are those throughout the kingdom. And along with the sudden shift of power, many non-Jewish people are converting, perhaps more from fear of the Jews than genuine faith (8:17).

TWO DAYS OF VICTORY

Nearly nine months pass, but the mood among the Jews remains jubilant. The new law enacted by Mordecai gave them the right to fight back when attacked by their enemies on the thirteenth day of the twelfth month. They are ready. Mordecai has become a powerful man in the king's administration, and the people are terrified of him and his people. The Jews have no trouble killing and destroying their enemies (9:5). In a single day they kill five hundred opponents in Susa alone, including the ten sons of Haman (9:6–9).

Interestingly, although the Jews had been authorized to acquire the plunder of those they defeated (8:11), they choose not to do so (9:10, 15, 16). So the only Jewish person to profit from the exposure of Haman is Esther (8:1).

The king is still willing to accommodate a request by Esther, so she asks for a one-day extension for the Jews in Susa to continue eliminating their enemies, and she wants Haman's sons to be hanged (their bodies publicly displayed). So while the Jews in other territories have a day of celebration and rejoicing, those in Susa kill another three hundred men and do their celebrating the following day.

THE ORIGIN OF PURIM

Letters go out one more time to all the Jews in Persia. But this time they aren't forewarnings of death to come or a call to take up arms and fight their enemies. This time the news is to celebrate their victory over their enemies (9:20–22, 29–32).

The celebration becomes an annual event among the Jews that continues today. The name, *Purim*, is taken from the plural of *pur*, the die that Haman had cast to determine what day the Jews would be annihilated. The holiday is still celebrated on one day in most places, but one day later in walled cities (9:18–19).

Demystifying Esther

Purim is different from most other Old Testament feasts and celebrations. It was not established by God, but by people (9:27). It is a celebration of human achievement rather than God's deliverance (9:22). And rather than centering on worship as most other feasts do, Purim involves generosity and gift-giving that can border on self-indulgence. There is no element of sacrifice—just celebration.

The book of Esther concludes with two tributes. King Ahasuerus (Xerxes) is king of one of the greatest empires of all time, yet all that is said of him is that he taxed his kingdom. Mordecai, on the other hand, is given lavish praise (10:2–3). Ahasuerus will soon be assassinated, which presumably ends Mordecai's influence as well. About 150 years later, the glory of Persia will come to an end at the hands of Alexander the Great.

The book of Esther is a picture—not a very pretty one—of Jewish people who choose to stay in Persia rather than return to Jerusalem. It is a story of God's wonderful providence for people who don't seem to make Him a priority in their lives. As wonderfully as things turned out, there is no mention of Esther, Mordecai, or Purim elsewhere in the Bible.

Take It Home

God's providence is evident throughout the book of Esther, even though Esther and Mordecai didn't return to Jerusalem. The book challenges modern readers to consider God's care and guidance even when we are not in the ideal situation. His mercies do not depend on our location or even our own faithfulness. They are an outpouring of who He is in our lives.

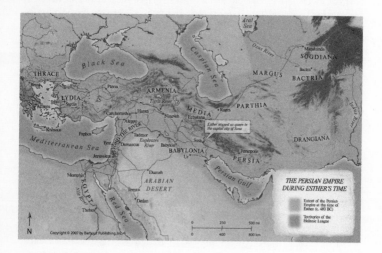

THE PERSIAN EMPIRE
DURING ESTHER'S TIME

JOB

INTRODUCTION TO THE BOOK OF JOB

Many people who read the book of Job miss the God-centered message because they are focused on the man-centered problems. Why the righteous suffer is never really answered in this book. As God shows Job, knowing the answers to life's problems is not as important as knowing and understanding the awesomeness of God and how wise He is.

AUTHOR

The author of the book of Job is unknown. Most likely, he was an Israelite, because he uses the Israelite covenant name for God (*Yahweh*, or the *LORD*).

OCCASION

We do not know when Job was written, though the account describes history around the time of Abraham—that is, around 2000 BC. The first 11 chapters of Genesis pre-date the story of Job, but they were not written down in a book form until the time of Moses, around 1500 BC.

HISTORICAL CONTEXT

Job was likely a contemporary with Abraham, around three hundred years or so after the Flood. The reasons for placing Job in this period of time are as follows:

1) *Long life*: Job lives another 140 years after the events of this book (42:16), which makes him around 200 years old at his death. After the Flood, human life span progressively decreased. Terah, Abraham's father, was 205. Abraham was 175. Isaac, 180. Jacob, 147. So Job fits in nicely around the time of Abraham.

2) *No law*: There is no mention of the Ten Commandments or any of the Mosaic Laws in the book of Job.

3) *Sacrifices*: Before the Mosaic Law, the patriarchal head of each family would offer sacrifices, just as Job does (see 1:5).

4) *Wealth*: Job's wealth is listed in terms of livestock and not money, as was the practice during the time of Abraham (see Genesis 12:16).

CONTRIBUTION TO THE BIBLE

The book of Job is one of the five Wisdom Books, comprising Job, Psalms, Proverbs, Ecclesiastes, and Song of Solomon. Much of these books is poetic, but in the Hebrew sense. While much of western poetry is associated with rhyme and meter, Hebrew poetry is associated with contrasting thoughts or parallel thoughts set against each other.

JOB 1:1–22

THE STORY BEGINS

Setting Up the Section

The book of Job has been called a masterpiece that is unequaled in all literature. The meaning of the name *Job* is "enemy" or "to be hostile toward." While this does not seem to typify Job's character, it does reflect his experience. When we look at Job's circumstances, we see his faith lived out in his life—he practices what he believes.

📄 **1:1–5**

PROLOGUE

In describing Job as blameless and upright (1:1), God is giving insight into the character of Job so that, as we read this story, we won't misinterpret what is going to happen to him. Job is a morally upright person—not perfect, but a good man who loves God. He fears God, meaning that he has a correct perspective of God as holy and righteous. Because he has this perspective, he shuns evil—literally meaning he turns away from it.

Demystifying Job

We are not entirely sure where the land of Uz (1:1) is located, but the Bible does give an interesting possibility. Lamentations 4:21 reads, "Rejoice and be glad, O daughter of Edom, who dwells in the land of Uz" (NASB). This seems to imply that the area of Uz was established before the Edomites came to dwell there. This area is located southeast of the Dead Sea.

Job is a wealthy man who is blessed with ten children (1:2). It is his number of animals that makes him wealthy (1:3). Money is not a part of his culture. The sheep are used for clothing and food, the donkeys and camels for transportation (the camels are the work horses of the desert. While donkeys are for short distances, the camels are used for cross country.) The oxen are for food, plowing, and milk.

It seems that Job's children like to party (1:4). With the wine flowing at these parties and clouding their judgment, Job fears that his children may have taken the name of the Lord a little too lightly (1:5). By their actions they are dishonoring God. So Job intercedes for his children, getting up early and offering ten sacrifices, one for each child.

🔖 **1:6–22**

JOB'S FIRST TEST

The interpretation of the Hebrew phrase *bene Elohim* is the cause of some controversy as to whether the phrase refers to angels or not. Some versions translate it as "sons of God," which can to some imply humanity. However, in Job 38:7, the phrase occurs in the context of creation, "when the morning stars sang together, and all the sons of God shouted for joy" (KJV). Angels were created before God created the heavens and the earth, and thus, they are the ones who shout for joy when the earth is created. So the "sons of God" reference is to angels and not mankind.

Critical Observation

The phrase *bene Elohim* is also found in Genesis 6, when we read of angels—sons of God—cohabitating with women and producing the Nephilim, or the fallen ones. Many suggest the ungodly men marry godly women and produce strange offspring. However, that is not what the scriptures say. Jude 1:6 tells us that "angels who did not keep their own domain, but abandoned their proper abode, He has kept in eternal bonds under darkness for the judgment of the great day" (NASB). These are the fallen angels, those who sided with Satan, whom God places in chains for the Day of Judgment. The rest of the fallen angels we call *demons*, and they are not locked up but are free to do the work of Satan.

Notice the restlessness of the accuser, going to and fro over the earth (1:7). Why? To see who he can destroy and what lives he can ruin. As 1 Peter 5:8 says, "Be on your guard and stay awake. Your enemy, the devil, is like a roaring lion, sneaking around to find someone to attack" (CEV). It's important to remember that Satan could *still* have access to the throne of God, the very presence of God, but he is *not* God, nor is he equal to God. Satan is not omnipotent, omnipresent, or omniscient, as God is.

God points out to Satan this man Job and his goodness (Job 1:8). The word *considered* is a military term that is used of a general who is studying a city before he attacks it so that he can develop a strategy to destroy it. So God is asking Satan if he has found any weakness in Job by which Satan might gain control or cause him to stumble. God's implication is that Satan can find nothing to cause Job to stumble.

Satan claims that the only reason Job loves God is because God is blessing him (1:9–11). Satan says the only reason Job (or anyone) serves God is because He pays well. The second indictment he makes is against God; he says God buys human love by giving blessings.

Satan can do nothing unless God allows it (1:12). Suddenly, over the course of a day, tragedies begin to fall upon Job's household (1:13–19). Verse 16 is interesting because the servant says that the fire of God fell from heaven. Yes God allows it, but Satan is behind it. The world likes to blame God for Satan's work.

After hearing all this bad news, Job begins to mourn (1:20), and who wouldn't? But then he begins to worship God (1:21). When things are going well, it is easy to worship God, but what if you lose everything? Could you still worship God as Job does?

Take It Home

When you have the right perspective of things, it is easy to worship God. Job realizes that all his material possessions, his wealth, and even his children are on loan to him from God. So when they are taken away, even though he is broken over it, he realizes he can't take them with him. Job does not understand why this happens to him, but he knows his God and thus, as we will see, he does not bring a foolish charge against God for what transpires.

Those who feel they are entitled to much are going to be angry and bitter toward God when their things are taken away. Nothing is ours to keep, for we are God's stewards, watching over that which He has entrusted to us.

Job passes the first test (1:22). Satan is wrong; it is not the material blessings that cause Job to worship God. But Satan is not going to give up easily, as we will soon see.

JOB 2:1–13

MORE TRIALS

Setting Up the Section

Chapter 2 opens with another board meeting in heaven, as the angelic hosts come before the Lord, and Satan also comes to renew his charges against Job. Many people have a hard time understanding why God allows this to continue, but Satan is serving the purposes of God at this time.

📖 2:1–10

JOB'S SECOND TEST

Job 2:1–3 are an exact echo of God's dialogue with Satan in Job 1:6–8, with the addition of the assertion that Job has remained faithful in the face of tragedy.

Critical Observation

The word translated *incited* in verse 3 means "to seduce, entice, persuade, provoke." Applied to God it seems confusing; we are trying to understand an infinite God with our finite minds and limited vocabulary. God is in control, and He is not pushed into situations by Satan.

Satan is looking for that Achilles' heel, that weakness in Job, so that he can get Job to turn from God. Surely when his health is gone, he will surrender to Satan (2:4).

What a pathetic picture we see here of a man who has everything and is now reduced to nothing; even his health has failed him now (2:6–8). We do not know for sure what disease Job has, but it is clear that it leaves him miserable and very ill.

Verse 9 gives us an indication as to why Satan does not kill Job's wife when he kills Job's children: She is more help to Satan alive than dead. Yet Job does not bring any foolish accusations against God. Job tells his wife that we are not only to accept good from God but also whatever else comes our way (2:10). Job is not giving up; he is placing his life in the hands of a sovereign God.

📖 2:11–13

JOB'S THREE FRIENDS

Eliphaz, Bildad, and Zophar are true friends to Job, who come to comfort him during this difficult time (2:11). Job must have looked a mess, for at first his friends do not even recognize him (2:12). For seven days they cannot say anything; they just sit and mourn with him (2:13). As later passages will show, this is the best thing they do for him.

These first two chapters now set the stage for the rest of the book of Job, as he tries to understand why all these things have happened to him. Job's friends will quickly interject their opinions.

Take It Home

As tough as things are going to get for Job, and as tough as things may be for us at times, remember what Paul says in 1 Corinthians 10:13: "No temptation has overtaken you that is not common to man. God is faithful, and he will not let you be tempted beyond your ability, but with the temptation he will also provide the way of escape, that you may be able to endure it" (ESV). We give up far too easily many times, for God is right there with us.

JOB 3:1–26

JOB SPEAKS

Setting Up the Section

The events of chapter 3 come on the heels of some tragic events in Job's life. In one day, Job, one of the wealthiest men in the area, loses all his material possessions. Not only that, but his ten children, who he loves very much, are all killed on the same day as well. And yet, in all this tragedy, Job is still able to worship God.

Some time after these events, Job's health is taken away. He develops boils from the top of his head to the tips of his toes. And yet in all this, Job does not charge God foolishly.

Job's friends Eliphaz, Bildad, and Zophar have gathered around him, mourning silently for seven days. And now Job is going to speak from his heart.

📄 **3:1–10**

CURSES FOR THE DAY HE WAS BORN

When Job at last speaks, he curses the day of his birth, wishing it would be wiped off the calendar (3:1–6). He is not cursing God, but it does sound like he is questioning why he was even born if he was going to have to live a life like this (3:7–10). Job is not a stoic, and God is not allowing these things to come upon his life to see if Job can sit there unmoved, emotionless. God has a purpose for all this: to increase Job's faith.

Take It Home

Our common modern stereotype of Job is that of an incredibly patient man. As you read the scripture closely, however, Job is more characterized by his perseverance than his patience (James 5:10–11). His prayers reveal many of the same thoughts and feelings that we all experience when we face suffering.

It is important that we not miss God's mercy and compassion in the message of Job as well. We do suffer in this life, but we can trust God's purposes and His character. Remembering this helps us to persevere in our own suffering.

WISHING HE HAD DIED AT BIRTH

Job wishes he had been born dead, for it would be far better than the life he has (3:11–12, 18–19). He says that in death there is peace not only for the righteous (3:11–16) but also for the wicked (3:15–17).

Job is here speaking out of frustration and not out of revelation. God later says to Job, regarding this issue, "Have the gates of death been shown to you? Have you seen the gates of the shadow of death? Have you comprehended the vast expanses of the earth? Tell me, if you know all this" (38:17–18 NIV). Job does not understand what he is talking about regarding death, for he has never experienced it.

Critical Observation

Seventh-day Adventists and the Jehovah Witnesses formulate their doctrine for soul sleep and annihilation of the wicked from Job 3:11–17. They say that the righteous will be resurrected when the Lord returns, but until that time the soul is asleep. The wicked are also asleep in death until the Lord returns; then He will cause them to cease to exist, to be in a state of nothingness, with no punishment at all. This even goes for Satan.

However, in Revelation 20:10 we read, "Then the devil, who had deceived them, was thrown into the fiery lake of burning sulfur, joining the beast and the false prophet. There they will be tormented day and night forever and ever" (NLT). No soul sleep or annihilation there.

THE MISERY OF LIFE

Job is at the point where death itself seems more precious to him than all the treasures of the world (3:20–22). He closes his monologue by questioning the meaning of life (3:23) and contrasting its harshness to the presumed peace of the grave (3:24–26).

JOB 4:1–5:27

ELIPHAZ SPEAKS

Blaming Job for His Troubles   4:1–5:7

Eliphaz's Solution   5:8–27

Setting Up the Section

Job has broken a seven-day silence to wish he had never been born. Now, after all these words from Job, Eliphaz wants to interject some of his own thoughts regarding this situation.

📖 **4:1–5:7**

BLAMING JOB FOR HIS TROUBLES

It seems that Job's friend Eliphaz can't hold back—he has to speak to Job about what Job has said and about what Job is experiencing (4:1–2). At first his words seem to affirm Job, as he reminds him of how Job has encouraged so many others in difficult times (4:3). But this affirmation turns to rebuke as he says, in effect, "Look, you have helped others through difficult times, but now you, the great counselor, can't even handle the difficult times you are going through. What's your problem Job?" (4:5–6).

Eliphaz says that the reason Job is going through these trials is that he is not innocent; only those who sin will go through times like this (4:6–7). This is a simplistic approach to Job's problem, but not a scriptural truth. But for the next thirty-six chapters, his friends are going to tell Job this very thing—that his sins have caused his suffering.

Critical Observation

The Bible has many examples of the righteous suffering, but the best, of course, is that of Jesus Himself. Peter says in 1 Peter 3:18, "For Christ also suffered once for sins, the just for the unjust, that He might bring us to God, being put to death in the flesh but made alive by the Spirit" (NKJV).

There is a measure of truth in that punishment will come for the wicked, but it is not always immediate. But this is not the only reason for suffering. Notice that Eliphaz comes across as being so spiritually insightful (4:8). Eliphaz's conclusion is that God will blast those who are evil just as He is doing to Job (4:9–11).

Eliphaz turns mystical as he builds up to the climax of his statement, claiming personal spiritual guidance (4:12–16), but his insight is less than profound. It doesn't take a mystic to recognize that God is more righteous than human beings (4:17). Eliphaz seems to suggest that Job ought to expect destruction because of his own wrongdoing (4:18–21).

Demystifying Job

Eliphaz bases his advice on this alleged vision. His advice does contain some truth, but ultimately God rebukes him for speaking untruth (see 42:7).

The holy ones to whom Eliphaz refers in 5:1 are angels, like those who gather in God's throne room (1:6; 2:1). Eliphaz's reference to those losing their homes and children (5:2–5) is a none-too-subtle parallel of Job's misfortunes which, Eliphaz contends, come to fools and simpletons—presumably like Job. After all, trouble doesn't spring out of nowhere (5:6), so clearly Job must have done something to bring it on himself.

Demystifying Job

The point of this book is that Job did not deserve the suffering he received. Thus, this book is associated with the question, "Why do bad things happen to good people?" While the Bible teaches that none of us is actually good (Romans 3:10–18), the question is still a relevant one. Keep in mind however that the book of Job does not carry the responsibility of answering that age old question. We can extrapolate our own reasoning about how Job's story reveals some purpose to suffering, but our best reasoning does not lead us to God's truth. Instead we need to understand what the scripture does teach—God's purposes continue even in our suffering. There is a bigger story happening outside of our own circumstances. And certainly elsewhere in scripture we find the truth that even in our suffering God's presence continues as well.

5:8–27

ELIPHAZ'S SOLUTION

Eliphaz turns holier-than-thou at this point, saying that if he were going through the things that Job is going through, he would repent before God (5:8–16).

It is true that God does chasten those He loves (5:17; see Hebrews 12:5–8). Eliphaz mixes truth with error, and that is always destructive. The problem here is that Eliphaz assumes Job is guilty of some sin and this is God's reason for chastening him. But we have already been told in chapter 1 that this is not the case. Eliphaz's glib assurances, that if Job repents all will again be well, only increase Job's pain (Job 5:18–27).

Take It Home

Here is an important lesson for us to learn from Eliphaz: When people are going through difficult times, it is not time to preach to them. In fact, the best thing to do is listen, comfort them, and simply show that you care. Giving pious platitudes is of no help to people in pain and will only bring them down.

JOB 6:1–7:21

JOB REPLIES

Setting Up the Section

After sitting with his friends in silence for seven days (4:11–13), Job pours out his anger and despair in a monologue (chapter 3), to which his friend Eliphaz feels compelled to reply (chapters 4–5). Eliphaz, after suggesting that Job has brought his troubles on himself through his own sin, suggests that Job plead his case (and presumably repent) before God. Chapters 6 and 7 contain Job's response.

📄 6:1–30

JOB REPLIES TO ELIPHAZ

Job responds to Eliphaz by saying that his grief, if weighed against all the sand of the sea, would be far greater (6:1–3). He has allowed the situations of life, and maybe even some of the words of his friends, to cloud his picture of God, for he now thinks that God is his enemy (6:4). Job has never experienced anything like this in his life, and now God is exposing him to his weakness so that his faith may grow out of these circumstances.

Animals make noise when their stomachs are empty (6:5). Job feels he has a right to complain because his life has become empty—even the so-called comfort from his friends is tasteless and sickening (6:6–7). He is so miserable that he asks God to end his life before his misery leads him to deny God's goodness (6:8–10). He has nothing to live for and no hope for his future (6:11–13); even his friends have failed him. They are like flooding streams in the winter, when no one needs them, and vanish in the dry season when they might do some good (6:14–17). Just as desert caravans look in vain for an oasis, so Job looks in vain for comfort from his friends (6:19–20). Instead of supporting him at the only time he has needed it, they shrink back from his tragedy (6:21–23).

If his friends had anything to say that was worth hearing, Job would have been more than willing to listen, but they are not speaking the truth (6:23–24). Rather, they are implying that Job is the dishonest one for not admitting that his troubles are his own fault (6:25–30).

📖 7:1–21

JOB REPLIES TO GOD

Job compares his life to what others face in their lifetime. One difference is that their problems last for days, and Job's problems last for months. He speaks of a military man, one who does hard service (7:1); he has a certain time to serve, and then it is over. There is an allotted time to serve even for the hired man (7:2). And yet for Job, the days turn into months, and still there is no relief (7:3). When night comes, there is still no comfort; he only tosses and turns with the pain and itching of his blisters and extreme loneliness (7:4). And as morning comes, it is another day of sorrow and pain.

Demystifying Job

Job compares death to the dissipating of a cloud (7:9), but the Bible does not teach that in death we enter a state of nothingness. Job's point is that, once dead, he is not coming back. There is no reincarnation, no recycling through life to become a better person, and no hope for a better earthly life next time (see Hebrews 9:27 and the Critical Observation at Job 3:11–19 on what happens after death).

You have one chance in this life, and if you reject Jesus Christ, you lose. God has done everything necessary for you to enter into abundant life, but if you don't accept it, you will suffer the fate of rejecting the truth.

As Job anticipates his life coming to a hopeless end (7:6), he addresses God directly. Not, however, in humble repentance as Eliphaz might wish (5:8–27), but rather in complaint (7:8–10). Job is going to pour his heart out, and he is not holding anything back (7:11).

Take It Home

Job is not the only person whose complaints against God are recorded in scripture. Many of the psalms express similar strong emotions. To be godly does not mean we express no negative emotion. God knows our complaints, whether we express them or not. We can bring our complaints to God and expect to hear honestly back from Him. In Job's case, we have examples of his heartfelt, honest prayers of complaint. But also later in the book (28–42:6), God takes exception with Job's complaints about his friends. When we come to God with our response to life, He is there to speak into our lives as well.

Job questions God, asking Him why He is watching over his life so closely, like a watchman standing guard on board a ship, watching out for sea serpents (7:12). Job sees God as an adversary, not only allowing physical and emotional pain, but also sending terrifying nightmares so that Job cannot find comfort even in sleep (7:13–14). When Job says he does not want to live forever (7:15–16), he is not making a theological statement about eternal life, but simply stating that his life on earth is not worth living.

Critical Observation

When Job asks, "What are people, that you should make so much of us, that you should think of us so often?" (7:17 NLT), he sees God's attention as a burden. David asks the same question, but in a positive light: "What are mere mortals that you should think about them, human beings that you should care for them?" (Psalm 8:4 NLT). Same words; two different perspectives of God.

Job feels that every step he takes, God is right there ready to strike out at him (7:17–19). He wonders why God has made him a target (7:20). Adversity can lead to a warped concept of God, and we see this happening with Job. He is unable to recognize God's forgiveness (17:21) because of the cultural assumptions Eliphaz has already expressed: If God loves you, you will prosper. Job even goes so far as to tell God that He will be sorry when Job is gone, because He will no longer have anyone to pick on.

JOB 8:1–22

BILDAD SPEAKS

Setting Up the Section

Job has poured out his complaints to God, and his friend Bildad is shocked that Job dares to speak to God in this way. Here he takes Job to task.

📖 8:1–4

BILDAD'S SHOCK

Bildad blasts Job and tells him to stop his pleas of innocence, for they are nothing more than a bunch of hot air (8:1–2). This, too, must have hurt Job. Bildad first tells Job that God is righteous and then says the reason for the death of Job's children is because of some sin in their lives (8:3–4). You see, it would be hard to refute Bildad without seeming to say that God is unrighteous. And yet we know that Bildad is wrong; he does not have the full picture. It is neither God's unrighteousness nor personal sin that brings tragedy on Job's children.

BILDAD'S SOLUTION

Like Eliphaz, Bildad has a simple solution to Job's problems: If Job will confess his sins, then God will make him healthy, wealthy, and prosperous (8:5–7).

Take It Home

Does Bildad's advice sound familiar? It is what many of the "health and wealth" teachers preach from their pulpits—and it is bad theology. Bildad is only speaking a half truth, and half truths are nothing more than lies. We again must understand that God does bless the just *and* the unjust. And we must also fall back on the sovereignty of God; He is in control.

Bildad points to history and the experience of former generations to bolster his point (8:8–10). He argues that the godless person will wither and die, just as the papyrus without the marsh, the reed without water (8:11–13). The implication, of course, is that since Job is experiencing all these troubles, he must be godless. The word translated *godless* in verse 13 means something like "hypocrite." To Bildad's way of thinking, Job is trusting his own (false, according to Bildad) reputation as a blameless man (see 1:1), but that trust is as misplaced as leaning on a spider's web or a rootless plant (8:14–19).

Demystifying Job

Job and his friends lived around the time of Abraham, which was only 250 to 300 years after the Flood. When Bildad refers to what previous generations learned, he is probably thinking of how God destroyed all the wicked by a flood. Now Job, presumably because of his sin, is being wiped out as if by a flood.

BILDAD'S SUMMATION

Bildad calls for Job to plead his case before God. If Job is innocent, he has nothing to worry about. If Job is not innocent, then God will deal with him appropriately (8:20–22).

JOB 9:1–10:22

JOB REPLIES TO BILDAD

Human Innocence vs. God's Power	9:1–35
Challenging God	10:1–22

Setting Up the Section

Job's friend Bildad has taken Job to task for questioning God. He has declared that God sends punishment to the wicked and brings blessing to the righteous, with the implication that Job will again be blessed if he lives righteously. This prompts Job to reflect on what it means to be righteous in God's sight.

📖 9:1–35

HUMAN INNOCENCE VS. GOD'S POWER

Job tells Bildad that his words are empty because, even if Job could go before God, he can't win. All this righteousness that Eliphaz and Bildad are touting is out of reach for mere mortals (9:1–2), and even if one were innocent, who could beat God in an argument (9:3)? Not only is God wiser and more powerful than any human being (9:4–10), but He is spirit and, as such, can be difficult for the human mind to comprehend.

Demystifying Job

The name *Rahab* (9:13) means "to press or to assail" and refers to a mythical sea monster.

If God is not as good as we think He is, then His having all that power is scary (9:12–13). And Job isn't sure that God is good. Job is allowing his circumstances to cloud his picture of God. He doesn't stand a chance with God (9:14–16); he can't even catch his breath and defend himself (9:17–20).

Critical Observation

Job's despair over his status before God brings to mind Paul the apostle, who said, "I know that nothing good lives in me, that is, in my sinful nature. For I have the desire to do what is good, but I cannot carry it out" (Romans 7:18 NIV). But rather than fall into despair, as Job does, Paul finds the answer to his problem: "Therefore, there is now no condemnation for those who are in Christ Jesus" (Romans 8:1 NIV). Christ alone can help us by His Spirit to do those things that are pleasing to God. It is not by the will of the flesh but submission to the Holy Spirit that this is accomplished.

To Job, it doesn't seem to matter if you are good or evil, because God destroys both equally (9:21–22). In fact, it seems Job sees God getting a kind of perverse pleasure in destroying people, especially the innocent (9:22–24). Job clearly knows the greatness of God and His power, but Job is struggling with the goodness of God. He is struggling because he sees the innocent suffer, including himself, which he can't understand. And his friends are not helping one bit.

Notice Job's conclusion: If he is going to be punished regardless of his innocence or guilt, then why bother to repent (9:25–31)?

How can Job go into heaven, go before God, and plead his case (9:32)? He is a mere human, and there is no one who can bridge that gap, no mediator (9:33). Job sees God as a cruel taskmaster with His rod of discipline ready to strike anyone at His will, and Job is terrified of Him (9:34–35). Notice, as Job's picture of God gets more distorted, it is harder for him to truly love God.

Take It Home

Job knows his desperate need for a mediator (9:33) but despairs of finding one. How rich we are who know that "there is one God, and one mediator also between God and men, the man Christ Jesus" (1 Timothy 2:5 NASB). There is no one else that can bridge the gap—no priest, no man, not even Mary—but only Jesus Christ who, being God, made Himself flesh to die for our sins in order to bring us to God (1 Peter 3:18).

📖 **10:1–22**

CHALLENGING GOD

Job is going to speak from his heart, and whatever comes out, let it be. He is not going to hold anything back (10:1). He knows that he is the work of God's hands, and yet it seems God despises him and loves the wicked (10:2–7).

Job now speaks of his own frailty, that God has created him out of the dust of the earth (10:8). Like a master potter, God has formed Job, and He has formed us, but these bodies of flesh will return to the dust of the earth (10:9).

Job sees himself trapped. No matter what he does before God, it won't be good enough and he will be judged (10:12–17). He asks why God allowed him to be born, if God is only going to torture him (10:18–19).

Job has had it; he can't take it any more. So he cries out to God, asking God to leave him alone, to give him a break, and let him try to enjoy the short time he has left (10:20–22).

JOB 11:1–20

ZOPHAR SPEAKS

Setting Up the Section

Eliphaz was eloquent with his words, but they were not encouraging, only judgmental. Bildad was brutal as he accused Job of not being as innocent as he tried to make others believe. And now Job's third friend, Zophar, comes on the scene and blasts Job with stinging sarcasm.

📖 11:1–12

ZOPHAR'S QUESTIONS

Zophar begins with rhetorical questions that let Job know he is not going to be able to justify himself (11:1–2). Zophar is not going to let Job get away with his empty words, for the things that have come upon Job's life show that Job is not pure (11:3–4). Zophar does not believe in Job's innocence. In fact, he is calling to God to show Job all the evil that is in him, that secret sin that has brought this upon his life (11:5). And just to let Job know how spiritual he is, Zophar tells Job that God has spoken to Zophar and has shown him that Job has only received half of what he deserves (11:6).

Next Zophar takes Job to task for trying to understand God (11:7–9). Zophar says that Job will obtain wisdom when a man is born from a wild donkey (11:10–12).

Critical Observation

In the King James Version, verse 7 asks if we can find God by our searching. The answer to that question may surprise you. No, we can't find God by our searching because He is not lost; we are! God is the good shepherd who goes looking for His sheep. Jesus said in John 6:44 that no one can come to Him unless it is through the work of the Father. God is the initiator; we are only responding to what He has begun.

📖 11:13–20

ZOPHAR'S ANSWERS

After all his rhetorical questions, Zophar offers his own simplistic answer: Get right with God, and the sun will once again shine on Job's life, a smile will return to his face, and he will be protected from his enemies just as a moat protects those living within the city walls (11:13–18). According to Zophar, Job's friends will also return if he gets right with God. But if he doesn't, his life will come to an end (11:19–20).

Take It Home

There is no way we can fully understand an infinite God with our finite minds (Isaiah 55:8–9). Things occur in our lives that we do not fully understand. Sometimes we can't intellectually understand what God is doing and why He is doing it. This is when we have to walk by faith and not by sight, trusting that God knows what is best.

JOB 12:1–14:22

JOB REPLIES TO ZOPHAR

Folly and Wisdom	12:1–25
Silence and Speech	13:1–28
Life and Death	14:1–22

Setting Up the Section

In response to Zophar's oration (chapter 11), Job again speaks.

📄 **12:1–25**

FOLLY AND WISDOM

Now it is Job's turn to use sarcasm. He tells Zophar that undoubtedly, when Zophar dies, so too will die all the wisdom in the world (12:1–2). Job lashes out at his friends' pride as he tells them that he understands just as much as they do; that he has not heard anything earth-shattering from their speeches (12:3).

It seems hard for Job's friends to be compassionate when things are going well in their own lives. They are making themselves out to be righteous, for they are blessed. And they are making Job unrighteous, for he is cursed. Those who come to comfort him are only mocking him (12:4–5). Notice Job's argument against their counsel. They have their theological answers to Job's problems, but Job calls for them to apply that to the real world and see if it still holds water. And he shows them that it doesn't, for the robbers are still prospering and the unrighteous seem to live in comfort (12:6).

Demystifying Job

The meaning of the phrase "those who carry their god in their hands" (12:6 NIV) is uncertain. Since it is mentioned in the context of marauders, perhaps the "god in their hands" refers to their plunder, or possibly it refers to their swords, on which they depend for means to power in battle. It also may refer to those who try to bring God under their control or power, a common meaning of *hand* in this kind of context.

Job says creation itself knows that God is free to do whatever He wishes with His creatures (12:7–12). Every breath is a gift of God (12:10). Job is saying that God is sovereign over nature, over nations, and over the lives of humans (12:13–25).

13:1–28

SILENCE AND SPEECH

Job has had it with his friends' worthless counsel and does not want to hear their empty words any longer. He only wants to hear from God (13:1–4). He calls for his friends to be silent—that is the best counsel (13:5).

Job's friends think they are speaking for God, and yet their counsel is wrong (13:6–9). God will reprove them for their false counsel and their empty words, for they are meaningless, of no help, and most important, they are not of God (13:8–12).

Job now wants to speak his piece (13:13). He is still in his cave of despair, living in self pity, but then, seemingly out of nowhere, he makes a solid statement: "Though he slay me, yet will I hope in him" (13:15 NIV). Even though Job has no idea why all this has happened to him, and as unfair as it seems, he is now going to trust in God with his life. Job is learning to trust God more and his faith is growing. He sees God as his salvation (13:16–19).

Job wants to talk things over with God, but first he asks God to remove all the adversity that has come upon his life and let him rest for a while (13:20–22). Asking for God to show him his error, Job reflects on his youth and concludes that God is getting back at him for something done back then (13:20–28).

Take It Home

As we go through difficult times, we tend to look back and blame our present situation on what we have done in the past, just as Job does. But God brings us through trials to stretch our faith, not for the purpose of revenge or intimidation.

14:1–22

LIFE AND DEATH

The human life is short when compared with eternity (14:1–2). God knows the number of our days (14:3–5). Job here again sees God as his adversary and asks God to leave him alone (14:6).

Job concludes by bemoaning what he sees as the ultimate fate of every human being: death, which in his mind means the end of existence (14:7–12). He expresses a beautiful longing for renewal and forgiveness (14:13–17) but then concludes that there is no hope (14:18–22).

JOB 15:1–35

ELIPHAZ'S SECOND SPEECH

Calling Job a Fool   15:1–16
The Wicked Get What They Deserve   15:17–35

Setting Up the Section

Each of Job's three friends has had his say. Now Eliphaz begins round two with his second speech.

📄 **15:1–16**

CALLING JOB A FOOL

Eliphaz questions Job's wisdom, saying that Job's words are nothing more than a lot of hot air (15:1–3). Eliphaz believes that Job is undermining people's piety by refusing to admit that his sins have brought his troubles on him (15:4–6).

Next Eliphaz attacks Job's credentials, asking Job if he is the oldest and wisest man around or if he has some private access to God's council that is denied to his friends (15:7–9). No, Eliphaz insists; the oldest and wisest men side with Eliphaz on this subject (15:10), and Job, far from being privy to God's wisdom, isn't satisfied with it (15:11). Eliphaz sees Job as a man who claims to be righteous but who is really entertaining sin (15:12). He sees Job's anger with God as another form of sin (15:13).

Take It Home

The Bible gives many examples of the anger and frustration that God's people feel when things go wrong. Anger itself is not the problem; the problem comes when that anger prompts people to do and say things they should not. For example, the prophet Jeremiah is angry when people do not respond to his preaching. He crosses the line into sin when he accuses God of deceiving him. God immediately calls him to account and repentance (Jeremiah 15:18–19).

Eliphaz is right to say that no one can attain righteousness on his or her own; even angels—holy ones—rebel against God (15:14–16).

📄 **15:17–35**

THE WICKED GET WHAT THEY DESERVE

Eliphaz falls back on what he has seen and the worldview he has been taught (15:17–19): that the wicked suffer their whole lives (15:20). He assumes that the converse is also true: If a man is suffering, he must be wicked. All of Job's prosperity has been taken away, just as happens to the wicked (15:21). Job has met the same fate as the wicked (15:26).

Demystifying Job

In Job's time, weight was a sign of wealth (15:27), because the rich were able to enjoy much more food than the common people. Job probably looked well-fed before his troubles began, but by the time his friends arrived, he was probably skin and bones—so changed that at first they do not even recognize him (2:12).

His prosperity is gone; his life is dark and hopeless (15:29–30). In Eliphaz's eyes, Job is deceiving himself by claiming that he has done nothing to deserve his troubles (15:31). Eliphaz's metaphors of vines stripped of their grapes before they have matured, and trees dropping their flowers before they have had time to develop into fruit (15:32–33), must have fallen hard on the ears of a man whose children died untimely deaths. All Eliphaz predicts for Job now is barrenness; the only "children" Job will father are evil and deceit (15:34–35).

JOB 16:1–17:16

JOB'S SECOND RESPONSE TO ELIPHAZ

Attacked by God and Men	16:1–21
Harassed Till the Very End	16:22–17:16

Setting Up the Section

Eliphaz has enumerated the bad things that happen to wicked people—things that are now happening to Job. The implication is clear: Job is a wicked person. Now Job replies, addressing Bildad and Zophar as well as Eliphaz.

🖹 **16:1–21**

ATTACKED BY GOD AND MEN

Job blasts his friends for their insensitivity to his condition and calls them miserable comforters (16:1–2). He wants them to realize what they are doing by imagining they were in his shoes (16:3–4). Job tells them that if they were in a similar situation, he would comfort instead of condemn and encourage instead of discourage them (16:5).

Demystifying Job

To shake your head at someone (16:4) is to say that their words are empty—the very thing Job's friends have been doing.

Job is not finding any comfort in his own words or in the words of his friends (16:6). He sees himself being eaten alive, wasting away to nothing, and God continues to cause havoc with his life (16:7-9). Job complains that God has given him wicked friends who are continually coming against him (16:10-11).

Take It Home

The phrase *Job's comforters* has come to mean "people who don't comfort at all." We are not called to be that kind of friend (see 1 Thessalonians 5:14–15).

As a lion or tiger goes after its prey and grabs it by the neck to choke the life out of it, Job sees God doing this to him. In fact, Job sees himself as nothing more than a target on God's practice range; his suffering is tearing his guts out (16:12-14).

Job doesn't understand why this is happening to him; he feels that he does not deserve all of this (16:15-17). He wants to sit down and talk with God face-to-face (16:18-21).

📖 **16:22–17:16**

HARASSED TILL THE VERY END

Again, Job sees his life coming to an end (16:22-17:1). His many friends have forsaken him, and no one will speak up for him (17:2-5).

Job had not only been wealthy but he had also been well respected. Others looked to him for help and direction (see 4:3-4). But now these same people look at him in disgust and begin to spit upon him (16:6). Job doesn't care what they say; he knows he is innocent, and he is not going to change his story (16:8-9). In fact, he gets a little sarcastic, telling his friends to come back and stick the knife in a little deeper (17:10).

Job wants to die. His children are gone, and now he claims death as his family, and he waits for them to come and take him away (17:11-16).

JOB 18:1–21

BILDAD'S SECOND SPEECH

Setting Up the Section

After hearing Job's complaint in chapters 16 and 17, Bildad steps up to the plate to have a second try at arguing Job into agreeing with his friends and their theology.

📖 **18:1–4**

CALLING JOB TO HIS SENSES

Bildad sees Job as long-winded (18:1–2), and he is upset that Job is speaking so harshly to his friends (18:3)—despite the fact that Bildad and the others are equally harsh to Job. He tells Job that it is not God who is causing his pain, as Job claims (see 16:13), but rather it is Job inflicting pain on himself because of his sin (18:4).

Take It Home

Bildad and Job's other friends are very sincere in what they are doing; the only problem is that they are sincerely wrong. May we learn to stop and bring things before God, asking for His wisdom before we speak out of our own foolish hearts and cause more harm to others than good (see James 1:19–20).

📖 **18:5–21**

METAPHORS OF DISASTER

Bildad now launches into a poetic speech intended to convince Job that he is wrong to believe that good things happen to evil people (see 10:3). He recites a litany of bad things that happen to wicked people—to all wicked people, according to Bildad.

Wicked people die, signified by the extinguishing of lamps and fires (18:5–6). This might seem rather obvious, since everyone dies, but the verb *snuffed out* suggests death at the hands of others. If that fate does not overtake a wicked man, perhaps his life will flicker out through weakness or illness, or even because his own schemes backfire (18:7).

Verses 8–10 enumerate the various ways that a wicked person can be "thrown down" (NIV), as verse 7 expresses it. He could wander into a net that is spread out on the ground (18:8)—maybe even a net that he has spread out to catch someone else but that he absentmindedly wanders into while plotting his next scheme. Even if he is alert to what lies on the ground in front of him, he could be caught from behind by a trap or snare (18:9). If his own schemes don't trip him up, then he may fall into a trap that someone else has set specifically to catch him (18:10).

Demystifying Job

The noose referred to in verse 10 is not a noose to hang a person by the neck. Rather, it is laid out on the ground as a trap. When the prey steps inside the noose, the noose tightens, the prey is caught by the ankle, and he is thrown off his feet. It is interesting that in all the ways described here that a wicked person might be thrown down, each trap catches the victim by the feet as he is walking. This calls to mind Psalm 1:1, "Blessed is the man who does not walk in the counsel of the wicked" (NIV).

Terror lies in wait everywhere for the wicked (18:11), and that terror is justified because calamity and disaster lurk around every corner (18:12). Job, with his blistered skin, must have identified with the wicked man whose skin is being eaten away (18:13) by "death's firstborn" (NIV)—probably a poetic name for a deadly disease.

There is no safety for the wicked man, even in his own home; he is torn from his home and delivered to death (18:14). Even if he were able to remain home, he would find it burning with sulfur—reminiscent of the destruction of Sodom and Gomorrah, those strongholds of evil (see Genesis 19:24).

Critical Observation

The king of terrors (18:14) is the frightening name for the Canaanite god that was death personified. Mot devoured his victims. Isaiah turns this imagery around and prophesies that the Lord will swallow death forever (Isaiah 25:8), and the apostle Paul explains that this prophecy is fulfilled in Jesus Christ's resurrection from the dead (1 Corinthians 15:54).

The wicked man's roots—his ancestors and his descendants—do not thrive (Job 18:16), and no one remembers him or his family once he is gone (18:17–18). He has no name, not only because his own name is forgotten, but also because his family name does not continue; none of his offspring or descendants survive (18:19). From east to west, a fate like this is viewed with horror (18:20). Quite possibly Bildad is thinking also of how appalled he and Job's other friends were when they first saw Job in his misery. It is easy for Bildad to see how many of these horrors reserved for wicked men have befallen Job, and he concludes that Job either does not know God or at least is on the way to becoming estranged by God because of his complaints against Him (18:21).

JOB 19:1–29

JOB'S SECOND RESPONSE TO BILDAD

A List of Complaints   19:1–20
A Plea for Pity   19:21–29

Setting Up the Section

Job responds to Bildad's poetic discourse on the fate of the wicked—and by implication, the fate of Job—with some well-chosen words of his own.

📖 **19:1–20**

A LIST OF COMPLAINTS

Words of hate and wrath that come from the heart of men and women are not of God and can hurt people. This is where Job is. He is broken, tormented by his friends' words (19:1–3). Job sees himself as innocent before God no matter what his friends say, no matter how much they make themselves out to be righteous. Job's conclusion is that God is wrong. He can't understand why all this trouble has come upon him (19:4–8).

In verse 9 Job is speaking of all that has been taken away from him. He has, in a sense, been laid out naked before all his friends and family.

Demystifying Job

Job speaks of his crown being removed (19:9). It may well be that Job was a king, and when this trouble came into his life, he lost his throne. Or the word *crown* might be a poetic way of referring to Job's honor, his wealth, or even his hair, which he had shaved off (see 1:20). No one knows for sure.

Again, Job perceives God as his enemy (19:13). He is about as low as a person can get. His friends and relatives have forgotten him and forsaken him (19:14). Even the few remaining servants have refused to listen to him anymore (19:15–16). No one is at his side any longer. Now even his own wife, who wasn't too supportive in the first place (see 2:9), is keeping her distance because of his offensive breath (19:17). All the children that used to gather around him, those that loved him, are now speaking against him and looking down on him (19:18).

Critical Observation

Job speaks of his own children ignoring him (19:17), which seems confusing when, in chapter 1, we are told that all his children were killed. The Amplified Bible helps clear this passage up. It says, "I am repulsive to my wife and loathsome to the children of my own mother." It could be that Job is speaking of his own brothers and sisters, who are ignoring him.

📄 **19:21–29**

A PLEA FOR PITY

Job cries out to his friends to give him a break (19:21). He feels as if his friends are persecuting him just as God is doing (19:22). Feeling that no one is really listening to him, he longs for his words to be permanently recorded (19:23–24), possibly so that more unbiased readers might judge him less harshly than his friends do. And those words have indeed been recorded and passed down throughout the generations.

Take It Home

Job believed that God had brought this trouble on him. But that is not the case. Satan is the one responsible for Job's misfortunes, even though God does allow it—for Satan cannot do anything without God's permission. And remember that when the enemy does something it is not to build up, but to destroy (see John 10:10).

Now Job speaks of resurrection (19:25–27). In contrast to his earlier descriptions of nothingness after death, he now says that, even after he has died and his body has gone back to the dust of the earth, he will be raised up and in his body. Since this is the only time Job mentions the resurrection, it may be that we are incorrect to interpret his words through our New Testament understanding of the resurrection of the body. But certainly with our perspective, affected by New Testament teachings, we find hope in these verses.

Job also knows that no matter how much evil his friends speak against him, he is innocent. And as much as it hurts now, he knows that he will ultimately be vindicated. So he tells his friends to watch out because God will take vengeance; His wrath will come upon them for what they have done to him.

JOB 20:1–29

ZOPHAR'S SECOND SPEECH

Short-Lived Joy for the Wicked   20:1–19
More Punishment to Come   20:20–29

Setting Up the Section

As we move into Job chapter 20, we are closing out round two of this verbal tongue-lashing that Job is receiving from his three friends. Zophar is going to respond to what Job has just said. Job accuses his friends of speaking lies and making up stories to prove their neatly packaged theology. They are accusing Job of hiding sin in his life and that is why all this calamity has come upon him. But Job tells them to be afraid of being judged themselves. He turns the tables on them now, and it is to this that Zophar is going to respond.

📖 20:1–19

SHORT-LIVED JOY FOR THE WICKED

Even in the poetic style in which it is written, it is clear in Zophar's reply that he is very upset with what Job has said against him and his friends. Zophar is not going to take this lying down. He is not going to let Job walk all over him (20:1–2). Why is Zophar so upset? Because Job has insulted his character, just as Zophar has insulted him (20:3).

Zophar returns to the refrain Job has heard from all his friends: comparing what happens to the wicked to what is happening in Job's life. The wicked may prosper, but only for a short time (20:3–4). Eventually, even the highest-ranking among the wicked will be valued no more than human waste (20:7); nobody will even remember them (20:8–9). Their children will be poor and have to beg for food (20:10). One moment the wicked may be young and full of life, but the next moment they could be dead (20:11).

Critical Observation

The idea of not enjoying what one has worked for (20:18) is common in wisdom literature in the Bible. (See, for example, Ecclesiastes 2:18–23.)

The wicked savor evil the way a child might savor candy, but ultimately they will be left with a bad taste in their mouths (20:12–17). They may have every luxury, but they won't enjoy it (20:18). All their hard work won't bring them satisfaction (20:19).

Demystifying Job

Honey and cream (20:17) represent a prosperous life. The land of Canaan was said to be a land flowing with milk and honey (Exodus 13:5).

When Zophar talks of how the wicked treat the needy (20:19), he is implying that Job has oppressed the poor and repossessed homes by force. He has no proof of this. Maybe there were rumors to that effect, but more likely Zophar simply assumes Job's guilt to account for Job's current suffering.

Take It Home

Why do Job's friends go to such extremes to make Job appear guilty? Because to them, sin equals punishment—so Job must be a sinner. God will deal with the unrighteous according to His timetable and His ways. In this life we see the wicked prosper and suffer. We also see the righteous suffer and be blessed. God is sovereign; He is in control. Think about it this way: There are more than five billion people in the world today, and God is orchestrating each and every one of their lives. Most of us have a hard time taking care of ourselves. We don't always know the ways of God, but we do know the character of God, which is the same yesterday, today, and forever (Hebrews 13:8).

📄 **20:20–29**

MORE PUNISHMENT TO COME

The fate of one who indulges his greed is to experience more greed—so much that he can never be satisfied (20:20). Ultimately, there will be nothing more to acquire (20:21). But the wicked are not going to get away with anything. Just when they think everything is okay, God will deal with them (20:22–26).

Zophar's summation of the fate of the wicked implicitly warns Job that if he continues to hide his sin, all these things that will happen to him—and there is worse yet to come on Judgment Day (20:27–29).

JOB 21:1–34

JOB'S SECOND RESPONSE TO ZOPHAR

Setting Up the Section

Not willing to let Zophar have the last word, Job responds to Zophar's speech.

📖 **21:1–16**

CONTRADICTING HIS FRIENDS

In verse 1, Job is basically saying, "If your speech is supposed to comfort me, then mine will do the same for you" (21:1–2). Job is going to say what is on his heart, and then his friends can mock him more if they want (21:3).

Job must have looked awful. In fact, it seems that his friends have a hard time even looking at him. So Job calls them to take a good look at him, even though his appearance is shocking to those who see him (21:4–5).

Job contradicts Zophar's litany of what happens to the wicked by pointing to what really takes place in life. The wicked don't die young; they are profitable and powerful (21:6–7). They have many healthy children (21:8), their homes are safe (21:9), their livestock breed and are healthy (21:10), and they enjoy good times (21:12). Job's life seems to drag on in pain, while he sees the wicked not only living long, prosperous lives, but when they do die, they go quickly (21:13).

Demystifying Job

Just as Zophar goes to one extreme in saying that the wicked are always punished, Job goes to the other extreme and says that the wicked are always blessed. Neither is true (see Psalm 37:35–36). God is sovereign and He has a purpose for everything. We must be careful that when we speak, we are not speaking out of our emotions but according to the Word of God.

People who have everything they want see no need for God (21:14). They have it all; what more do they need? God is of no profit to them, or so they think (21:15–16). But when all is taken away, they tend to look up to God.

Critical Observation

Jesus makes the same point that Job makes here (21:14–15) when He says that it is easier for a camel to go through the eye of a needle than for a rich man to enter heaven (Matthew 19:23–24). The point is not that rich people won't go to heaven but that wealth can blind our eyes to our need for God.

21:17–34

CONFUSED BY GOD'S WAYS

Job's friends have been blaming Job and his hidden sin for the death of his children. Job argues that God should punish the wicked and not their children (21:17–21). But then Job seems to backtrack, acknowledging that it is presumptuous to try to teach God what to do (21:22). Still, God's ways are incomprehensible to Job. Why should one person live happily right up until his death, while another has nothing but misery in his life (21:23–26)?

Job is fully aware that his friends are trying to prove that his hardships are evidence of his wickedness (21:27–28). He challenges them to ask anybody, from any part of the world; anyone will agree that the wicked prosper (21:27–30). Even in death the wicked are honored; they are treated as heroes (21:31–33).

Job's friends are speaking nonsense, Job insists, and how can nonsense be of any comfort (21:34)?

JOB 22:1–30

ELIPHAZ'S THIRD SPEECH

Direct Accusation   22:1–20
A Call to Repentance   22:21–30

Setting Up the Section

The third round of this three-on-one conversation between Job's friends and Job now begins, with Eliphaz, as in the previous two rounds, taking the lead and speaking first.

22:1–20

DIRECT ACCUSATION

Eliphaz reminds Job that Job's actions do not benefit God at all (22:1–2). Job is not doing God a favor by being good (22:3). But the point is moot, Eliphaz implies, because obviously Job is not being good—God wouldn't allow all these troubles to happen to a good man, Eliphaz claims (22:4). Clearly, to Eliphaz's way of thinking, Job is unendingly sinful (22:5).

Take It Home

God desires us to do good because it is what is best for our lives, and we are blessed by it. But it doesn't add or take away from God at all. Yes, our unrighteousness grieves God, but it doesn't harm Him.

Up until this point, Eliphaz and the other friends have been satisfied to list the consequences of sin and let Job draw the conclusion that, since he is suffering those consequences, he is obviously a sinner. But Job hard-headedly refuses to draw that conclusion, so now Eliphaz comes out and accuses Job directly. Eliphaz has no proof that Job did any of the things Eliphaz is about to accuse him of, but he is trying to figure out the ways of God by applying life's situations to them. So he has come to the conclusion that Job has become wealthy by strong-arming the poor—taking their clothes, refusing to give them food and water, and disregarding the plight of the widowed and fatherless (22:6–9). That is why, Eliphaz says, everything is going wrong for Job now (22:10–11).

Eliphaz accuses Job of trying to get away with some kind of evil when God isn't looking (22:12–14). Ironically, God *has* been looking at what Job does and has decreed Job blameless and upright (1:8; 2:3). Eliphaz evokes the image of the Flood, as Bildad had done earlier (8:11). Just as God swept away the wicked with the Flood, so now He is deluging Job with judgment (22:15–16).

Demystifying Job

There was a belief that when clouds covered the earth people could do what they wanted because God, up in heaven, couldn't see through them (22:13–14).

Eliphaz now quotes Job's own plea for God to leave him alone (22:17; see also 7:20) and piously asserts that he, Eliphaz, has nothing to do with such wickedness (22:18). He goes on to say that the innocent rejoice in the suffering of the wicked (22:19–20). Since he has just identified Job as wicked and himself as innocent, the implication is that Eliphaz is happy about Job's downfall.

📖 22:21–30

A CALL TO REPENTANCE

As the friends have done before, Eliphaz tells Job to get right with God and he will be blessed (22:21–28). He calls on Job to submit to God, lay up God's words in his heart, turn from wickedness to God, delight in God rather than in wealth, pray and obey, and be concerned for sinners. Perhaps Eliphaz sees himself in the role of the one through whom God will extend deliverance to Job (22:30).

JOB 23:1–24:25

JOB'S THIRD RESPONSE TO ELIPHAZ

God's Omnipotence   23:1–17
The World's Injustice   24:1–25

Setting Up the Section

Eliphaz has exhorted Job to return to God (22:23). Job replies that that is just what he wants to do—not because he has wickedness to confess but because he wants to present his case to God.

📖 23:1–17

GOD'S OMNIPOTENCE

Job wants to meet God face-to-face so that he can plead his case before Him. Job believes that if he can talk with God, he will be vindicated and God will relieve him of his troubles (23:1–8).

But search as he may, Job cannot find God (23:8–9). He is confident, however, that God can find him. And he is confident that he will not be found lacking. Job understands that trials are used to purify us, just as gold is refined in the refiner's fire so that it can become pure and all impurities removed (23:10). He maintains that he is innocent before God: He has followed God's ways (23:11) and treasured God's Word (23:12).

Critical Observation

When Job talks of testing (23:10), deep down he knows the truth about what God is doing, but it has been clouded at times by his recent experiences. The apostle Peter puts it this way: "In this you greatly rejoice, though now for a little while, if need be, you have been grieved by various trials, that the genuineness of your faith, being much more precious than gold that perishes, though it is tested by fire, may be found to praise, honor, and glory at the revelation of Jesus Christ, whom having not seen you love. Though now you do not see Him, yet believing, you rejoice with joy inexpressible and full of glory, receiving the end of your faith—the salvation of your souls" (1 Peter 1:6–9 NKJV).

Job speaks of the sovereignty of God (23:13). Unfortunately, this knowledge does not comfort Job; it makes him afraid (23:14–16). He is afraid because he thinks that this all-powerful God is out to get him (23:14–16). Job acknowledges God's sovereignty, but his circumstances have led him to forget God's love. Nevertheless, he will not be silent (23:17).

Take It Home

Job is right when he says that God does whatever He pleases (23:13). This does not negate our responsibility to pray, however, as some would have you believe. They say, "God is going to do whatever He wants, so why pray?" We pray because God tells us to pray. It is through prayer that God conforms our hearts to His.

God does answer our prayers, but we don't fully understand how it all works. When God was going to destroy unbelieving Israel, Moses stepped in and interceded for them, and God spared them. Did God change His will? Or was Moses' heart so conformed to God's that his request was in line with God's will? We don't understand these things, but we do know that God invites, even commands, our prayers.

📖 24:1–25

THE WORLD'S INJUSTICE

Having affirmed God's knowledge and God's power, Job now questions why God doesn't provide, in essence, a court room in which people might urge God to use that knowledge and power to correct injustices (24:1). In short, why does a powerful God allow bad things to happen to good people? Job lists some of these injustices (24:2–9).

Demystifying Job

Moving boundary stones (24:2) was property theft. It effectively moved the lot lines to expand one person's property at the expense of his neighbor.

Job has seen the wicked do all these things. He has seen how the poor must work hard without getting the rewards of their labor (24:10–11). He hears their cries for help—surely God must hear them, too. But God does nothing (24:12).

Job continues to list charges against the wicked. The wicked run from the truth, the light, because it exposes their evil deeds. They love the dark because they can get away with murder (24:13–15). Darkness is the natural environment of the wicked, just as daylight is the natural environment of the innocent (24:16–17).

Strangely, Job seems to agree with his friends about the fate of the wicked. He lists many of the consequences that his friends have already described: early death, being forgotten after death, losing all that they have (24:19–24). Where Job differs from his friends is in turning the equation around. Job's friends say that because the wicked suffer, anyone who suffers is therefore wicked. Job disagrees; he persists in claiming innocence. Some suggest that these verses are not so much statements of fact as they are Job's desire for the wicked to receive their deserved punishment.

Job concludes with a challenge to his friends to prove him wrong, if they can (24:25).

JOB 25:1–6

BILDAD'S THIRD SPEECH

Setting Up the Section

We are in round three of the verbal tongue-lashing given to Job by his friends Eliphaz, Bildad, and Zophar. As Bildad begins to speak, he doesn't have a lot to say. It seems that he is running out of material with which to condemn Job. This may also be the reason that Zophar does not speak for a third time; we would expect him to take his turn after Bildad, but there is really nothing left to say; it has all been said before. Chapter 25 records the shortest speech in the book of Job, but it will lead to the longest speech in the book—from chapter 26 through chapter 31.

📖 25:1–6

BILDAD'S THIRD SPEECH

Job has just concluded his previous speech with a challenge for his friends to disprove him if they can (24:25). Bildad does not take on this challenge, but instead he agrees with the first part of Job's previous speech: There is no one more powerful than God (25:1–2). Human kings may have large armies, but God's forces—the angels and heavenly armies—are too numerous to count. A wealthy man may illuminate his home with candles, but that is only a pale reflection of God's light, the sun (25:3).

If the contrast between divine and human armies and divine and human light is great, how much greater is the contrast between divine and human righteousness! In the face of God's righteousness, no mere human can measure up (25:4). In comparison with the brilliant moon and stars—which are infinitely less glorious than their Creator—human beings look like maggots.

Critical Observation

Bildad is right in what he has to say here in chapter 25. No one can be righteous before a holy God apart from Christ (see Romans 3:10–12). It is only because the penalty for our sin has been paid for by Christ that God can look on us with acceptance. It is only because the spotless Son of God, who chose to be born of a woman, has imputed his righteousness to us that others can stand before God as pure.

Take It Home

We don't much like to think of ourselves as worms (25:6). Some preachers have openly refuted this worm theology. The argument goes something like this: "You would only pay what something is worth; thus, because God gave His only begotten Son to die for us, we must be worth a lot! We must be valuable!" But Bildad's point here is not that people aren't valuable; his point is that we aren't, on our own, righteous material. There is no one God is not willing to save. God saves us by His grace and mercy alone, and not because we have some kind of redeeming quality in us. What God long ago said to Israel, we can easily apply to our own lives (see Deuteronomy 9:6).

JOB 26:1–31:40

JOB'S FINAL RESPONSE

On Power	26:1–14
On Justice	27:1–23
On Wisdom	28:1–28
On Former Happiness	29:1–25
On Loss	30:1–31
On Innocence	31:1–40

Setting Up the Section

Job's three friends seem to have run out of steam. After two or three rounds of arguing with Job, they have little left to say—as evidenced by how short Bildad's final speech is (chapter 25). Job, on the other hand, is just getting warmed up. What follows is his longest speech in the book.

📖 26:1–14

ON POWER

Job's words drip with sarcasm as he responds to Bildad. (The *you* in verses 3 and 4 is singular, not plural. Apparently Eliphaz and Zophar have already been silenced.) What a comforting friend, wise and insightful, Bildad has been, Job says—meaning exactly the opposite (26:1–3). To speak so wisely must require inspiration—but from what spirit (26:4)? Clearly Job is not buying his friends' implication that they (and not Job) speak for God.

Perhaps in contrast to belittling Bildad, Job now exalts God. Nothing escapes God's notice and God's control. God created and still upholds (notice the present tense in verses 7–10) the skies; the earth stays where He put it, even though it seems to be suspended with nothing to hold it up (26:7). The water cycle is no less amazing: We take its transformation from liquid to vapor to liquid again (26:8) as a matter of course, but if a rock did the same thing, we would be amazed!

Demystifying Job

The Bible is not intended to be a scientific workbook, but it is remarkable how fitting verses 7–8 are to our current understanding of the cosmos. The science of Job's day up until the recent past includes some strange theories of how the earth is held. Some say it was on the back of an elephant, others on the back of the giant Atlas, and some even on the back of a turtle. But Job tells us that God hangs the earth on nothing. It is suspended in space.

The most commonplace of daily events are under God's control, Job says. When a cloud passes between earth and the moon, God is in control of it (26:9). When the sun rises over the eastern horizon and sets over the western horizon, God is in control (26:10). Storms that seem to shake the heavens (26:11) and churn the waters (26:12) are as nothing to God; He can blow them away with a single breath (25:13).

Demystifying Job

Rahab (26:12) is the name of a mythical sea monster—as is the "gliding serpent" (called Leviathan in Isaiah 27:1) mentioned in Job 26:13. In the Bible, these monsters are poetic representations of storms and other wild forces of nature.

All this evidence of God's power can be seen in creation, and yet it is only the tiniest fragment of what God is doing. What we know of God's power is like a whisper compared to thunder—far too great for us to comprehend (26:14).

📖 27:1–23

ON JUSTICE

Although Job believes that God has denied him justice (27:2), he is committed to remaining truthful (27:3–4). A good part of that truthfulness, in Job's mind, is standing by his statement that he has done nothing to deserve the troubles that have come on him. To give in to these charges, Job says, *would* be wicked, because it would be a lie (27:5–7).

Demystifying Job

The breath of God that Job refers to (27:3) simply means life. At Creation, God breathed life into Adam (Genesis 2:7). Even while arguing that God has misjudged him, Job recognizes that life lasts only as long as God chooses to give it.

Job's friends have become his enemies through their false accusations, and now Job wishes they would be punished for their lies about him (27:7). He envisions Eliphaz, Bildad, and Zophar in the hopeless situation of begging God for help, as Job has, and getting no response (27:9–10). "I've listened to all your talk," he says in effect. "Now let *me* tell *you* a thing or two about how God works" (27:11–12).

Quoting what Zophar has said to him (20:29), Job begins a long litany of the things that a wicked person (in this case, perhaps his former friends) can expect from God (27:13). Their children will suffer (27:14), their wealth won't last, (27:16–18), and they will eventually vanish (27:20–23).

Critical Observation

When Job claims that the righteous will receive the wealth of the wicked, he is stating a principle of ideal justice. Ultimately, Job is convinced, God will punish evil and reward good. Although Job's experience at this point does not bear this happy thought out, Job knows enough of the character of God to cling to the conviction that justice will one day prevail.

📖 28:1–28

ON WISDOM

Job now talks about those who go down into the earth to dig for precious stones and metals and bring them back up to the surface. It is dangerous work, but for those who are successful, the rewards outweigh the risks (28:1–11).

Wisdom is harder to find and harder for people to value, as well (28:12–13). One can't mine wisdom from the ground like silver or gold, nor gather it from the ocean depths, like pearls or coral (28:14). Nor can one buy wisdom with the riches that can be mined—with gold, silver, precious stones, coral, or topaz (28:15–19). As precious and valuable these stones and metals may be, they are worthless when compared to wisdom.

Take It Home

We live in a world that is vastly more intelligent than it was a hundred years ago. We have more information coming at us today than we know what to do with. And yet, for all that intelligence, we are unwise. Intelligence, in the Hebrew mind, is the accumulation of knowledge. Wisdom, on the other hand, is taking what we know and applying it to our lives—it is the application of knowledge.

Wisdom originates from God. Thus, as we apply the Word of God to our lives, we are exercising wisdom (see Proverbs 2:1–9). Do we as Christians dig into the Word of God as much as men dug into the earth looking for treasure? In the Word of God are riches that are more important than anything we can dig from the dirt.

Finding wisdom begins to seem hopeless (28:20). God alone knows the way to wisdom; He is the One who determines what wisdom is (28:23–27). And He defines it for human beings: The fear of the Lord is wisdom, and to shun evil is understanding (28:28).

Critical Observation

God Himself approved Job as a wise man when He described Job in exactly the terms used in verse 28 to define wisdom: Job is a man who fears God and shuns evil (1:8; 2:3).

📖 29:1–25

ON FORMER HAPPINESS

Job now reminisces about his past, about the good times and joy he had before all this trouble came upon his life (29:1–2). Job walked in the light of God (29:3–4). His children, who are all dead now, used to run around his feet, and what joy their voices brought him (29:5). Luxuries like cream were as common as the dirt beneath his feet (29:6). Goodness at one time seemed to follow him wherever he went. But now that is all gone.

Job had been a respected man who sat at the gate of the city as part of the city council (29:7). The young deferred to him and the aged stood in respect of him (29:8). We get the idea that when Job talked it was so quiet you could hear a pin drop. Everyone wanted to hear what he had to say (29:9–10).

Earlier, Job's friends had accused him of oppressing the poor and taking advantage of the fatherless and widows. But Job contends that the opposite is true: He had a reputa-tion as a good man (29:11) because he helped the poor and fatherless (29:12), comforted the dying, and brought joy to the widow's heart (29:13). When people looked at Job, they saw righteousness and justice (29:14). He helped the disabled (29:15), befriended strangers (29:16), and stood against the wicked (29:17). He was a good man who practiced what he believed.

At that time, Job had it all figured out. Since he was doing good, he expected to live to an old age, and his life would continue to be blessed (29:18). He would be like the righ-teous man described in Psalm 1, who is like a tree planted by streams of water (29:19). His reputation as the greatest man among all the peoples of the East (see 1:3) would be constant (29:20). But things are not working out as he has planned.

People used to gather and wait in line to hear the wisdom of Job (29:21). His words were refreshing to them; they stood drinking in his words (29:22–23). They were delighted when they won his approval (29:24). Job received a lot of respect from the multitudes of people that came to hear him (29:25). That is the way it was, but now things have changed dramatically.

📖 30:1–31

ON LOSS

In Job's day there were people roaming the streets who were nothing more than thieves and troublemakers who no one wanted around. Now even these people mock Job. The lowest of society are putting Job down—a man who was at one time held in high esteem and highly respected (30:1).

These people live off the land and are not physically healthy. They basically take what they can find, even the garbage that people throw out (30:2–4). These people are hated by society and run out of town. No one wants them around, for they are troublemakers (30:5). These are the ones who now mock and spit upon Job. They make up songs to taunt him and treat him as if he is the outcast to be avoided (30:9–10).

Demystifying Job

Twice Job uses the imagery of a bow—in the good old days, his bow was always new (29:20), but now God has unstrung his bow (30:11). Bows and arrows were the main weapons for hunting in Job's time, and they represented a man's strength and status. A bow with no bowstring, however, was useless—a sign of weakness and humiliation.

Since God has taken away all Job's wealth, people no longer feel the need to show respect to him (30:11). While young men once stepped aside on the path to let Job pass (29:8), now they block his way (30:13–14). Where, before, people were eager to win Job's approval and feared his disapproval (29:21–24), now it is Job who is afraid and humiliated (30:15).

Previously, Job enjoyed the material luxuries of wealth and the blessing of God's friendship (29:4–6), but now he is in physical pain, and God's presence is like a straitjacket that chokes him and trips him up. Job's distress is so great that he feels he has become like dust and ashes, the symbols of remorse and grief (30:18–19).

It seems that God has closed His ears to Job's cry (30:20). Job is crying out for help, but things just seem to be getting worse and worse for him (30:21–22). He is certain now that he will be miserable for the rest of his life (30:23).

It seems unbelievable to Job that he, who has helped those in difficulty so often, should have no one to help him now (30:24–25). Yet this is the case; every hope for relief is disappointed (30:26), and his suffering goes on (30:27–30).

For Job, there are no more songs of joy; the only songs in his life are dirges (30:31).

📖 31:1–40

ON INNOCENCE

Job contends that he has not looked with lust at any woman. Now this is not just by accident; Job made an intentional decision—a covenant with his eyes—not to look at a woman this way (31:1). This covenant, this conscious decision, affects all areas of Job's life, because he knows that God knows his every thought and action (31:2–4).

Take It Home

Job knew that resisting temptation took an act of will. This is true for us today, as well. Certainly, we can stand only in the righteousness that has been imputed to us by Jesus Christ. This is called *positional righteousness*—referring to our position or status before God—and many times that is as far as Christians go. But the New Testament abounds with instructions to make a conscious decision for holiness (see 1 Peter 1:13–16). This is *practical righteousness*—where we purpose in our hearts not to let lust (or anything that would incite temptation) enter our eyes and our minds, causing us to stumble in our relationship with God. We should have that desire to walk in righteousness. We need to make a conscious decision on our part to live as God wants us to live.

Job is willing to have his life actions be placed in the balances of God, and if it comes up short, he is willing to be judged accordingly. But Job feels that he has tried to do good and that his life has reflected that (31:5–8). He gives specific examples of his innocence, couching each in the same "if/then" structure: "If I have done this, then let me be judged for it."

"If I have been involved in an adulterous relationship," says Job, "then let me be punished by my wife's unfaithfulness" (31:9–10). Adultery is a shameful sin that brings destruction with it (31:11–12).

Job contends that he doesn't treat people differently because of their social status, the color of their skin, or their nationality (31:13). He acts this way because he acknowledges that God has created every human being in the same way, reflecting His own image (31:14–15).

Job says that he has never walked away from anyone in need but has come to their aid and given to them what they needed to live—be it food, clothing, even help against their enemies (31:16–22). Job does this because of his fear of the Lord. The "fear of God's splendor" speaks of reverence and respect for God (31:23).

Job does not worship his wealth or place his confidence in it (31:24–25), nor does he turn to horoscopes or other astrological enticements (31:26–27), because he recognizes that both are idolatry and unfaithfulness to God (31:28).

Demystifying Job

The worship of the heavens—the sun, moon, and constellations—was very popular and, of course, of pagan practice. That worship included kissing one's hand and throwing that kiss to the sun or moon.

Job claims that he has not gloated over his enemies' troubles (31:29) or cursed them (31:30), and he has offered hospitality to household staff and strangers alike (31:31–32).

He lived his life in the open for all to see. He is not a hypocrite, trying to hide his sin (32:33–34).

Job underscores the seriousness of his claims by putting his name to them—possibly literally signing a document, or perhaps symbolically. And he wishes that his accuser—God—would put His charges in writing as well, so that Job could refute the charges one by one (31:35–37). So confident is Job of his innocence that he again invites scrutiny of his behavior in another of his "if/then" statements (31:38–40).

With this, Job rests his case. In the remainder of the book of Job, we will hear only two brief statements from him (40:3–5; 42:2–6).

JOB 32:1–37:24

ELIHU SPEAKS

Setting Up the Section

Job's three friends Eliphaz, Bildad, and Zophar have run out of gas. They have nothing left to say, for they have said more than enough to Job already. By this time a crowd has gathered to watch the confrontation—a confrontation that is loud and animated. And in this crowd is Elihu, a young man who has heard all these words and now has something to say.

📄 32:1–22

COMPELLED TO SPEAK OUT

The three friends see the futility of arguing with Job more. Because Job will not admit that he has been wrong, that he has sinned, they see him as self-righteous (32:1). By now a large crowd has gathered to hear these encounters between Job and his friends, and within that crowd is a man named Elihu. Elihu is angered by Job's words (32:2), and he isn't too happy with Job's three friends, either, for they have condemned Job with no proof of sin. Elihu sees their reasoning as faulty (32:3). Out of respect for men older than himself, Elihu remained silent, but now that the three friends are giving up, Elihu can remain quiet no longer (33:4).

Demystifying Job

Abraham's brother, Nahor, had two sons, Huz and Buz (Genesis 22:21). Elihu was a descendant of the family of Buz, making him a Buzite (32:2).

Elihu begins respectfully enough, acknowledging the older men's right to speak first. But he points out that age does not always equal wisdom; wisdom is given by the Spirit (or breath) of God, and the young can receive that wisdom as well (32:8–9). Elihu is eager to share his wisdom (32:10).

Elihu has listened patiently to the words of the three friends, but they have come up short and not convinced Job of his error (32:11–13). All they have done is put Job on the defensive. Elihu hopes that Job will listen to him because he has not been part of the earlier arguments—and because he has something new to say (32:14). He doesn't see why he should be forced to remain silent just because the three friends have given up (32:15–16). Elihu has so much to say that he is ready to burst (32:18–20). He promises not to stoop to flattery or favoritism (32:21–22).

📖 33:1–33

A VARIATION ON AN OLD THEME

Some time earlier, Job had expressed a desire for a mediator between him and God (9:33). Elihu says that he is that man who can stand in the gap and bring Job and God together. He claims to be righteous, sincere, and Spirit-filled (33:1–5)—in other words, someone God will listen to, but also someone Job doesn't need to be afraid of (33:6–7).

Critical Observation

Elihu is here describing the perfect mediator: truly righteous and truly human (see, for example, Hebrews 2:17; 7:26). What he gets wrong is the identity of this mediator, who is not Elihu, but Jesus Christ.

Elihu accuses Job of falsely claiming to be sinless (33:8–9). Here he is misrepresenting Job, who has readily admitted that he is a sinner (7:21; 13:26). Further, he regularly offers the appropriate sacrifices for sin (1:5). What Job has claimed is to be innocent of the kind of wickedness that deserves the punishment (as he perceives it to be) that he has received (33:10–11).

Elihu also accuses Job of claiming that God does not speak to humans (33:12–13). He lists many ways that God does in fact communicate: through dreams and visions (33:14–15), audibly or through the warnings of godly people (33:16–18), and even through pain, which can focus one's thoughts on God and on self-examination (33:19). What Elihu has to say is a little different than what Job's three friends were saying. Job's friends had maintained that the things happening to Job were a direct result of sin in his life. Elihu is saying that God has brought this upon Job because He is chastening him in order to confess his sin and get back on track (33:20–22).

Critical Observation

God does indeed sometimes use what C. S. Lewis calls "the megaphone of pain" to get our attention and lead us back to Him. But Elihu is wrong in assuming that Job's suffering is God's rebuke and call to repentance; Job 1 and 2 have already made clear that the reason is quite different. In the same way, we would be wrong to assume that suffering is always God's rebuke for wrongdoing. (See Luke 13:1–5 for Jesus' warning against that kind of judgment.)

Elihu tries to encourage Job with the possibility that one of the angels will intercede with God on Job's behalf (33:23–24). Ironically, Job's troubles result from exactly the opposite: Satan's accusations against him.

The appropriate response, Elihu instructs Job, is to confess first to God (33:26) and then to people that he has sinned (33:37) and that God has given him another chance (33:38). In fact, Elihu says, Job's suffering is actually evidence of God's love, as it gives Job a chance to repent and be restored (33:29–30).

Elihu pauses to ask whether Job needs any clarification before he continues with his instruction (33:31–33). Presumably Job does not, because Elihu continues his lecture.

📖 34:1–37

REPENTANCE VS. REBELLION

Elihu now turns to address those around him, inviting them to be partners in the process of assessing Job's situation (34:1–4). He summarizes Job's claims of injustice (34:5–6) and then plays "good cop" to the three friends, saying Job has taken all their abuse, but Elihu is not going to do the same (34:7–8).

Despite what Elihu claims (34:10), Job knows that the wicked will be punished and there is a profit in doing good. Once again, Elihu is misrepresenting what Job has to say. Then Elihu begins to defend God, asserting that God does justice, not evil (34:10–12). No one supervises God (34:13); He holds us together and gives us the very breath we breathe (34:14–15).

Now Elihu turns back to speak directly to Job. The Hebrew for the verbs in verse 16 is singular. He accuses Job of condemning God as unjust in His dealings with Job (34:17). He contends that Job honors those in high positions, like kings, and yet he puts God down (34:18–20).

Evildoers can't get away with anything; God knows what they are doing (34:21–22), Elihu reminds Job. Although Job has been asking for a hearing before God, Elihu argues that hearings are unnecessary for a God who already knows everything (34:23). God will mete out justice, and that justice will be made public so that everyone can see what happens to people who reject God's laws (34:24–27) and mistreat the poor. Job has complained that God is silent when Job calls to Him. Elihu says that it's God's right to remain silent (34:28–29); God maintains justice over the nations even when He is silent (34:30).

Elihu sets out a model of behavior for Job to follow, first with a hypothetical situation (34:31–32), and then more directly with a rhetorical question about Job's apparent refusal to repent (34:33).

Elihu seems to be thinking aloud as he summarizes Job's position: Everyone knows (so Elihu believes) that Job is a fool (34:35). Job deserves even more troubles than he has already received, because not only is Job a sinner, but he refuses to confess that sin and thus rebels against God's chastisement (34:36–37).

📄 35:1–16

GOD'S AUTONOMY

Elihu points out what he sees as an inconsistency in Job's complaint. Job claims that there is no benefit for not sinning, and yet he expects God to vindicate him for not sinning (35:1–3). Elihu points out that God is far above human beings (35:4–5). God does not owe Job anything. Nor is God affected by how good or how bad Job is (35:6–7). While Job can't hurt God by his actions, he can very much hurt or help himself and others by what he does and what he says (35:8).

Many cry out for help during difficult times, but they look for their help in all the wrong places (35:9). They don't look to God, who will put a song in their heart and give them hope and joy again (35:10).

🏠

Take It Home

We are not so different from the people Elihu refers to in verse 9. Like them, we look for help in all the wrong places. We look to drugs, alcohol, relationships, and so on—those only bring more difficulty in our lives. But during difficult times it is God who can put a song in our hearts and give us peace through the storms. Many of the great hymns were born out of these difficult times, and many of the psalms were also written from this vantage point. God gives us songs of hope and joy.

Many people speak boldly about things they don't know (35:11). But God does not respond to them, because they are arrogant (35:12–13). Job is equally arrogant, Elihu says, and that is why God doesn't answer him (35:14–16).

📄 36:1–37:24

GOD'S POWER

Elihu has elevated himself to the position of spokesperson for God (36:1–2)—but God has not given him this position. Elihu claims he has obtained perfect knowledge through direct revelation from God, so Job had better listen (36:3–4). Because of His great power, God's justice will be fulfilled (36:5–6). Earlier, Job had complained that God would not leave him alone (7:17–19). Elihu considers it a comfort to know that God's eyes are continually upon His people (36:7). The righteous God exalts, but the arrogant He afflicts (36:8).

Job is angry because God has brought a clear charge against him (31:2), but Elihu argues that God does warn people of their sins (36:9) and brings trouble on them to get them to repent (36:10). If they do repent, they will prosper (36:11); if not, they will perish (36:12).

Elihu warns Job not to be like those who rebel against God's discipline (36:13-14) but instead to recognize it as God's loving way of bringing Job out of sin and misery and into joy and comfort (36:15-16). He sees Job in danger of choosing evil rather than submitting to God's discipline (36:17-21).

There is no one who teaches as God does (36:22). He is not wrong and He will never be wrong (36:23). We can know God because He has revealed Himself through scripture and through His creation (36:24-25). But we cannot understand God's thoughts and ways, nor can we fully grasp the truth that God is eternal. He has always existed (36:26).

Elihu points to the earth's atmosphere as an exhibit of God's wisdom, power, and provision. What follows is an accurate description of evaporation and distillation of water as rain (36:27), clouds (36:28; 37:11), and cyclones (37:12). Many feel that, as Elihu is speaking to Job, in the distance is a huge storm forming. As Elihu is trying to make his point, he sees this storm and begins to draw illustrations on the power of God and His awesomeness (36:30-27:13).

Elihu again asks rhetorical questions as he challenges Job to reflect on God's power and control over creation (37:14-20). Just as we find it difficult, almost impossible, to stare at the sun with our naked eyes, so, too, is it impossible to stand in the brightness of a holy and righteous God in our own righteousness (37:21-23). The only reasonable response is to revere Him (37:24).

JOB 38:1–42:6

THE LORD SPEAKS WITH JOB

God Speaks of His Power in Creation	38:1–40:2
Job Replies to God	40:3–5
God Speaks of His Justice	40:6–41:34
Job Confesses	42:1–6

Setting Up the Section

As Elihu is finishing his words against Job, a huge storm is forming in the distance. Elihu draws some illustrations from this storm and relates them to God. For some thirty-five chapters, Job and his friends have spoken, but now it is time for God to speak. For thirty-five chapters mankind has attempted to understand the how's and why's of God with finite minds—and no one has come to an understanding of these things. Now God is going to speak out.

What is interesting in this section is that God does not explain to Job—or us—exactly why He has done these things to Job. In fact, He asks Job a series of some seventy questions, and in the end, God's *answer* is far more important than an understanding of His *ways*. Simply speaking, God gives Himself as the answer.

📄 38:1–40:2

GOD SPEAKS OF HIS POWER IN CREATION

Job has wanted to ask God questions, but God turns the tables and begins asking Job questions (38:1–3). This is probably to get Job refocused. Job has been looking and developing his ideas of God through life's situations instead of falling back on the truths of God. His picture of God has been clouded by life's circumstances, and God is going to clear things up.

God asks Job whether he was around when the earth was created (38:4). Today we do know the measurement of the earth (38:5). It is 24,901.55 miles in circumference at the equator, and its diameter is 7,926.41 miles at the equator. And yet we still know so little, as God is going to show us.

God is actively involved in creation and everything that has taken place since that time (38:6). The angels were present at earth's creation and shouted for joy at what God had done (38:7). But Job was not around. God set the boundaries for the waters without the help of Job (38:8–11). Job was not around when God created the days and the light (38:12–15). Again, God is trying to get Job to take his eyes off of the circumstances he finds himself in, and to look back to his Creator, where true help and hope come from.

The ancients were not aware of the fresh water springs that are on the ocean floor, nor the channels and pathways located in the depth of the oceans, but God knew (38:16).

Job had wanted death to come upon him, for he saw death as a place of nonexistence (3:11–17). But Job is wrong about that. God rebukes Job for speaking about something he knows nothing about (38:17–18).

What happens to the darkness when the lights go on? God knows (38:19–21). Who understands how God controls the weather to influence the outcome of battles (38:22–23)? We know today that light can be divided into the light spectrum (38:24), but how did they know this back then? God knew because He created the light.

Critical Observation

God uses the elements of nature to bring about His will. Remember in Judges 5, Barak defeats the army of Sisera when God causes a torrential rainfall, causing their chariots to be stuck in the mud so that they have to flee on foot. God causes hailstones to fall from the sky, destroying the Amorites in Joshua 10. And in 1 Samuel 7, God uses thunder to confuse the Philistines, giving Israel the victory.

God reminds Job that He waters the wilderness, causing the vegetation to grow (38:25–27). He did not just create life and sit back and watch what happens, as the deists believe (38:28–30); He is actively involved in sustaining His work.

The Pleiades and Orion (38:31) are winter constellations. The Great Bear (38:32), or Arcturus, is the fourth brightest star in the sky. Obviously, Job has no control over them (36:33), nor can Job make it rain (38:34–35, 37–38), but God can and He does.

Demystifying Job

Arcturas, the Bear of Job 38:32, is some thirty-six light years away from us. Now that sounds pretty close, but when you calculate out that light travels at 186,000 miles per second, and one year it would travel around six trillion miles, you realize that it is actually very far away. Our sun is 864,000 miles in diameter and contains 335 quadrillion cubic miles of violently hot gases with a core temperature of twenty-seven million degrees Fahrenheit. Arcturus is thirty times larger than the sun and eighty times brighter. It travels at 250,000 miles per hour.

God provides food for the various animals—even those Job will not go near (38:39–40). God points to nature and how the animals give birth without the knowledge of Job, but God is aware (39:1–4). The onager (39:5) is a wild donkey, and God is saying He cares for all of them (39:5–8; Psalm 50:10–11).

Demystifying Job

The mountain goat of Job 39:1 may be the Nubian Ibex, who does hide when it gives birth. Even today very few have seen the birth of an Ibex.

The wild ox (39:9) could be the Auroch, which became extinct in 1627. This creature refused to be domesticated. It was fierce and it was huge, just a little smaller than an elephant. And God is saying to Job, "If you can't stand before my creation, if you can't handle him, how can you stand before me?" (39:9–12).

The ostrich can stand seven to eight feet tall, weighing up to three hundred pounds. But they are flightless, unlike the stork (39:13). And they are without sense. But even though God did not give the ostrich wisdom, He gave it the ability to run (39:17–18).

It is God who made the horse for battle (39:19–25) and gave hawks the instinct for migration (39:26). God equipped the eagle to make its nest high up where it can see its prey from great distances (39:27–30).

Demystifying Job

The migration of birds, such as the hawk mentioned in Job 39:26, is an interesting subject. The Golden Plover travels some eight thousand miles from the Hudson Bay region and winters in Argentina. The Barn Swallow migrates a distance of nine thousand miles from northern Canada to Argentina. The Arctic Tern migrates a distance of fourteen thousand miles, traveling from pole to pole and back. And even in storms they can travel without getting lost. How do they know where to go? God has given them a way to know what they are doing.

God now calls on Job to respond to all these questions He has put to Job (40:1–2).

📄 **40:3–5**

JOB REPLIES TO GOD

Job had much to say before, when his eyes were focused on his situation. But now that God has his attention, he has very little to say. He rightly recognizes his error and is ready to listen to God (40:3–5).

📄 **40:6–41:34**

GOD SPEAKS OF HIS JUSTICE

Out of the storm, God again challenges Job to answer Him (40:6–7), using the same words He used earlier (38:3). This time, God addresses Job's primary complaint: that He has been unjust to Job (40:8; see 19:6). Job has claimed to be just, so now God challenges Job to demonstrate his power to administer that justice (40:9–13). If Job can do that, then Job can vindicate himself (40:14).

Verses 15–24 make up the first of two poems that God speaks to Job, returning to the themes of chapter 39 and God's control over nature. Here God describes the behemoth. This is an animal that God created (40:15), not a mythical being. It is one of the most powerful of all God's creatures, but God is even more powerful (40:16–19). The area described as its habitat (40:21–23) is probably the region north of the Sea of Galilee. The idea of any human capturing the behemoth is laughable (40:24), but God can certainly control it.

Demystifying Job

Scholars aren't certain exactly what kind of creature the behemoth (40:15–24) is. It is variously considered to be an elephant, a rhinoceros, a water buffalo, or a hippopotamus. It is a land animal that also lives in the water. It is also an herbivore—in other words, it eats grass. It is a massive creature that has a tail (or possibly a trunk) like a cedar tree. From the description that is given, it seems that the behemoth could be a dinosaur—possibly either a Brachiosaurus or an Apatosaurus.

Next God speaks a poem about the leviathan, asking Job if he would bring this creature home as a pet and play with it (41:1–5). The idea is obviously absurd; even professional fishermen armed with harpoons can't bring the leviathan down—one only needs to look at the creature to know the futility of such a task (41:6–9). If Job can't stand against this creature, God asks, then how can he stand against God who created this creature (41:10–11)? He can't!

God elaborates on the fearsomeness of the leviathan. It is powerful and untamable, with scary teeth—perhaps like a crocodile's (41:12–14). Apparently, it is a reptile with a scaly back that is like a protective shield (41:15–17). To get within breathing range of the leviathan is to court disaster (41:19–21). Its muscles are as hard as rocks (41:22–24), and it can take down ships with its thrashing (41:25). Swords and spears can't pierce its scales (41:26), and metal gives way under its biting (41:27). Even its underbelly—usually the most vulnerable part of an animal—is as hard and as sharp as broken pottery (41:30).

When the leviathan takes to the water, its thrashing can cause seas as rough as a storm would, complete with whitecaps (41:31–32). Nothing on earth—and certainly not Job—is its equal (41:33–34).

Critical Observation

The last verse of this poem about the leviathan (41:34) shifts from speaking of physical prowess to speaking of attitude and rank. It seems that the dragon that God is speaking of here is the same dragon found in the book of Revelation, Satan (see Revelation 12:3–4, 7–9).

📖 42:1–6

JOB CONFESSES

Notice the perspective that Job now has of God and the situation he finds himself in. First of all, Job recognizes the sovereignty of God and that He is in control of everything (42:1–2). God shows Job that He not only created the heavens and the earth and all that dwells in it, but He sustains them also. Everything is subject to His sovereign rule.

Secondly, Job recognizes the foolishness of his words. Job has spoken about issues he knew nothing about (42:3), and yet he sounded so sure of himself. God redirects Job to fall back on the things he knows about God instead of coming up with foolish conclusions about life's situations.

It is one thing to hear God but quite another thing to *encounter* God (42:4–5). It is Job's encounter with God that causes him to see himself as a sinner, and he repents of his sin (42:6).

Take It Home

Many times, when we are hurting or we find ourselves in difficult situations, we take our eyes off God and what His Word has to say, and we come up with foolish words. If we will let God redirect us to fall back on the things we know about God through His Word, we, like Job, will find it is full of wonder, hope, and comfort.

JOB 42:7–17

EPILOGUE

Setting Up the Section

God's dialogue with Job is concluded, but God has two more things to do before the case is closed. First, He has a few things to say to Job's three friends. And second, He restores justice to Job.

📖 42:7–17

EPILOGUE

God now turns from Job to Eliphaz and the other two friends. These men had not represented God correctly, and God held them accountable for their actions (42:7).

Critical Observation

God was angry with Job's three friends because they did not speak the truth about God. They had reduced God to a cause-and-effect God, and they assumed that they could both understand and predict all God's actions. In essence, they denied God's sovereignty by declaring that God must respond in a certain way to certain situations.

The three friends had spent much energy trying to convince Job of his sin and of his need to repent and offer sacrifices for that sin. How ironic it must have seemed when God told them that *they* were the ones who needed to offer sacrifices—and that God would accept those sacrifices for Job's sake and because of Job's righteousness (42:8–9).

When did God bless or restore Job? When he prayed for his friends who blasted him (42:10). Then all the friends and relatives who had abandoned Job (see 19:13–19) came rushing back, eager to comfort Job—and to eat his food (42:11).

Take It Home

Why did God wait to bless Job until after Job prayed for the friends who had attacked him? Job had some bitterness toward his friends, as his replies to them have shown. But to pray for them he had to let go of that bitterness.

God wants to bless us, but what are we holding onto? What bitterness, or anger, or whatever is keeping God's blessings from being bestowed upon us?

God blessed Job with even more wealth than Job had before—twice as many sheep, camels, oxen, and donkeys as before (compare the numbers listed in 42:12 with those listed in 1:3). It seems that Job had the same number of children (42:13), but the reality is he has twice as many, for seven sons and three daughters were with the Lord. Job treated his daughters with the same kindness as he treated his sons, even giving them an inheritance, which was unusual in those days (42:14–15).

Despite his friends' dire warnings that Job would die young (see 36:14) and leave no heirs (see 18:19), Job lived 140 more years and saw not only his grandchildren but his great-grandchildren and great-great-grandchildren as well (42:16). He died old and "full of years" (42:17).

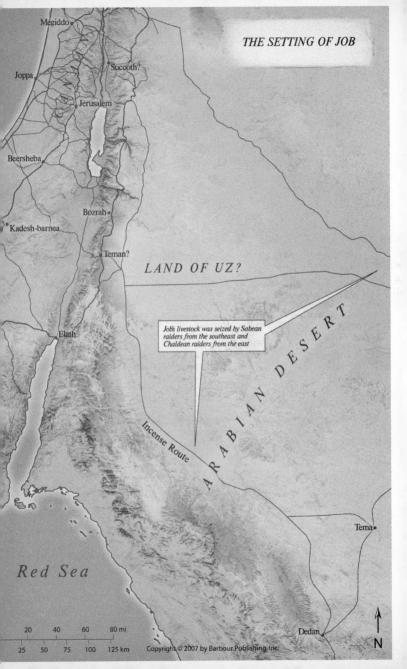

THE SETTING OF JOB

Megiddo

Joppa

Succoth?

Jerusalem

Beersheba

Bozrah

Kadesh-barnea

Teman?

LAND OF UZ?

Elath

Job's livestock was seized by Sabean raiders from the southeast and Chaldean raiders from the east

A R A B I A N   D E S E R T

Incense Route

Red Sea

Tema

20   40   60   80 mi

25   50   75   100   125 km

Dedan

N

CONTRIBUTING EDITORS:

Dr. Ralph Davis is the Teaching Pastor of Woodland Presbyterian Church in Hattiesburg, Mississippi. He is well known for his excellent Old Testament commentaries, and his book *The Word Became Fresh: How to Preach from Old Testament Narrative Texts*. He is formerly the professor of Old Testament at Reformed Theological Seminary in Jackson, Mississippi.

Bob Deffinbaugh, Th.M grew up in Washington state where he attended Seattle Pacific University. Since then, he graduated from Dallas Theological Seminary and has taught as a national seminar instructor for Prison Fellowship, served on various missions boards, and has taught the Bible in India, Africa, and China. In the 1970s, he helped plant Community Bible Chapel where he has served as an elder and Bible teacher for nearly thirty years. He lives with Jeanette, his wife of forty-four years, in Texas. They have five grown daughters. Many of Robert's original teaching transcripts can be accessed through *Bible.org*.

Pastor Joe Guglielmo is the Senior Pastor at Calvary Chapel of Manitowoc, in Manitowoc, Wisconsin. His passion is to teach, to equip the saints to grow in their relationship with the Lord, through a verse-by-verse study of God's Word. Over the past fourteen years he has completed a verse-by-verse study through the Bible and is starting his second time through. Pastor Joe has been married to his wife Julie for thirty years and have two sons, Joe and Tony and their wives, Ashely and Kara. Tony and Kara have two sons, Liam and Kaine. You can check out Pastor Joe's Bible studies at *www.ccmanitowoc.org*.

CONSULTING EDITOR:

Tremper Longman is the Robert H. Gundry Professor of Biblical Studies at Westmont University. He has taught at Westmont since 1998 and taught before that for eighteen years at the Westminster Theological Seminary in Philadelphia. Dr. Longman has degrees from Ohio Wesleyan University (B.A.), Westminster Theological Seminary (M.Div.), and Yale University (M.Phil.; Ph.D.). He has also been active in the area of Bible translation, in particular he serves on the central committee that produced and now monitors the New Living Translation.

NOTES

NOTES

NOTES

NOTES

NOTES

NOTES

_____
_____
_____
_____
_____
_____
_____
_____
_____
_____
_____
_____
_____
_____
_____
_____
_____
_____
_____
_____

NOTES